SYLVIA PLATH

SYLVIA PLATH

THE WOMAN AND THE WORK

Edited with an Introduction
by Edward Butscher

DODD, MEAD & COMPANY
NEW YORK

Dedicated to

HOWARD *and* MURIEL HIRT

dear friends, warm hosts, Boston's true elite

1 2 3 4 5 6 7 8 9 10

The authors have quoted passages, for the purpose of illustrating their own discussions of Sylvia Plath's life and works, from the following works by Sylvia Plath: *The Colossus and Other Poems*, copyright © 1957, 1958, 1959, 1960, 1962 by Sylvia Plath; published by Alfred A. Knopf, Inc. *Ariel*, copyright © 1961, 1962, 1963, 1964, 1965 by Ted Hughes; published by Harper & Row. *Crossing the Water*, copyright © 1971 by Ted Hughes; published by Harper & Row. *Winter Trees*, copyright © 1972 by Ted Hughes; published by Harper & Row. *The Bell Jar*, copyright © 1971 by Harper & Row; published by Harper & Row.

Library of Congress Cataloging in Publication Data
Main entry under title:

Sylvia Plath : the woman and the work.

Includes bibliographical references.
1. Plath, Sylvia. 2. Authors, American—
20th century—Biography. I. Butscher, Edward.
PS3566.L27Z92 811'.5'4 77-24700
ISBN 0-396-07497-9

Contents

Preface

The unique advantage of an anthology of this sort resides in its ability to bring together a host of various, sometimes contradictory perspectives. In the case of Sylvia Plath, the advantage is enhanced, I think, by the great complexity and controversial nature of her achievement, not to mention the relative paucity of similar collections. Equally important, perhaps, is the fact that Plath's dramatic biography has assumed almost the stature of myth, which is why it seemed necessary to include personal memoirs as well as professional critiques. Indeed, a poet's life and art have never appeared so intimately related before, with the possible exception of Edgar Allan Poe's own horror tale. Thus, despite the inevitable, inevitably profound division between woman and work, the memoirs and critical pieces tend to complement one another in fruitful ways.

Besides providing a morality lesson for future writers intent upon pursuing recently departed artists, my introductory essay tries to supply a broad biographical and literary outline, touching upon the major events in a career shaped around basic Freudian dilemmas, without shortchanging the central role of imagination and cultural traditions. The memoirs that follow are naturally more restrictive in locus, but have the intrinsic merit of immediacy, of individual personalities working through retrospection, not analysis. They create their own *raisons d'être* along the way, as does the poem by Richard Wilbur, who knew and understood Plath before postumous fame had distorted her reality. Paula Rothholz's poem has the different value of isolating and defining the heart of the poet's depressive state during her final year, bringing a specifically feminine sensibility to bear.

In selecting the critical essays I was motivated by two considerations: literary excellence and comprehensiveness. I wanted to preserve what I felt were authentic contributions to Plath scholarship, but I also wished to cover the whole range of available Plath literature in some organized fashion, from *The Colossus* through *Crossing the Water* and *The Bell Jar* to *Ariel* and *Winter Trees*. The essays by Pamela Smith, Gordon Lameyer, and Marjorie Perloff seem to do this admirably, while the critiques by Constance Scheerer, Robert Phillips, and Joyce Carol Oates deal with the entire *oeuvre*, though in their very special ways. Arthur Oberg's and Irving Howe's pieces, on the other hand, struck me as essential for other reasons. Also fascinating and well written, they have the additional gadfly worth of contemplating the poet and her art from a negative vantage point, raising important questions about the less attractive aspects of Plath's accomplishment.

And yet, in the end, if this anthology truly attains its main objective, it will send the reader back to Sylvia Plath's literature, a wiser, if not always a sadder, man or woman.

Flushing, New York

Acknowledgments

I wish to thank Gordon Lameyer, Dorothea Krook, Jane Baltzell Kopp, Clarissa Roche, and Elizabeth Sigmund for their acute memoirs, which were specifically commissioned for this anthology.

"Architectonics: Sylvia Plath's *Colossus*," reprinted by permission of *Ariel: A Review of International English Literature*. Copyright © 1973 by The Board of Governors, The University of Calgary.

"Death Throes of Romanticism," reprinted from *New Heaven, New Earth* by Joyce Carol Oates by permission of the publisher, Vanguard Press, Inc. Copyright © 1974 by Joyce Carol Oates.

"The Plath Celebration: A Partial Dissent," reprinted from *The Critical Point* by Irving Howe, copyright © 1973, by permission of the publishers, Horizon Press, New York.

"Sylvia Plath and the New Decadence," reprinted with permission of *Chicago Review* from *Chicago Review*, Volume 20, Number 1. Copyright © 1968 by *Chicago Review*.

"On the Road to *Ariel*: The 'Transitional' Poetry of Sylvia Plath," reprinted by permission of Marjorie Perloff, copyright © 1973 by the University of Iowa, copyright transferred to author March 1, 1976.

"The Deathly Paradise of Sylvia Plath," reprinted by permission of Constance Scheerer and *The Antioch Review*, copyright © 1976 by *The Antioch Review, Inc.*

"The Dark Funnel: A Reading of Sylvia Plath," reprinted from *The Confessional Poets* by Robert Phillips by permission of the publisher, Southern Illinois University Press. Copyright © 1973 by the Southern Illinois University Press.

"Outside the Bell Jar," reprinted by permission of Laurie Levy and *The Ohio Review*. Copyright © 1973 by Ohio University.

"Cottage Street, 1953," reprinted by permission of Richard Wilbur.

"For Sylvia at 4 A.M." has been dedicated by Paula Rothholz to Dr. Martin Lubin, with thanks.

Special thanks has to go to Joan Robinson for her typing aid, and, as usual, to warm friends and students who made the author's writing life so much easier, especially Jodie Arrington, Donna Wolz, Marian Madden, and Julia Leeds. Gratitude of a different, if no less warm, nature must also go to Godfrey, Pudding, and Miss Boo (née Pussywillow).

And, of course, Amy Rothholz once again contributed her stellar distractions, and her mother Paula was practically a coeditor in her efficient assumption of so many tedious details. To both my deep appreciation and affection.

A Sylvia Plath Chronology

1932   Born on October 27 in Boston's Memorial Hospital, the first child of Otto and Aurelia (Schober) Plath.

1934   Father's book, *Bumblebees and Their Ways*, is published.

1935   Brother Warren is born on April 27.

1936–1937   Parents buy a house on Johnson Avenue in Winthrop, Mass., the same suburb of Boston where her maternal grandparents already lived.

1938   Winthrop was struck hard by a disastrous hurricane on September 21. Earlier in month, she had entered Winthrop's public school system.

1940   Father died on November 5, after months of painful illness and loss of leg.

1940–1941   First poem and first drawing published in Boston newspapers. Also attended first wedding, acting as a flower girl for an aunt. Grandparents sell home to move in with the Plaths. Mother begins teaching at Boston University's School for Secretarial Studies.

1942   Family moves to Wellesley, Mass. She and brother enter Marshall Perrin Grammar School.

1944   Enters Alice L. Phillips Junior High School, where she will maintain "A" average and publish poetry in *The Phillipian*, the school's literary magazine.

1947   Graduates from Phillips, winning Honorable Mention in *National Scholastic*'s Literary Contest, and is only student in the school's history to earn a sixth letter, as well as an Achievement Certificate from the Carnegie Institute. In September enters Bradford High School.

1950   Appears in school play, *The Admirable Crichton*, as Lady Agatha during senior year, graduates from Bradford and wins a full scholarship to Smith College. In August, *Seventeen* publishes her short story, "And Summer Will Not Come Again," and the *Christian Science Monitor* publishes "Bitter Strawberries," a poem.

1953   Spends the month of June in New York City as a Guest Editor for
        Mademoiselle. On August 24, tries to commit suicide by swallow-
        ing sleeping pills and hiding in a crawl space under the porch of
        her house, but is found two days later and rushed to hospital. Will
        spend five months at McLean's, an expensive private institution in
        Belmont, paid for by Mrs. Prouty.

1954   Returns to Smith, having lost a year.

1954–1955   Wins several poetry contests at Smith and writes her honor's
        thesis on Dostoevsky's use of "doubles" in two of his novels.
        Graduates *summa cum laude* and wins scholarship to Cambridge
        University, England.

1955–1956   First year at Cambridge marked by continued academic success,
        some further acting experience, and association with *Varsity*
        (school newspaper) and other Cambridge publications. Maternal
        grandmother, Aurelia Greenwood Schober, dies of cancer on
        April 29. Weds Edward Hughes in London on June 16, a private
        service attended by Mrs. Plath. Newlyweds spend summer honey-
        moon at Benidorm, small fishing village in southern Spain.

1956–1957   Fulbright renewed for second year; husband teaching drama at
        secondary school; find a small flat near Grantchester Meadows.
        In March, Ted notified that *The Hawk in the Rain* had won the
        New York Poetry Center Award, would be published in America
        and England. They sailed for United States in June and spend
        summer at Cape Cod, a wedding gift from Mrs. Plath. Began teach-
        ing at Smith in September, but Ted unable to secure a post.

1958   Ted secures teaching position at University of Massachusetts at
        Amherst. They decide teaching and poetry are incompatible, giv-
        ing Smith and U. Mass. notice, determined to survive in Boston
        on grants, prizes, earnings from writing.

1958–1959   Lives in apartment on Beacon Hill; she works briefly at hospital;
        audits Robert Lowell's writing class at Boston University in Feb-
        ruary with Anne Sexton and George Starbuck; consults doctor
        about inability to become pregnant; goes with husband on camp-
        ing trip across the country and becomes pregnant. The period be-
        tween September 9 and November 19 spent at Yaddo in upstate
        New York. Returns to England in December.

1960   They move into Chalcot Square flat on February 1. *Lupercal* pub-
        lished in Spring. Frieda Rebecca Hughes born at home on April 1.
        In November, Heinemann publishes *The Colossus*. Gives first BBC
        reading on November 20.

1961   Loses second child through miscarriage in February; has appendix
        removed in March; edits *American Poetry Now* supplement for

The Critical Quarterly. On September 1 they move into Court Green house in Devon. According to Plath's notebooks, *The Bell Jar* had been finished by August.

1962   Nicholas Farrar Hughes born on January 17. *Three Women: A Monologue for Three Voices* is completed in May. Period covering June, July, and August characterized by family tension, discovery of Ted's adultery, arrival of Mrs. Plath, accident in Morris station wagon, and Ted's eviction. In September comes trip to Ireland and Ted's final departure for London. Poetry of *Ariel* and *Winter Trees* being written at rapid pace. Moves to London flat in December.

1963   London hit by snowstorm and freeze from December 25 to middle of January. *The Bell Jar* published on January 14 under Victoria Lucas pen name. Commits suicide by gas on morning of February 11.

I

SYLVIA PLATH:

THE WOMAN

1   In Search of Sylvia: An Introduction

Edward Butscher

> *Day now, night now, at head, side, feet,*
> *They stand their vigil in gowns of stone,*
> *Faces blank as the day I was born.*
>
>   "The Disquieting Muses"

My initial contact with the work of Sylvia Plath came in the 1960s, while taking a summer course (under an NDEA grant) at Stony Brook. As conducted by Professors Edward Fiess and Thomas Rogers, it was a stimulating course with a dreadfully long title that taught textual criticism within the confines of rigid deductive principles. Each week involved the production of a full-fledged essay on some literary enigma, usually a short story or longish poem, and I reacted with a poet's traditional love of structural challenges to the weekly assignments, particularly when presented with Plath's "The Moon and the Yew Tree."

The poem was and is a stunning experience. Supported throughout by a magnificent literary intelligence, its pervasive, haunted, haunting, often powerful sense of despair and alienation seemed to tap the same dark roots feeding my own baroque aesthetic at the time. After completing the required paper, I visited the university library. There I discovered that little biographical material on Plath was available, beyond the sensational sketches that had appeared in *Time* and *Newsweek* upon publication of *Ariel* in America, and not much more in the way of critical commentary. Even the poet's three published works, *The Bell Jar* and the two poetry collections, *The Colossus* and *Ariel*, were not easy to obtain. *The Bell Jar*, in fact, had appeared only in England, due to the efforts of Ted Hughes (as I learned much later), who was naturally concerned about the negative effect this satiric, autobiographical novel would have on his mother-in-law, Mrs. Aurelia Plath.

The library did have copies of *The Colossus* and *Ariel*, and I read them with about equal degrees of admiration and amazement. It was difficult to believe that the same poet had written both. *The Colossus* was patently the polished product of an extremely clever but almost repellently remote poet who seemed intent upon disguising some hidden self, her own emotional reality. Not that any of the poems lacked talent. Far from it. The very best of them, such as "Two Views of a Cadaver Room," "Night Shift," "All the Dead Dears," "Watercolor of Grantchester Meadows," "The Disquieting Muses," "The Beekeeper's Daughter," "The Stones," [1] and the title poem itself, were genuine poetic achivements, potent, complex, rather formal, brilliantly orchestrated performances that took full advantage of their author's rich literary background and penchant for original metaphors. What appeared missing from all of them, especially after exposure to the passionate outcries of *Ariel*, was a distinct personal voice. The intense, surreal confessionalism of the *Ariel* poems, as well as their conversational ease, was eons removed from the neoclassical rituals embalmed in *The Colossus*.

What had happened to Sylvia Plath in the several-year gap between the publication of the two books? More important, what did this have to do with her ability to create an entirely new poetic idiom? These related questions were obviously central, and I was determined to find the answer or answers, deciding that a critical biography offered the best possible approach. At any level, literary criticism only has value insofar as it can illuminate either the process of creation or its less evident referential foundations. Evaluation must play a crucial role as well, of course, but is, I believe, innately implied by the other two. After reading a smuggled-in copy of *The Bell Jar*, which tended to confirm the familial anguish motoring the persona behind *Ariel*, I secured Mrs. Plath's Wellesley address and wrote for assistance. A kindly reply note informed me that an "official biographer" (Lois Ames) was already engaged in extensive research and had been for quite some time.

In light of her daughter's undeniable genius, Mrs. Plath's news was not entirely unexpected. I believed that my own efforts could begin after Miss Ames's biography was published, since my primary aim remained critical in nature. It was two years later, after the appearance of Charles Newman's excellent anthology, *The Art of Sylvia Plath*,[2] and after my discovery that the official biography was no nearer completion, that I initiated my own research project, contacting whatever former friends, teachers, and classmates of Plath's could be tracked down. Most of them were amenable enough and frequently provided leads to other witnesses—"witnesses" is appropriate as I soon came to view myself as a literary Lew Archer in pursuit of another violated little girl, another doomed Oedipal victim, who had been as contradictory as she had been gifted.

The official or institutional profile of Sylvia Plath that emerged was consistent to the point of redundancy. Teacher after teacher from elementary through junior and senior high school attested to her academic brilliance and conventional sweetness, though, here and there, crept in small reservations regarding her social life outside school, suggestions that she might have been a "loner," despite many surface friends, who frightened off boys with her mental gymnastics. But these were intimations at most, vague *gestalts*, if you will, that were never sufficiently concrete to warrant any major alterations in the early sketch of Sylvia as a strongly motivated but uncomplicated over-achiever.

The first significant indication of subterranean corridors came from an interview with Wilbury Crockett, a later friend and Plath's English teacher during her three-year stay at Bradford High School in Wellesley. He spoke with intelligence and genuine warmth about the brainy, beautiful young girl he had introduced to so many classic authors, emphasizing the unique, almost breathless enthusiasm she had brought to bear upon the works of T. S. Eliot, Dylan Thomas, Thomas Mann, Leo Tolstoy, and others. And yet, his granitelike honesty demanded the further admission that he had always been aware of a certain amount of play-acting behind her extroverted personality, a feeling that she was "going along for the ride even then," that she was probably manipulating people to suit some private need and design. In retrospect, this was the first crack in the elaborate mask or masks Sylvia had labored over the years to perfect. I also learned from Mr. Crockett about a subtle strain of tension that had existed between the poet and her mother, a strain that suggested much deeper family chasms than hitherto suspected by adolescent companions.

Having recently suffered a heart attack and ordered by her doctor to avoid all future interviewers, Mrs. Plath herself was not available for comment, and Warren Plath, the beloved younger brother, never responded to any of my letters. This was frustrating, to say the least, but did save us a great deal of subsequent embarrassment, since my researches ultimately resulted in a number of conclusions about the poet and her home environment that proved highly objectionable to the Plaths.

Truth is ever a pluralistic phenomenon, and when confronting the vast array of prosaic material that sustains each human configuration— i.e., family myths, personal myths, cultural and religious myths, the artifices of a deliberately distorted past—the biographer of a poet must be concerned with distinguishing between objective structures and less visible supportive illusions, between "facts" and the effect of those facts upon the subject's central myth of identity, her own life. Facts as such are relatively easy to come by in a society where growing complexity has spawned a growing network of official institutions. Schools, librar- ies, newspaper files, governmental agencies, and the like are there for the plundering, as every credit house and FBI investigator well knows, and the laziest of biographers can still construct a reasonable collage from the bits and pieces resurrected from these bureaucratic mauso- leums.

They provide a spare but accurate portrait of Sylvia Plath and her world as it roller-coastered from the time of her birth on October 27, 1932, in Boston's Memorial Hospital to the early morning suicide thirty years later in a London flat. Her father, a German immigrant named Otto, was a respected professor at Boston University, where he taught entomology and German, and had written a scholarly treatise on bees, *Bumblebees and Their Ways*[3]—actually a slightly revised version of his Harvard thesis. Her mother Aurelia (née Schober) was the daughter of Austrian immigrants, who had seemed content to play the role of academic wife and homemaker. The Plath family owned a house on the bay side of Winthrop, a peninsula suburb of Boston, and the Scho- bers lived at their own home on the ocean side, near Point Shirley. With the arrival of Warren Plath on April 27, 1935, the Plath family seemed complete.

The records of the Winthrop public schools indicate that both Sylvia and Warren did extremely well in scholastic matters, and one teacher recalled the loveliness and cheerful demeanor of Sylvia.[4] She also re- called the day when the Plath children had to leave school and Win- throp soon after the death of their father, paying a farewell visit and giving her a copy of their father's book. Otto Plath had died on November 2, 1940, less than a week after his daughter's eighth birthday, but the painful diabetic condition had been stalking him for months, wrecking his hard body, turning him eventually into a bedridden invalid.

Here official records are insufficient. The atmosphere must be imagined in that house with a dying father and a fearful, timid mother, imagined from the literature that would come years later and from Sylvia's own memoir of her childhood, "Ocean 1212-W." [5] In the memoir, which makes no mention of Otto's lingering illness and death, the poet envisions the move from Winthrop as the end of a "fine white flying myth," and it was probably no accident that Sylvia's first printed poem appeared in a Boston newspaper when she was eight and a half years old.

What seemed imperative was some insight into Otto Plath, the father figure who looms like a huge deity—albeit a hateful and/or impotent one—over the bleak landscape of Plath's art. Various official agencies and libraries again supplied valuable background data: schools attended, the death of a blacksmith father, divorce from a woman named Lydia, and immediate remarriage to Aurelia Schober (a former pupil) in Reno, academic success at Harvard, and a teaching career at Boston University, but the personal element was lacking. What kind of man had Otto Plath been? Was he anything at all like the German tyrant, the Nazi panzer man, villified in poem after poem by his ambivalent daughter, who had felt betrayed by his death?

Fortunately, I was able to interview a former student and colleague of his, who confirmed his stubborn streak, a certain rigidity about organizational matters, but insisted upon his general congeniality and well-known devotion to entomology. Another colleague, who had known the Plaths on a more intimate basis, supported this impression in the main and recalled how vehemently Professor Plath, an immigrant from the Polish Corridor, had detested his Calvinistic schooling in the Midwest and the rise of Adolph Hitler in Germany. If he had been a tyrant, he had been a petty, rather benevolent despot who restricted his tyranny to the home, a somewhat typical *pater familias* far more interested in writing monographs and his book on bees than in the existence of a precocious daughter. The daughter, for her part, had gone out of her way at an early age to impress and please him, earning his praise. The tragic nature of his death and his odd refusal to take proper precautions against diabetic complications after a toe became infected—I did not know then that he had convinced himself he had a case of incurable cancer—suggested arrogance, but hardly on a scale to justify "Lady Lazarus" or "Daddy."

The mother was the truly vague figure, nestled so snugly in her husband's large shadow, although she had also suffered disguised attacks in her daughter's literature, had been castigated for failing to honor Otto's memory, and for implied criticisms about his lack of foresight in financial affairs. But Aurelia Plath, many of her friends and neighbors readily agreed, was an urbane, congenial, hard-working woman totally dedicated to giving her two children the best of everything in this best of all possible Americas—the move to Wellesley in 1942 had represented a social and cultural advance over the minority-riddled environs of Winthrop. Piano lessons, literary evenings, dance lessons, Scout camps, sailing lessons, and the proper athletic exercises, such as tennis and bike-riding, were but a few of the advantages bestowed upon Sylvia and Warren by a widowed mother who labored long hours in a series of poor-paying academic jobs to support a household that now included a set of aged parents. Again and again, friends and neighbors alluded to the "happy face" she had put upon her ordeal; they did not hesitate to use the term "martyr" in describing her constant sacrifices.

The mystery deepened. Where lurked the monster, the maternal ogre deprecated in *The Bell Jar* and poems like "The Disquieting Muses" and "Medusa"? And she was, she was a monster, this sincere Aurelia Plath of Wellesley, a vampire of the unconscious as fatal as Dracula himself, albeit an unwitting creation, another well-intentioned road-paver. With a sort of desperate love, she had drawn her precocious daughter to her bosom like a threatened mother mouse and never let go, feeding her fat, true, but feeding upon her as well.

This is very normal, of course, in a gross surface way, the inevitable giving and getting involved in any close human union, but the intense parent-child matrix does demand much more from the parent in the end, more giving and, ultimately, unconditional surrender. But Mrs. Plath could not comply when it came time for her daughter to assert her own identity, could not release her emotionally, and used the blanket of "love" to disguise her intentions. Hungrily, vicariously, she lived through her daughter, sucking up her life to fill the empty sack of her own dull existence, a fair exchange, so fair, but their crucial symbiotic relationship evolved (through high school and college) into a dangerous anaclitic tie as Sylvia's world demanded greater and greater perfection: her mother wanted and needed it; her father had always possessed it; she admired and imitated it and him, driving herself to achieve, to achieve what Mrs. Plath had been denied—a gay social life, many ultra-eligible boy pursuers, superior academic standing, recognized creative productions, the American Dream come alive as it only can in the mind and soul of immigrants' offspring.

Others saw this in Mrs. Plath, contemporaries of her daughter at college and elsewhere. Marcia Brown, Sylvia's best friend during her early years at Smith and later in Boston, saw it. She characterized it with penetrating frankness: "Mrs. Plath overreacted to everything . . . she gushed all over the place, everything was sweet and dear and touching, tears in her eyes all the time. I just had the feeling she was breathing on her [Sylvia] every minute." Years afterward, David and Elizabeth Compton, friends of Sylvia's in Devon to whom *The Bell Jar* would be dedicated, recalled how embarrassed and upset she became over the ceaseless barrage of letters from her mother, how she regarded them (and presumably Aurelia herself) as a "great weight" that had to be borne for the sake of family harmony—Sylvia was not about to admit aloud that she needed her mother still, needed her love and middle-class reassurances that a human ordering of events remained plausible, important.

The psychological entanglements are complex and deep, and I can see no sense in covering ground already touched upon in my critical biography.[6] Suffice it to say that the eternal trinity of father-daughter-mother provided Sylvia Plath with her art's obsessive core and shaped her life into another American tragedy, another sad tale of the nascent artist discovering that "going home again" was both impossible and absolutely essential. Psychic undercurrents are by nature vague and contradictory, not to mention almost beyond verification, and only a return to details permits the poet's career (and my search for her) to reassert its pattern.

The search, of course, continued to center on the artist, and no amount of detail could alter the huge discrepancy that seemed to exist between the Sylvia Plath who moved with effortless grace through Bradford High School—winning prizes, amassing perfect marks, helping edit the newspaper, earning the praise of teachers and peers alike—and the Sylvia Plath who wrote "A Family Reunion" in her senior year, publishing it anonymously in the school paper but not bothering to change the names of relatives caught within its poisonous folds. Mrs. Plath was stunned and hurt by the poem when she read it, as her daughter must have known she would be. "A Family Reunion" is a delightfully vicious exercise in caricature, by far the best piece of verse Sylvia had yet written, suggesting that negative emotions tapped the richest lode of her multilayered talent.[7] It also made clear, I believe, that the configuration behind the art (which I eventually labeled "the bitch goddess") was a repressed creature of awesome Freudian dimensions, a conscious persona and unconscious reality that would transform method into creative madness to carve out a unique female power myth.[8]

Sylvia's years at Smith, punctuated again by awards, high marks, and a growing reputation as a prize-winning poet, were preserved in school records, in yearbooks and literary magazines, in copies of the school newspapers, in written comments by teachers and personnel interviewers. But the flesh and blood depth of this extraordinary presence emerged most vividly from the living memories of the men and women who had been her closest companions at the time, friends such as Marcia Brown, Gordon Lameyer, Myron Lotz, Peter and Jill Davison, and Nancy Hunter,[9] buttressed by the many Plath letters they had been able to save. The official records, particularly the comments of Sylvia's teachers, stress the positive aspects of the mask, the "sweetness and light" haloing Sylvia's peaks of success, which appeared to possess no background crevices, no hints of jealousy or vanity or that worst of all Ivy League gaucheries: naked competitiveness. In a letter to me and other researchers, Professor George Gibian (Sylvia's Russian Literature teacher and subsequent advisor for her honor's thesis on Dostoevsky) remembered her dedication and amazing thoroughness as a student, along with her lack of neurotic tics, although he also recalled how peculiarly she had gazed upon his infant son when she babysat for him, as if the boy "were some strange creature, someone from another world."

But contemporaries who knew Sylvia more intimately recollect a more complex and credible personality, a driven girl obviously torn between a constant need for public admiration and a less acceptable compulsion to leave her mark upon the world at any cost, an occasionally neurotic, usually affected young lady with an enormous ego and an imagination to match. The most sympathetic of her friends, Marcia Brown, whom

Sylvia had adopted as a positive double or "alter ego" from the very beginning, felt that Sylvia rarely "acted" in her company, but she did relate two incidents in which her friend's remarkable control faltered. The first involved Sylvia's initial trip to New York City in 1952, when the vast city caused her to lapse into gushing public relations. The second, far more serious episode came about during Marcia's wedding, when Sylvia wept, drank too much, and played pathetic seducer to the males in attendance, though she survived the actual ceremony with aplomb.

It was apparently in her relationships with men that Sylvia's façade was put to its severest tests. The former boyfriends and lovers whom I interviewed seemed fairly unanimous in their descriptions of Sylvia's dramatic manic-depressive shifts, appreciating her wit and beauty while ever aware that she was using them, as they were undoubtedly using her. To them, she was exciting, she was literate, she was a genuine "golden girl," but one who required delicate handling. As for sex, it appeared to swell behind the mask like a pulsing volcano, but did not emerge fully until after the suicide attempt in the summer of 1953 and Sylvia's five-month treatment at McLean's, the latter paid for by Mrs. Prouty.[10] Davison believed, however, that much of her newfound freedom in the sexual arena, which had been encouraged by her psychiatrist, did not accurately reflect her own desires, and was but another aspect of a mask's performance. I tend to agree, especially in light of Sylvia's father obsession and pervasive narcissism.

Whatever their import for personal growth, the brilliant career at Smith, the suicide attempt, the incarceration in a mental home, where electric shock treatments left a permanent scar on her psyche, and the triumphant return to Smith comprised years of plodding apprenticeship as far as Sylvia's poetry was concerned. Reading and rereading the reams of verse turned out during this period—"turned out" is an apt adjective for the relentless, masonlike approach to aesthetic questions evident before 1959—I could discern the foundation of the Gothic vision that would frame her later work, a vision welded together from intense reactions to Poe, Freud, and Nietzsche, among others, and an agnostic conviction that the universe was essentially all malevolent process. Her imagination was dominated by a Darwinian hellscape, which presented an odd contrast to the sunny popular platitudes and middle-class conformity that governed her daily life.

Although all the Smith poems reflected a technical allegiance to W. H. Auden, Wallace Stevens, and Dylan Thomas, a preference for linguistic and metaphorical complexity (which impressed academic judges), none of them expressed sufficient emotional power to make them worth saving in their own right.[11] But they served their crucial function as exercises, permitting Sylvia to explore the luxurious literary tradition inherited from a long line of British and American ancestors. Poems such as "Two Lovers and a Beachcomber by the Real Sea," "Doomsday," "To Eva Descending the Stair," and "Lament" did move form closer to content, while other poems, e.g., "Second Winter," "Ice Age," and "Winter Words," emphasized a persistent fondness for winter images, icons of an arid stasis, intimating where the wellsprings of her art were buried.

After winning her Fulbright scholarship and departing for Cambridge by ship, Sylvia began a much more serious apprenticeship over the next two years, eventually utilizing the greater emotional and thematic freedom urged on her by Ted Hughes (whom she would marry in June, 1956) to create the first of her genuine poetic achievements, poems on the order of "All the Dead Dears" and "Black Rook in Rainy Weather." And this would be accomplished while Sylvia searched with desperate dread for the perfect mate, determined to wed a man in the image of her dead father, whom she could both love and intellectually stand in awe of, a fellow artist whose talent had to match, if not surpass, her own. This much I gleaned from what Cambridge letters were available and from the comments of Marcia Brown and Jane Kopp, a classmate of Sylvia's at Cambridge.

For my first research trip to England, I had arranged to interview Miss K. T. Burton, Sylvia's Cambridge supervisor, and Mrs. May Targett, another classmate who had also known her at Smith. I also had been in contact with George MacBeth, the Scottish poet who had produced many of the programs Sylvia and her husband had appeared on for the BBC. To facilitate matters, I had written to Olwyn Hughes as well, Ted's sister, who was managing the Plath Estate on her brother's behalf. Many of the people interviewed in America, along with a number of British poets to whom I had written, had warned me against Olwyn, claiming she was a tough, penny-pinching business woman and obsessively devoted sister who was determined to rewrite literary history by wielding her power over the Estate to censor any material which might place the Hugheses in a bad light. In fact, several well-known

English authors had reluctantly refused to see me on the ground that they could not reveal the truth of Sylvia's last years and still maintain social and/or business ties with Ted and Olwyn Hughes.

I tried to keep an open mind, however, having grown almost immune to the herd of sensational rumors that were released by the mere mention of Plath's name. Most of these stories struck me as absurd in the extreme, but I did take the simple precaution, which I have never regretted, of not quoting from available Plath letters, restricting myself to published material and personal interviews. I reasoned that Olwyn could thus be circumvented, since quoting from printed sources would entail, at most, the payment of a few permission fees.

Even this precaution seemed unnecessary, as Olwyn's prompt reply could not have been kinder or more generous. Though she regretted that a previous contract with Lois Ames prevented her from aiding me with biographical details, she did promise to provide whatever help she could concerning Sylvia's work and unpublished manuscripts. She also invited me to visit her apartment office after my arrival in London— her letter identified her as a "Literary Agent." I was both relieved and cheered by this refutation of those nagging rumors, one of which had come from a respectable book dealer, who insisted that Olwyn was "an animal to deal with" in business matters.[12]

It was spring 1973 when I finally reached London and began researching Sylvia's English sojourn in earnest. One project was to locate and photograph the two townhouse flats in the Primrose section of town where Sylvia had once lived (and died). They belonged to a series of well-maintained buildings located not far from the London Zoo in neighborhoods that can only be depicted as quaint, pretty, and comfortably middle class. It was easy to imagine Sylvia walking these streets, first as a young wife and mother pushing a pram toward the zoo or strolling hand-in-hand with her tall, handsome husband, then as a lonely winter figure hunched against a suddenly harsh wind. Here she had returned with two young children to confront separation from her idolized husband, growing melancholia, and one of the worst winters in London history. Here she had finally surrendered to a womblike oven, but only after a heroic struggle to establish herself as the first major woman poet in American literature.[13]

I felt myself drifting nearer and nearer to the elaborate complex of selves, the fierce mixture of life and art, that had been Sylvia Plath.

This feeling was intensified over the next two weeks as I interviewed people who had known her at Cambridge and read her own words in the scripts preserved at the BBC Library. May Targett had much to tell about the famous British university, what it meant to be an American female student there during the 1950s. She had inherited Sylvia's room at Whitstead—one of Newnham's newer dormitories—when the poet left to join her new husband, whom she had wed without Cambridge's official permission. She also expressed her distaste for Ted Hughes, emphasizing that Ted had needed Sylvia much more than he had ever realized or admitted, needed her practicality, tireless energy, and literary knowledge. Mrs. Targett's comments were amplified by a subsequent session with Miss Burton, who had been struck by the apparent incompatibility of Ted and Sylvia, at least on the surface; his rough provinciality presenting a stark contrast to what she claimed was Sylvia's superior social sophistication, although she conceded that she had no idea how large poetry loomed in Sylvia's mind and life. Like other of Plath's teachers at Cambridge, i.e., Dorothea Krook and Valerie Pitt, Miss Burton had sensed no deeper, darker undercurrents, remembered clearly thinking that Sylvia needed little help from her or anyone else, being so remorselessly the stereotyped, cheerful, efficient, all-American coed.

My meeting with George MacBeth was less successful, though stimulating in its own way. After a long period of reflection, he had concluded that he would prefer not to talk about Sylvia again, having already granted Lois Ames an extensive interview, which she had taped. He did not wish to recover familiar territory, wanted to avoid the possible confusion engendered by two separate statements on the same subject. There was a certain hesitancy about his attitude that put me a bit on guard, recalling the odd refusal of other literary figures in London to get involved, but we spent a pleasant hour together, discussing contemporary poetry, the horrible situation in Northern Ireland, and the profound differences between English and American sensibilities. I departed with the impression that Mr. MacBeth might be more open in the future. Both of us, of course, assumed that Ames's overdue opus was on the horizon.

As for Olwyn's invitation, our meeting never did materialize. I had telephoned soon after arrival, and she graciously asked me over for tea one afternoon two days later. I showed up on time, knocked on the door, waited for a good half hour, then caught a cab back to the hotel. When I contacted her next morning, she was profuse with her apologies, and immediately arranged another appointment. Again, I appeared promptly, beating on the same battered door, cooled my heels for almost an hour, and departed in a rage. This time I did not call her, determined to pursue the search for Sylvia without outside (inside?) assistance, as originally planned. But Olwyn sent around a note of sincere regret, claiming the recent loss of a secretary was responsible for her seeming impoliteness and enclosing a tattered, typewritten copy of "Snow Blitz" as a peace offering—Sylvia's lightly fictionalized sketch about her harrowing experiences during the 1963 snowstorm, which she had hoped to sell to a popular magazine.

Facts, poems, impressions, recollections, Sylvia's own letters, all continued to provide important background terrain for the human being who had begun, at last, to acquire more than one dimension. The Sylvia Plath who gushed and pedaled her way through Cambridge on a bicycle imported from Smith, embarrassing her fellow American students with her gauche extravagances and easy candor about sexual matters, was not far removed from the Sylvia Plath who wrote poems each morning with the dogged persistence of a drone and had enough literary sophistication to realize that the sparsely published, rough and tumble Britisher named Ted Hughes was destined to emerge as England's foremost poet. Her selves were distinct, equally real, but they did emanate from the same narcissistic basement where the bitch goddess remained in chains.

That was the crux of it, I thought, Sylvia's potent, limitless narcissism, that and her acute literary intelligence. They provided the dynamic binding of life to art, fusing them, ultimately, into a unique voice and poetic vision. As Norman Mailer has written on Henry Miller: "One can detest oneself intimately and still be a narcissist. What characterizes narcissism is the fundamental relation. It is with oneself. The same dialectic of love and hate that mates feel for one another is experienced within the self. But then a special kind of insanity calls to the narcissist. The inner dialogue hardly ever ceases. The two halves of themselves exist like separate animals forever scrutinizing each other." [14]

While at Cambridge, Sylvia had written two of her finest poems. Both "Black Rook in Rainy Weather" and "All the Dead Dears" demonstrated an inclination toward taut leanness that boded well for any future aesthetic. More pertinent, they let the tormented inner self speak, for a space, in her own lizard tongue, not so much to rage against a universe without pity or hope as to define the antagonistic extremes of her own split existence: the vulnerable daughter doomed to repetitions and making *memento mori* mudpies poised against the nascent artist awaiting "rare and random descents" of transcendent significance and beauty. Interestingly, after her marriage to Ted, amid the clutter of coy bridal bouquets like "Snowman on the Moor" and "Wreath for a Bridal," she also began slowly to shape a satanic myth to replace the lost Christian totem of Lucifer, perhaps influenced by her husband's own myth-making tendencies.

In "Hardcastle Crags," the female persona had (by poem's end) transformed simple flight into a courageous first step, refusing to be ground down to a skull by the mindless processes of an annihilating cosmos. Not long after, stepping off the literal platform of a visit with Ted to a country fair in Yorkshire, she had used "Sow" to suggest a mythical equivalent for *angst*, an analogue for modern evil, though not without recourse to a Biblical past. Later, the whole fascinating business would be worked out through "Bull of the Bendylaw" and "Night Shift," among others, including "Electra on the Azalea Path," until the complete Oedipal myth of the father was articulated and found wanting, until "The Colossus" himself lay in silent ruins, while his abandoned daughter hid, cupped like a fetus, inside his huge dead ear.

The structure was cogent and insistent, the linear development, the steady march toward an obsessive core, the deliberate use of myth-making to explore an inner imago and chart the failures of modern civilization, but its human cast demanded further trips to England. Biographically, the pattern continued its ordinary "hill and dale" approach. After a brave decision to abandon Smith and a lifelong teaching ambition—she had taught there for a year upon leaving Cambridge—Sylvia headed for Boston with Ted, where they soon secured a small flat on Beacon Hill, struggling over the next year to master their poetry and their bills. Ted became involved with Stanley Kunitz and other local poets, and both of them played host to a variety of Sylvia's old friends. Marcia Brown (now Marcia Plumer), who had recently given birth to twins, lived not far away, and Sylvia often showed up to help with the babies; as usual, her external reaction to infants was positive in the extreme, and she was upset that she herself had not yet conceived.

But for Sylvia the central event of the stay in Boston had to be her decision to audit Robert Lowell's course in poetry-writing at Boston University with Anne Sexton and George Starbuck. It was 1959, another watershed year for modern American poetry, a year in which Lowell, Sexton, Snodgrass (a former pupil of Lowell's), and Ginsberg utilized very private, often humiliating aspects of their own lives to illuminate and revitalize the romantic projections of self initiated by Wordsworth generations earlier. Called "confessionalism" by admirers and detractors alike, this new mode was indeed Catholic in its fundamental commitment to the concept of salvation through agonized purgations of a naked ego, although its fictions of self were certainly more important than its apparent concern for clinical revelations. With the exception of Ginsberg, whose obsessive *Kaddish* relied upon a collage effect for narrative unity, all the so-called confessional poets remained quite traditional in their approach to problems of craft, the "excesses" of content rarely violating well-learned lessons of technical restraint.

Poetically, Sylvia's exposure to Sexton's and Lowell's greater psychic honesty was decisive in demonstrating the need for her own verses to break through their disguises, their remoteness, their ironic Audenesque rationalities. Besides promoting the advantages of a conversational voice, they also left little doubt that true emotional intensity, which her poems largely lacked, would emerge only when she plunged into the cauldron of childhood. Obsession still beckoned to her, the compulsion to deal with her father and her ambivalent relation to his ghost, but now she could contemplate a different, more efficient way of handling it, could meld method with madness in such a fashion as to transform poetry, hitherto a chore, into a joyous, "absolutely fulfilling" experience.[15]

This change did not come about immediately, but the seeds were planted by Lowell and Sexton, and their harvest lacked only the completion of the last steps in her dual aesthetic task of (1) providing a poetic analogue for modern evil, and (2) erecting a myth upon the grave-altar of her father, *the* father. The climax arrived, appropriately, near the end of 1959, in an autumnal setting amid decaying relics from a lusher era. Summer had been spent on a camping tour across America, during which time she had become pregnant at last, due, apparently, to an earlier consultation with a Boston doctor. Upon their return in September, Sylvia and Ted entered Yaddo, the New York estate given over to artists, for a welcomed two-month stay, a pleasant hiatus before their permanent return to England. It was at Yaddo that Sylvia brilliantly brought the first phase of her artistic development to a close.

While there, Ted had suggested she reread Theodore Roethke's poetry with care, which she did, particularly the "greenhouse poems," and husband and wife shared deep psychic experiences, chants, meditations, invocations. The ultimate result was "Poem for a Birthday," the dazzling, if uneven, autobiographical sequence about the creation of the bitch goddess, her artist persona and secret self. Before that, "The Colossus" had imaginatively carried both aims into a bleak fruition: the analogue for modern evil envisioned as the ruined colossus of her dead father; the inherited myths, classical and Freudian, mummified inside a stillborn Titan, incapable of further art. Now myth-making could encompass a direct Nietzschean drive for control, the erection of a deity of *self*, not father, a female self with a very masculine will to power. In "Poem for a Birthday," the father figure is contemptuously dismissed more than once, tossed into a dustbin, puppet-master turned puppet.

When the young couple left for England in December, Sylvia was on the verge of a major expression. England was to be the cradle for her new art. It was time for my own follow-up voyage of discovery. During this second excursion, I took the train to Cambridge and shared vicariously in the thrill Sylvia herself must have felt when following the same route. I retraced her steps around Newnham College and the town of Cambridge, finding the archeological museum and the grisly tableau that had inspired "All the Dead Dears." I also visited the Cambridge library, which had since been redesigned inside to resemble Alcatraz, and read what materials were available, including Sylvia's vapid contributions to *Varsity*, the school newspaper.

A much more significant journey was the subsequent bus ride to Aldermaston, where I interviewed the poet Paul Roche and his wife Clarissa, who had known Sylvia well at Smith (1957-1958) and later in England. They gave me further insights into the young woman who had undergone a subtle but far-reaching metamorphosis upon returning to her husband's country in the winter of 1959. Clarissa remembered and understood the extreme oscillations in behavior, the endless play-acting and the genuine anguish behind its brittle manifestations, while her husband talked about Sylvia's relative philosophical innocence, her beauty, her sensitivity, the distaste they had shared at Smith for tedious departmental meetings. Clarissa also recalled her friend's great obsession with her children's safety during the last year of her life, her nervous intentness and constant complaints about the lack of writing time, her bitterness against Ted after the break-up (and against the entire Hughes clan), her determination to produce great poems and a brood of children.

The testimony of the Roches, which struck me as balanced and perceptive, tended to support the general portrait of Sylvia already etched in my mind, despite many bare spots and a few opaque corners. I returned to London in a confident mood, certain I was on the right track but needing more solid information about that last year. There was still too much room for mere speculation, contradictory interpretations. Thus, I was glad to reach Olwyn's flat and finally find her at home. She ushered me into the living room with casual warmth, apologizing again for our last misadventure, but I have to admit that I was uncomfortable. The large room was incredibly messy, streaked by grime and an oppressive sense of neglect, the sofa and its ill-matching chair bulging with lopsided weariness, ripped and threadbare in places, smeared by years of hard use to a sort of subway grayness that depressed my middle-class veneer.

And yet, the entire Dickens-like scene had the opposite effect as well, relieving any fears entertained about a closet mind. Its bohemian openness promised a reasonable attitude toward matters of literary taste and biographical candor—an effect that was enhanced by the reassuring clutter of books, magazines, and records, not to mention an armada of unwashed cups and glasses. The meeting itself, despite frequent interruptions for phone calls and a visit from some fawning record-company salesman, went very well. We shared intimacies. Olwyn was quite candid about Sylvia's "nastiness," the difficulties Ted had encountered trying to live with her, and let me meander on about my researches. She mentioned an earnest attempt on her part to sell Sylvia's manuscripts and annotated books to an American university, where all scholars might benefit from them.

It was near the end of our discussion that she alluded to the Alvarez affair. "If only he had shown the article to us first, none of it would have happened," [16] she claimed more than once. I caught the hint but continued to wear the guise of naïve professor (without portfolio). We talked about poetry in general, both of us having just finished

Larkin's *High Windows* and Merwin's selective translations of Osip Mandalstam's verses, and I felt my spirits soaring. Surely such a literate, cosmopolitan woman would have no serious objections to an honest treatment of Sylvia's last years. We parted amicably with promises to keep in touch, and, shortly prior to my actual departure, she had let me read three of Sylvia's unpublished short stories, none of which deserved public print, as it turned out.

Olwyn still could not give me any biographical assistance, although she had touched upon a few minor items that helped put Sylvia's work habits into better perspective. As a result, even as I returned to America, I knew that another trip to England was essential. Fortunately, I had been able to make contact with Elizabeth Sigmund in Devon, who had been acquainted with Sylvia during the last year and was willing to talk. Furthermore, after several letters, I had finally convinced George MacBeth that he should share his recollections of Sylvia with me, stressing the woefully incomplete nature of Lois Ames's planned biography—Olwyn herself had told me, with a hint of exasperation, that the official biographer remained far behind schedule.

Sigmund appeared to hold the key. I needed Devon, needed to see and feel the Devon Sylvia had experienced, and needed to pick the brain of someone who had known her there, especially someone not influenced by the Hughes family. In one of her letters, Elizabeth had mentioned a recent visit to Ted at his home—he and his new wife, a nurse, continued to live in the house once shared with Sylvia—in which he had intimated that she would never be able to tell what she knew, not until she was at death's door. It sounded like a threat, at least as recounted by Elizabeth, and promised another slant. Perhaps the mystery was about to be solved, the mystery that no British writer had been willing to discuss.

Clarissa Roche had been frank about Sylvia's marriage and the reasons for its failure, emphasizing the inevitable misunderstandings on both sides of the British-American ledger and interjecting her own view that professional jealousy, Ted's jealousy of his wife's growing literary powers, might have played a significant role in the estrangement, which he had precipitated by having an affair. But supportive details were notable by their absence. Sylvia's poetry alone, however literal its original locus, could not provide enough answers.

Again, surface events were readily available for inspection, and the close interaction between life and art knitted its own design, but the tapestry broke, became entangled with other designs after the move to Devon in September, 1961. Before that, upon returning to England, Sylvia and Ted had found a tiny but cozy flat on Chalcot Square, and Sylvia gave birth to Frieda Rebecca Hughes at home on April 1, 1960, an easy birth despite the lack of hospital accommodations. All seemed to go well. The married pair were publishing more and more of their work, though Ted maintained his superior reputation, and Sylvia had the pleasure of seeing *The Colossus* in print by November of 1960. As poems such as "Tulips" and "In Plaster" would soon indicate, Sylvia's new voice was still struggling but had acquired a greater willingness to articulate her negative vision of the universe, one in which a no-longer-passive female speaker pounced almost joyfully upon vicious insights.

Disaster came early in 1961. In February, Sylvia was rushed to the hospital, where she lost her second child in a miscarriage. There had been no warning, no apparent cause. Fate had never seemed so capricious, and, six weeks later, its capriciousness assumed larger proportions after another mad dash to the hospital, this time to have an inflamed appendix removed. A room had been arranged for the new infant, baby clothes bought. Announcements had been sent out to friends and relatives. It is no wonder that deep doubts arose in Sylvia about her own ability to bear and sustain life, that the bleak landscapes of her earlier poetry returned to haunt her again with their winter sense of implacable doom. As a number of poems collected in *Crossing the Water* make clear, her awareness of a cosmic menace at work, the threat of extinction hanging over and deforming every human act of will, returned to images of a vulnerable female lost among the stone tokens of hostile nature.

But youth itself was a temporary savior, as were the routines of a shared future with her child and husband. What was required was a permanent home, a genuine house like her grandmother's sturdy dwelling in Winthrop, preferably in the country (Ted was fretting to escape the urban prison of London), where roots might be planted and cultivated, where a sense of place and history might confound the demons of Sylvia's Gothic imagination. Yorkshire was out, since she could not abide Ted's relatives and desired a warmer climate. When the opportunity came to buy a Devon cottage—more manor than cottage, containing, as it did, over two acres of rich land in the center of a small village—Sylvia and Ted jumped at the chance, borrowing from their mothers to help meet the costs involved.

It was September 1, 1961, when the Hugheses moved into Court Green, and Sylvia's again being pregnant at the time made the move appear only that much more sensible. Over the next year, Sylvia would have a second child, a boy named Nicholas, would lose her husband to another woman, and would write many of the poems that have established her as a major poet. Her own letters from the period, Alvarez's memoir, the testimony of Paul and Clarissa Roche, and the poems themselves had given me a rough outline of that year, but the forthcoming interviews with George MacBeth and Elizabeth Sigmund promised a more certain chronology, a sharper focus.

I returned to England in the summer of 1974 and, as before, paid a call on Olwyn Hughes at her request. She received me with the easy grace of an old friend, and we were soon chatting comfortably about the state of Plath scholarship. I felt compelled to bring up the matter (and manner) of publishing Sylvia's work, alluding to the outcries then being raised because the poetry was appearing in slender volumes, one after another, as if the poet were still alive, rather than in a single collected edition. At first, Olwyn seemed insulted by the implication of commercial opportunism, pointing out that she and Ted only managed the Estate on behalf of the children, that all profits would eventually accrue to Frieda and Nicholas. She asked if I was parroting the drivel spouted by Eric Homberger, whom she castigated as "a little twit." When I said no and defended Professor Homberger as a highly respected scholar, she changed her tune and reassured me that a collected edition was definitely in the works and should appear within a year, along with a selected edition of the short stories.

When I then mentioned casually that I would be heading for Devon in the morning to interview Elizabeth Sigmund, there was a flutter of protest. After suggesting a hotel in Exeter, she went on to warn me against accepting anything Elizabeth said at face value, stressing that Elizabeth was a genuinely warm woman who was, alas, apt to say anything to gain attention, a woman of great imagination and emotional kindness who found it difficult always keeping fact and fantasy separated. I thanked Olwyn for her advice and prepared to leave, but she was not quite finished. She suddenly insisted that I should also talk to David Compton, Elizabeth's husband during the time she had known

Sylvia, in order to get a saner, less hysterical view of the events Elizabeth was bound to distort.

I agreed and Olwyn immediately made a phone call. In a few minutes she was talking with David and arranging for me to interview him at his London home the day after my return from Devon. Upon hanging up, Olwyn said, "You realize, of course, that I am violating my contract with Lois by helping you in this fashion, but it is important that you get a balanced picture of what went on in Devon." I nodded and smiled, thanking her again for her efforts, and made my escape. Though truly grateful, I was unsure about her real motives at this juncture.

The train ride the next morning was pleasant, but upon arriving in Exeter I discovered that reaching North Tawton, the small town where Sylvia had lived, would involve taking a bus that ran only a few times each day—the original rail link used by Sylvia and Ted had since been discontinued. I spent the rest of the afternoon and evening exploring the beautiful cathedral town, which, like most of England, was undergoing grotesque processes of modernization, and caught the bus to North Tawton early the following morning. The half-hour journey was enjoyable and revealing as the gleaming new bus navigated serpentine country lanes with careless skill, passing a number of quaint villages and field after sun-splashed field of lush farmland. I could understand Sylvia's having been drawn to this rural serenity, appreciating the ways her New England mind must have reveled in the familiar touchstones of an ancient ancestry, sudden groves, neat furrows, Tudor houses, narrow cobbled streets, old stone churches.

North Tawton itself was a delightful surprise, nothing at all like the gray nonentity described in Alvarez's memoir. The shops and town hall were sufficiently antique, at least on the surface, and the church, though thickish and unadorned, imposed a gloomy medieval grandeur that held everything together. I called upon the only taxi driver in town, a congenial old chap who supplied relevant historical data during the trip to the primitive farmhouse where Elizabeth Sigmund lived with her husband and two children. He dropped me off, gave the children candy, and promised to pick me up in time to catch the last bus.

Elizabeth was an attractive, middle-aged woman whose full figure, soft features, and friendly directness accented a maternal sensuality that was near impossible to resist. I saw why Sylvia had been drawn to her.

Her husband, a younger man of easy charm, soon left to earn a few pounds cutting grass, and the children departed for school. In the large country kitchen, Elizabeth made us mugs of coffee and then slowly unwound the threads of Sylvia's life in Devon. As she talked, her eyes often misted over with tears, and I realized that Olwyn's warning had been partially on the mark. There was a distorting sentimentality at work here, but it never dealt in pure fantasy, only in a certain melodramatic intensification of events. Elizabeth had not seen, or perhaps had not wanted to see, the repressed Sylvia Plath, the Sylvia Plath who spent much of her life giving a performance, although she had comprehended her friend's drive to mythify experience, to "celebrate" the rustic dream world she had tried to maintain for herself and her family.

According to Elizabeth, Sylvia and Ted had been a perfect pair, their marriage a close, unique conjunction of vital life forces, which supported Alvarez's account, and the destruction of that marriage had been cataclysmic for Sylvia, because she had invested so much in its survival, had "given her whole heart away" in such a manner as to leave her virtually defenseless. Elizabeth also sensed the terrible weight of this on Ted, how smothered he must have felt under this kind of blanket devotion. She believed that his affair with Assia G. had been involuntary, reluctant. To Elizabeth, Assia was the villainess from beginning to end, having seduced Ted in his own home on a social visit, under Sylvia's nose. I was skeptical. Surely, Sylvia must have sensed the implications behind Assia's blatant flirting?

But Elizabeth insisted not, stressing Sylvia's total faith in Ted and her belief that mere sex, vulgar sex, could never pry him away from her. For the better part of the day, Elizabeth continued her story, also letting me read two letters Sylvia had written to her from London shortly before her death, and the picture that emerged—once edited of obvious exaggerations and a romantic inclination toward moral caricatures—fit the poetry and stitched together many biographical loose ends. I understood why Olwyn had been upset by my proposed visit, since she herself played a major, but negative, role in Elizabeth's recollections. Like others, Elizabeth noted the extreme closeness that had always existed between Ted and Olwyn, and remembered Sylvia feeling left out in the actual presence of the brother-sister union, an observation reinforced by Clarissa Roche's comments about Sylvia's bitter attacks upon Ted and Olwyn after the break-up. She described a dramatic Christmas scene in Yorkshire, where Sylvia and Olwyn had engaged in such a fierce struggle that Sylvia had eventually fled the house, remaining on the moors for hours before Ted finally drove out to fetch her.

The incident struck me as paramount because it, along with Sylvia's painful reaction to her miscarriage and her innate conviction of doom, helped define the arid terrain of the transitional poems in *Crossing the Water*. It also amplified the basic lack of empathy that had developed between Ted and Sylvia, which Elizabeth traced back to the Hugheses' working-class background and Sylvia's American naïveté regarding English folkways, another observation supported by Clarissa's testimony. My central concern remained anchored to the interior wedding of life and art, the fulcrum of self versus self or selves. I had already decided to leave out many biographical items, however sensational, that did not contribute to a further illumination of the literature, but this particular scene and reality was too relevant to ignore.

Two days later I was sitting in David Compton's parlor listening to his side of the story. Recalling Olwyn's eagerness for me to see him, I was not too sanguine about his candor. David, however, was far from being anyone's stooge and related what he knew of Sylvia's last year or so with refreshing frankness. His keen writer's eye made him a perfect source, and his entire account paralleled Elizabeth's almost point for point, including her negative profiles of Olwyn and Assia. More important, he also remembered Sylvia's mother and the odd reaction Sylvia evinced toward her personally and her endless stream of letters.

According to David, Sylvia had been embarrassed by Aurelia, by her heavy Germanic sentimentality and utter dependence upon bourgeois platitudes. He also, like Peter Davison and others, sensed that Sylvia inevitably gave a "performance" for her mother, could never communicate with her about any of the things that really mattered to her. Further, David's narrative elaborated upon many details Elizabeth had merely mentioned. For instance, he went into Sylvia's growing allegiance to the arcane, to black magic—Elizabeth had told me about her letters to a Jesuit group in Cambridge, seeking belief—and spoke about the morbid streak in her personality that had led her to pin up old clippings from American newspapers and magazines over her desk, clippings which dealt with bizarre murders and other extremes of behavior.

I left Compton's home convinced that the configuration had reached the edges of aesthetic completeness, that most of the bare spots were now sketched over, although those opaque corners remained, and always would. Sylvia had been too complex a person to be captured in any ultimate way, but I did believe that the general structure of her life had assumed a proper, dynamic relation to the art, that the drive toward greatness had a governing logic behind its rocket trajectory.

My meeting with George MacBeth later that same day was similarly informative, although he would not permit me to tape our conversation. He spoke easily about his first contact with Sylvia, whom he had been interviewing for possible reading spots on radio, and recalled being put off by her transparent attempts to impress him through lush praise of his own poetry and by the affected, "gushing" manner of her attitude in general. Out of nervousness, she had apparently reverted to the worst features of her Smith mask.

He had hired her anyway, sensing her genuine distinction as a poet. One of her remarks that day made a deep impression: while discussing his poetry, she had noted, "I see you have a concentration camp in your mind too." He and Sylvia never became close friends, but she did work for and with him several more times over the next year or so. MacBeth had spoken to her only a week before her suicide, finding her cheerful and relaxed, though she had commented with sardonic humor that she was now writing poems "as long and as lean as myself."

After leaving MacBeth, I wandered across town to St. James Park, immersed in that curious blend of relief, satisfaction, and nagging depression that seems inevitably to haunt the last stages of any literary project. Sitting on a bench and contemplating the squadrons of ducks and geese lumbering across the grass, my mind's eye sought out its own nourishment, swirled around lines of lightning from *Ariel*. Gothic morbidities, shrill rage, violent images, cool detachment, acid witticisms, childish stubbornness, the deity-control of genius, they all danced like shadows around the figure of a tall, slender, defiant woman striding angrily across the blasted moors of *Wuthering Heights*. I knew what had to be known and tried to intuit the rest, my personal egotism and literary absorptions responding readily to those same qualities as they had sculpted the features of one Sylvia Plath. At times, the portrait was still far too romantic and vague, more art than biography, but that also suited the pattern of a career founded upon masks, nurtured in myth-making, hammered true by the adolescent vortex where artifice has its forge.

The last year of Sylvia's life had seen the culmination of a Keatsian drive to become a major lyric poet, the incredible production of a whole string of poems—i.e., "Purdah," "Fever 101°," "Mary's Song," "Lady Lazarus," "Berck-Plage," "Death & Co.," "Ariel," "The Moon and the Yew Tree," "Edge," "Mystic," "Thalidomide," "Winter Trees," and most of the bee sequence—that deserve the title "masterpieces," because their multichambered hearts never stop pumping the "blood jet of poetry," never settle for less than a total corpus of experience. Echoes emanate from them, references to other realities, learned and felt, but confessional and surreal trappings, the demands of technique, enhance their intense air of traditional lyricism. For years to come, eager young critics will mine these (and lesser works) for lodes of secondary significances, and their labors will not be in vain: as "Cut" amusingly demonstrates, Sylvia's cool wit permitted her to retain absolute control over her creations, their forms and content, which she never hesitated to mock.

The most moving aspect of that year's steady outpouring of superb lyrics was the occasional alternate current that appeared, particularly in the poems written about the children, the pulsating yearning for normalcy. Looking at the poems directed toward Nicholas, for example, one can discern a distinct progression from an almost inhuman artistic playfulness to genuine emotional involvement. In "Morning Song" the child's "bald cry" signifies its entrance to a museum, where its mother refuses her role: "I'm no more your mother / Than the cloud that distils a mirror to reflect its own slow / Effacement at the wind's hand." This encapsulates poetic truth at the level of Dante's Lucifer: precise but icy. And in "The Night Dances" the process remains remote, though the persona is aware of her child as something human trying to penetrate "the black amnesias of heaven." But in "Nick and the Candlestick" mother and child have finally achieved a human relationship. "Love, love, / I have hung our cave with roses," one that permits the realization that Sylvia's son was her last resort, her last religion: "You are the one / Solid and spaces lean on, envious. / You are the baby in the barn."

This is still myth-making, of course, in a different way, an extension of ego into a mirror-child, but love has softened the inevitable metaphors of menace. Salvation, a search for belief in a reality outside mere phenomena, has found a living icon, and the poem entitled "Child" becomes its summary statement. The opening three lines are perhaps among the most touching Sylvia ever wrote, articulating the desperate poet's maternal, heart-stricken yearning to be normal:

Your clear eye is the one absolutely beautiful thing.
I want to fill it with colors and ducks,
The zoo of the new

But it too trails off into a reflection of a much harsher reality, where the persona sees the truer self in her son's lucid eye, "this troublous / Wringing of hands, this dark / Ceiling without a star." Christ was never born.

Dream deteriorated into reality in Sylvia's last year, a dangerous situation at best, then assumed nightmare aspects, and the price seems high, very high indeed if we accept the absurd proposition that the nature of her art unleashed repressed material that her conscious self could not handle, a view proffered by two of modern poetry's finest critics, A. Alvarez and M. L. Rosenthal. Research into Sylvia's last year supported an opposite conclusion: poetry kept her alive and sane during a time when the forces of daily existence were threatening to overwhelm her frail defenses. After her split with Ted, after the ruin of her Eden in the summer of 1962, she fought back against the tide of depression with the only method she knew, the method of madness, not clinical madness, but the madness of poetry itself, inspiration mated to craft.

Depression might have thrust Sylvia out of bed each morning at 4 A.M. or so, but it was not depression that compelled her to take advantage of this quiet time to shape a new power myth, a female spasm of sperm glory: "dew that flies / Suicidal, at one with the drive / Into the red / Eye, the cauldron of morning." And if writing *The Bell Jar* did summon up disturbing memories from an earlier suicidal despair, they too were absorbed into method by the cunning madness of art as the novel moved from naturalism into tart satire, shifted ground from the narrow, romantic, partly fictionalized dilemmas of a schizophrenic college girl to the much larger arena of a *Candide*-like adventure where the American Dream could be confronted directly and its built-in flaws exposed, including, always, a pervasive sexism.

Facts again must prevail, however, feeding different myths perhaps, cult myths that tend to debase the more fruitful myths the poet herself had sown through literature. Trapped in Devon with two small children, abandoned by a man she had imagined a giant, Sylvia did more than complain about her plight, although self-pity was a constant companion. She perfected her art. She ran her large house and mothered her children. She began to plan a new life for herself and her family in London, where she thought the loneliness would be less intense, never realizing that loneliness was a disease of the spirit, art's permanent disability. But the fate that overtook her in a flat located a few blocks from Chalcot Square, her first London home, was human in nature, not aesthetic.

Aggravated by the city's worst winter in over a century, her growing depression was something she believed she could still handle, a familiar enough enemy to invite contempt. When she no longer felt this way near the end of January, 1963, she wisely consulted a doctor, who tried to find her a hospital bed but could not. As in 1953, schizophrenic melancholia was transferring her fierce rage against both the world and Ted dangerously inward, against herself, increasing her sense of worthlessness, causing panic. In the early morning hours of February 11, when poetry was beyond her, she knew it was time once again to gamble against the gods. She lost.

Sadness, isolation, family conflict, art in the face of enormous odds, a climactic metamorphosis, the story of Sylvia Plath had encompassed them all with dramatic thoroughness, despite the brevity of her life, and I returned to America more aware than ever of the fundamental paradox of biography: it does slay as it revives. I also knew that my biography would displease and possibly enrage many readers, especially those feminist extremists who had come to Plath's work as if to an altar, deifying her life and being beyond recognition. Understanding neither what fuels the machine of art nor the self-parody at work behind Sylvia's masks, they would undoubtedly resent the "negative" facets of Sylvia's obsessive drive for success, which I could hardly afford to ignore since it gave Freudian breath to the bitch goddess construct.

My vision of Sylvia Plath has not changed much since, although I do not pretend to have limned her in any definitive fashion. Her art remains on its own terms, and the woman who produced it will always waver between shadow and self, between reality and myth—the myth she herself delighted in creating.

2   Cottage Street, 1953

Richard Wilbur

Framed in her phoenix fire-screen, Edna Ward
Bends to the tray of Canton, pouring tea
For frightened Mrs. Plath; then, turning toward
The pale, slumped daughter, and my wife, and me,

Asks if we would prefer it weak or strong.
Will we have milk or lemon, she enquires?
The visit seems already strained and long.
Each in his turn, we tell her our desires.

It is my office to exemplify
The published poet in his happiness,
Thus cheering Sylvia, who has wished to die;
But half-ashamed, and impotent to bless,

I am a stupid life-guard who has found,
Swept to the shallows by the tide, a girl
Who, far from shore, has been immensely drowned,
And stares through water now with eyes of pearl.

How deep is her refusal; and how slight
The *genteel* chat whereby we recommend
Life, of a summer afternoon, despite
The brewing dusk which hints that it may end.

And Edna Ward shall die in fifteen years,
After her eight-and-eighty summers of

Such grace and courage as permit no tears,
The thin hand reaching out, the last word *love,*

Outliving Sylvia who, condemned to live,
Shall study for a decade, as she must,
To state at last her brilliant negative
In poems free and helpless and unjust.

3 Sylvia at Smith

GORDON LAMEYER

Graduating from Gamaliel Bradford High School in Wellesley in 1950, Sylvia Plath entered Smith College the following fall in the Class of 1954, an excited but anxious over-achiever, ready to take on the collegiate world. Sylvia loved Smith—the stimulating classes, the visiting lecturers, the challenge of academic excellence. However, because of her nervous breakdown, her suicide attempt, and her recovery in the summer and fall of 1953, Sylvia did not graduate with her class. After four months at McLean's Hospital in Waltham, Sylvia was allowed to return to Smith to repeat the second semester of her junior year. The authorities urged her to take a reduced schedule, a condition to which Sylvia could hardly hold. As most of her readers know, Sylvia graduated *summa cum laude* from Smith in 1955 and continued on to Cambridge University for her master's degree in English. Near the end of the fifties, she returned to Smith for a year to teach English while her husband, Ted Hughes, taught for a semester at the University of Massachusetts in Amherst.

I know nothing about Sylvia's early years at Smith or about her teaching year. Others have recalled that she was an intensely competitive student and an inspiring teacher. My close friendship with Sylvia began at the end of her first junior year, spanned the time she spent in the mental hospital, as depicted in her novel, *The Bell Jar,* and continued until near the end of her senior year. Sylvia called me "the major man in my life" between the person who was the original for Esther's boyfriend, "Buddy Willard," and Ted Hughes. For three years I corresponded with Sylvia, from 1953 to 1956. For one of those years I was in love with her, but, even after we had broken up, I briefly traveled with her in Europe on her spring vacation from Cambridge, just two months before she was married.

At Smith there were nearly sixty girls in Lawrence House who could probably give a more objective impression of Sylvia than I. Her roommate senior year, Nancy Hunter, has already written such a memoir, *A Closer Look at Ariel*, which retells incidents from their senior year and from the previous summer when they shared an apartment in Cambridge, Massachusetts, with two other Smith girls. My memories of her are necessarily more subjective. From me she tried to hide her fiercely competitive, academic nature. I do not recall that she ever told me that she made Junior Phi Bete. I did not at first see the side of her seen by most of her contemporaries—the no-nonsense scholar, the writing grind, the quick-to-get-angry moralist when others were breaking study-hour rules and making noise. I suspect that Sylvia did not mix with too many girls in her house except in compensatory spurts; she was too wrapped up in her own world. As if possessed by a demon, Sylvia drove herself to succeed academically. But then, feeling the violent need to experience life outside of books, even to live dangerously, she threw herself with a vengeance into dramatic experiences, such as vacation trips to New York City or her first airplane ride in a small biplane over Hamp.

From my mother I had learned of Sylvia a half year before I met her. My mother had heard Sylvia speak at a Smith Club meeting in Wellesley and thought I might enjoy meeting this attractive English major. At the time I was dating another Smith girl and hence did not follow up on the suggestion until later in the spring. Out of the blue in April I called Sylvia on the phone at Smith, made a date, and met her for a coke and a sandwich at Toto's, an intimate den of wooden cubicles, carved with student initials, across Garden Street from Lawrence House. Sylvia was overly apologetic because her left ankle was in a cast, due to her skiing accident two weeks earlier in the Adirondacks with "Buddy Willard." I didn't know what to make of her effusiveness, her abundant energy. She seemed to effloresce about everything, especially poetry. She loved Dylan Thomas then almost more than life itself. I was not immediately attracted to her, because I felt she came on too strong with her enthusiasms, as if a little too sophomoric and immature

Several weeks later I ran into Sylvia, still on crutches, coming back to Lawrence House from Sage Hall where W. H. Auden had been reading some of his light verse. Ecstatic, she told me that she had just heard that she had won the *Mademoiselle* contest and would be spending June in New York City, working on the magazine as guest editor. I was disappointed that I would not be able to see her until early July, following my graduation in June from Amherst College. As it turned out, we lived about a mile apart in Wellesley on streets just off Weston Road. I was entering the Naval Reserve O.C.S. program at Newport, Rhode Island, on July 13, and I had hoped to see a lot of her since I discovered that she was as fascinated as I with Joyce's *Ulysses*.

When Sylvia returned to Wellesley at the end of June, I did not see— even if I had been trained to recognize them—any of the signs of incipient schizophrenia, such as the insomnia found in the heroine of *The Bell Jar*, following her return to a Boston suburb. If, like Esther Greenwood, Sylvia could not sleep, I think it must have started after I left for O.C.S. For those two weeks in early July, I saw Sylvia every day. We took trips to the mountains and the ocean; we talked about Thomas's poetry and about *Finnegans Wake;* we listened to Beethoven and Brahms symphonies on my record changer. Since I was an English Honors student and had read some books she had not, Sylvia seemed to idealize me, to my embarrassment, at least in the two letters I received while first at O.C.S. I had no clue that she was unable to sleep, that she felt she was losing her mind. Hence, in mid-August, it was a staggering shock when my mother called to tell me of Sylvia's attempted suicide. I had come to think of Sylvia as my girl and wondered if I in any way were responsible for what happened.

During the next two and a half years, I received over fifty letters from Sylvia, some of them eight to ten pages long, most of them typed and single-spaced, a few written in her neat printed hand in black ink. I wrote to her all during her hospitalization to try to lift her spirits but did not hear from her until Christmas, except for two letters written from the Newton-Wellesley Hospital a week or so after the event.

When Sylvia returned to Smith in February of 1954, I was on a European cruise on my destroyer, having received an Ensign's commission in November. A week after she returned to Smith, Sylvia wrote me a letter, dramatizing her reentry into college life. Her brother, Warren, had driven her back to college in a whirling snowstorm. As they descended the steep hill by Paradise Pond, leading to Lawrence House, the car skidded sideways and turned 180°, barely missing a car parked in front of a greenhouse on one side and, on the other, the steep banking down toward Paradise Pond. Ever seeking a chance to dramatize her life, this escape for Sylvia had become just one of her several flirtations with death.

Tired of double-crostics and of the routine at McLean's, Sylvia was more than happy to throw herself whole-heartedly back into the academic regimen, which included Russian Literature, European Intellectual History of the Nineteenth Century, Medieval Art, and Early and Modern American Literature. In this last course she loved the insightful lectures of Robert Gorham Davis, under whom I later studied at Columbia Graduate School. Sylvia found too pleasurable to be called assignments the readings in *Crime and Punishment, The Scarlet Letter,* and *Sister Carrie.* In her art course she loved delving into the pagan origins of Christian iconography. She wrote of renting modern art masterpieces for her wall, sitting on the floor playing "reckless" bridge with friends, and lounging over coffee with friends to catch up on the events of the past semester.

Sylvia never missed an opportunity to meet and cultivate the writers on campus and the guest lecturers. She was an admirer of Elizabeth Drew, who often asked her to tea. In her letters to me from Smith, Sylvia tended to write in hyperbole, gushing on, for instance, about "the whole enormous and quite spectacular universe." Everything was upbeat. But Sylvia had not fully regained her stride. She had done no creative writing since the previous spring, which rather depressed her. She felt she had to lie fallow, like a barren field, for further growth.

In February Sylvia sent me a Valentine, telling of her evening at the Hampshire Bookshop, hearing the English novelist Esther Forbes lecture. Afterward Sylvia took the opportunity to chat with her. I was glad to hear that Sylvia was back in the swing of things, going to interesting places, seeing shows like the dance drama, *Green Mansions.* Most important for her, she was meeting other writers such as Mary Ellen Chase, who was then novelist-in-residence at Smith.

That spring of 1954 the course which meant the most to Sylvia was George Gibian's Russian Literature course, where Sylvia had her introduction to Tolstoy and Dostoevsky. The latter she finally decided to focus on when she came to write her English honors' thesis the following fall. (In *The Bell Jar* the part about Shem and Shaun in *Finnegans Wake,* the warring twins, came from our reading of Joyce's cryptic book the previous summer.) Following Gibian's course, Dostoevsky became Sylvia's obsession. She carried his volumes on weekends to Yale or with her to the beach in the summer. I believe that Sylvia learned more about herself from reading *The Brothers Karamazov* and *The Idiot,* not to mention *The Double,* than from any sessions with her psychiatrist, Ruth

Breuscher, whom Sylvia continued to see regularly at about bimonthly intervals through the following summer.

That spring Sylvia's letters to me were mostly filled with news of the literary stars she was hearing, such as I. A. Richards, but occasionally she gave me glimpses into her relationship with friends such as Nancy Hunter. On a jaunt down to Joe's, obstensibly to talk about their history assignment, Sylvia found Nancy both brilliant and eloquent. As they quaffed a bottle of red Chianti, they exchanged ideas, Sylvia told me, in every area "from sex to salvation." An Apollonian at heart but a Dionysian or a Bacchanalian occasionally, Sylvia wrote puckishly of later enshrining and encircling my navy photograph on her bureau with two "pagan" wickered wine bottles made of "voluptuous" green glass.

By the middle of the semester Sylvia had already decided to write her thesis the following year on Dostoevsky, either on the idea of the Christ and the Anti-Christ or on the recurrence of the split personality. She wrote that she really loved her thesis advisor, George Gibian ("an exquisite young Czech"), whose penetrating, vital, and stimulating mind she felt would be a good counter to her own euphoric outbursts of metaphysical prose. By this time she had also talked Alfred Fisher, the Shakespearean and contemporary poetry man, into giving her a special course in writing poetry the following year during the spring term.

Near the end of this repeated semester, while Gibian had Sylvia reading *War and Peace* and *Anna Karenina*, Newton Arvin, who shared the American Literature course with R. G. Davis, had Sylvia reading Henry James for the first time: *The American, Portrait of a Lady*, and *The Ambassadors*. At the end of the semester Sylvia was reading on her own Christopher Frye's *The Lady's Not for Burning* while reveling in Sherwood Anderson's *Winesburg, Ohio*. While some girls were sunbathing on the roofs and decks of houses during spring semester, Sylvia indulged the libidinous side of her nature, bathing in the sunlight of her reading, underlining her books in black ink, and turning down the corners of pages "as is her bad bad habit."

During her exams Sylvia wrote that she enjoyed a comprehensive question on egoism, given her by Newton Arvin, but mainly she felt the strong need stoically to plunge back into her readings in Intellectual History: Nietzsche, Marx, and Hegel. She was simultaneously writing a paper on Fromm's *Escape from Freedom* while preparing for her Tolstoy-Dostoevsky exam. Although I did not see it at the time, escape from egoism was, I believe, Sylvia's major problem. In retrospect, it is interesting to note that critics have pointed out Sylvia's inability to create characters unlike herself, that the real subject of all her writing was the feelings of a speaker or persona very much like herself.

Because our relationship had become strained after ten months of not seeing each other, our letters toward the end tended to be rather literary, exercises in description or narrative accounts of shore leave in Europe or of vacations in New York. I tried to give Sylvia a vicarious account of my foreign adventures, while she gave me watercolor sketches of her life at Smith. While she was at McLean's, I thought my kind of therapy would help to speed her back to the world we both loved. After two letters from the Newton-Wellesley Hospital a week following the suicide attempt, I did not hear from Sylvia until Christmas. Now, back at Smith, she seemed to be galloping along, devouring ideas and writers at a great rate.

By the time I returned home in early June, Sylvia appeared entirely cured. There was no trace of melancholia; in fact, she seemed just like the previous summer, bubbling with enthusiasms, laughter breaking through her conversation like an overflowing fountain. The only thing which disturbed me about her was that she had begun to bleach her hair. To take attention away from the scar beneath her left eye was the way she rationalized it to me.

The events of the succeeding summer I have recorded in my longer memoir, *Who Was Sylvia?* (to be published by Stemmer House). Nancy Hunter Steiner recorded her memories of Sylvia that summer when they both attended Harvard Summer School, living in an apartment on Commonwealth Avenue in Cambridge. In that book, using pseudonyms for names of acquaintances, Nancy refers to me as "Jeffrey McGuire." I suppose "Jeffrey" derived from her association of me with Lord Jeffrey Amherst! As she relates there, by the end of the summer Sylvia and I were unofficially engaged, despite Sylvia's run-in with "Irwin" while I was off on a two-week cruise. I might say, parenthetically, that I do not figure as a character in *The Bell Jar*, because our relationship was really outside the material developed there and, in the main, took place after the events depicted in that *roman à clef.*

When Sylvia returned to Smith for her senior year, she told me that she felt like a long-ripening, slowly maturing wine, taking five years to come to fruition. Busily she set to work submitting her applications for fellowships for the following year to the proper authorities.

In her Shakespeare course, Sylvia found Miss Dunn a virtual "dynamo."

When I visited Hamp one weekend and went to one of Miss Dunn's classes, I felt she was altogether oblivious to modern criticism. I spoke to Miss Dunn after class and found that, when the New Criticism came in during the thirties, she had decided to keep to her old pattern, largely a verbal picture of the man and of his times, a "history of ideas" approach. I was unimpressed, because Amherst English teachers had been heavily influenced by the New Criticism, and I had not yet learned to judge writers or approaches on my own. But, brought up in an academic family, Sylvia tended to adore her teachers. Either they were models for herself or surrogates for her father.

Back in the traces of academic life, Sylvia that fall dyed her hair a walnut brown to rid her appearance of the flighty, platinum-blond effect. She put a straight-jacket on her mind and concentrated with full might on her thesis. Most of the weekends she was too busy to see me, primarily because of the rigid demands she made of herself while writing her thesis. Also, she felt somewhat haunted, because she was taking German again, having taken it also in summer school; she was determined to wipe off her record the only B she had gotten during the second semester of her first junior year, lest it prevent her from making *summa*. Actually, having more credits than she needed, she dropped German during the second semester of her senior year in mid-semester so that she could concentrate on her poetry and not worry about German grammar.

Not such an avid student myself, I did not like this excessive attention to grade excellence, which I felt to be Sylvia's chief aim. In her letters to me at this time she spoke, it seemed to me, rather superciliously about the dilettantes in her house who she felt wasted their time playing bridge, knitting, and going to movies. By contrast, Sylvia drove herself through her work like a whirling dervish, sometimes failing to make meals. Our relationship began to falter. Sylvia seemed to need to know that I was there, in the distance, as a sustaining force, but she sometimes had to suggest strongly that I not come up from Boston for the weekend, where my ship was in the Charlestown Naval Shipyard. Or, if I came up, she wanted me to limit my visit to one night, staying in my fraternity house at Amherst. Apparently I provided Sylvia with a sense of security for the future and with a very sympathetic ear. As her major correspondent, I gave her an outlet for her prose. Only twice did she send me poems, because she did not get the chance to sit down and write them until she took that course with Mr. Fisher. Fisher had her reading Joyce's *Cham-*

ber Music and turning out batches of poems each week, which she served up to him like a batch of toll-house cookies. More and more she had to apologize for having to hibernate for eight months of the year, promising at the end to emerge like Alice in Wonderland, stepping through her magic mirror and becoming a sun-worshipping summer queen. Metaphorically, Sylvia was fond of trying on new roles and personas as if they were actresses' costumes.

Visiting Professor of American Literature at Smith that year, Alfred Kazin gave Sylvia tremendous encouragement in her writing, urging her to spill out all her ideas, learning to give them form, to write creatively. For his American Literature course he even allowed her to write creative papers, rather than critical ones. He made her feel it was her holy duty to write. Sylvia thanked her stars that she had interviewed Kazin for the *Alumnae Quarterly*, causing her to want to take his course in the spring semester. Kazin became her idol, the omnivorous reader, as well as the ubiquitous and seemingly omnipotent critic. Although his field was American Studies, he was more pleased with his introduction to the *Portable Blake*, she wrote me, than anything else he had written up to that time. That winter Kazin introduced Sylvia to Peter Davison, who the following summer for a short while became involved with Sylvia after we had broken up, as retold in his pretentious autobiography, *Half Remembered*.

Life was always full to the brim for Sylvia at Smith in those days and cresting over the brim, "overflowing." If she had been a Marlovian heroine, she would have been an "overreacher," because she could not stick by the golden mean, nothing too much, but was always anxious to experiment *in extremis*, with Blake, to find out what "enough" was by indulging herself in "too much." Her letters were filled with purple passages. In retrospect, I would have to say that at times she was whistling Dixie, telling herself she was extremely happy in an effort to mask her anxiety over future possible scholarships to Oxford, Cambridge, and Harvard, not to mention the possibility of marrying me after a year or so, following her year in graduate school and my three years in the Navy.

Mary Ellen Chase and Alfred Kazin wrote strong recommendations for Sylvia to the Fulbright Committee. They were largely responsible for her winning the fellowship, because they assured the committee that Sylvia was fully recovered and, despite her medical history, would be able to perform with imagination and zest. With her twinkling eyes and verve, Sylvia had a way of charming people and getting them to do things for her. For instance, Mary Ellen Chase made Sylvia cookies during exam time. Despite the way the sick heroine of *The Bell Jar* pillories the woman novelist at her college, Sylvia, when healthy, felt very differently about Mary Ellen Chase, "that magnificent woman."

During Sylvia's last semester at Smith, while I was on a shake-down cruise in Guantanamo, Cuba, Sylvia wrote of the encounter with the Woodrow Wilson Committee ("a hideous committee of 4 smug men"). They grilled her on English literature and on her reasons for wanting to be a teacher. As Nancy Hunter Steiner recalls in her memoir, Sylvia was overwhelmed that one of the men was very surprised that she had not heard of C. P. Snow, whom this inquisitor thought to be one of the major contemporary writers in English. I am sure that Sylvia took consolation the following year at Cambridge in F. R. Leavis's haughty put-down of C. P. Snow as hardly worth reading, certainly not part of "the great tradition."

With her closest friend of this year, Sue Weller, Sylvia flirted with the idea of teaching English at the American School in Morocco. Located in a Sultan's palace in Tangier, this school had the romantic aura of three continents with its bazaar and its babel of languages. Sylvia was then beginning to hunger for an international orientation. With Sue she also made plans to drive to New Orleans and possibly on to Mexico City.

When I returned from the shake-down cruise in March, Sylvia told me over the phone that she could not see me for a couple of weekends. Although her thesis was behind her, she was writing stories now for the *Ladies' Home Journal* in hopes of keeping her, as she said, out of "debtors' prison." Earlier I had felt that Sylvia had begun to use me as a crutch for her wounded ego. Like Nancy Hunter, she needed to know that there was always a man around, ready to come at her beck and call when she waved her magic wand. I did not want to play that role. With my destroyer alongside the dock in Providence, I drove up to Cannon Mountain to go skiing with two girls from Pembroke College.

Several weeks later, my hand in a cast from a skiing accident, I drove up to Smith. There we finally "broke up." The wheel had come full circle, with one of us symbolically broken and in a cast. On this weekend, as if I had lost my bearings, I can remember straying into a bush in front of Lawrence House. Sylvia apparently wanted to retreat into her pristine shell of winter, as she says in her poem, "Spinster." There the speaker is going to erect defenses against the advances of any male, hostile or loving. Basically, I think Sylvia wanted someone to replace the father she had lost in childhood. After coming close to me—as she had and later did to others—she rejected this suitor as not godlike enough to be both father and lover. I later came to feel that Sylvia's narcissism, a fixation caused at the time of her father's death, prevented her from loving anyone else fully. Although I resented the way she had treated me, nevertheless, after we split, Sylvia and I still wrote each other for nearly a year.

At the end of that summer of 1954 I saw Sylvia just before she sailed for England. I drove her back from Baltimore to Wellesley after her visit in Washington with Sue Weller. Twice we went to the beach together, one of her favorite locations. During the first ten days of a thirty-day leave I spent in Europe, Sylvia and I traveled together like sister and brother from Paris to Munich to Venice and finally to Rome.

Sylvia always seemed to fluctuate between great contrasts, to be coming about like a sailboat or even jibing in the wind. She seemed to be trying to compensate for a sense of missed life, to swing from books to "living," and then back to books. By contrast, I always felt more on an even keel. I wouldn't let the events of my life rock my emotions so. I felt that her sudden shifts, her intensities, her ravenous appetite for life, were, in their painful aspects, masochistically self-induced or self-inflicted as if to make her feel more acutely so that she could use these painful experiences as grist for her writing mill.

In her last weeks at Smith as an undergraduate, Sylvia garnered all the poetry prizes, as well as sharing with a Wesleyan boy the Irene Glascock Poetry Contest award at Mount Holyoke. The judges for this contest were John Ciardi, Wallace Fowlie, and Marianne Moore. She wrote that she loved drinking Scotch afterward with John Ciardi, who greatly encouraged her to send her poems to various magazines.

Obviously, Sylvia thrived under the kind of conditions and pressures set up by a high-powered faculty such as the one attracted to Smith College. My own feeling at the time was that Sylvia, driven by her demons "to succeed," neglected aspects of her life other than the academic. I'm very glad things worked out as they did, however, because it was through Sylvia that I met my wife, Betty, who was President of Lawrence House in the class that graduated a year later. The differences in outlook between Sylvia and Betty are like night and day. The former was essentially brilliant and egocentric; the latter essentially warm and magnanimous.

4   Outside the Bell Jar

Laurie Levy

> . . . to be an adult meant to be
> a survivor . . .
>
> A. Alvarez

We are very verbal survivors.

We invoke stasis with interpretation, achieve catharsis in disclosure. Like reluctant travelers aboard electronic sidewalks—clinging to railings as if to deny propulsion toward the inevitable, we stave off loneliness and keep a grip on immortality by relating ourselves to our mutual loss: Sylvia Plath.

Do we explain what we were/are to Hecuba only to affirm our own surviving? (A game of literary cryogenics?) Does the artist-survivor tame the tension by releasing his child's curiosity to grapple with his identity, vis-à-vis her whom he's survived? (Is he then grown up? In-grown? Predacious?)

The more essays and memoirs, the more frequently and intensely she haunts us, the greater our need for abreaction, the more memoirs. . . .

*   *   *

I survive in limbo, at the rear of a line in the supermarket. Drugged in an aisle by fluorescence. I leaf through a magazine, a marshmallow monthly for the young, and Sylvia is back again, the subject of another nervous paean . . . but extinguished . . . I blink past it; focus on an old photo across the page. A reprint of twenty young women smiling insincerely, their forty arms extended to form a human star. They seem unaware that in twenty years they will return, parodying my survival.

Maybe the fault is not really in ourselves, but in our stars . . . my watch ticks frantically, like a bomb or a pulse . . . I see that Sylvia Plath is still at the top of the star and I'm still at the bottom.

> Although the horoscopes for our ultimate orbits aren't yet in, we guest editors are counting on a favorable forecast . . .
> —Sylvia Plath, *Mademoiselle*, August, 1953

As I bear my anonymity and my grocery bags to my car, I wonder if Sylvia is haunting the other eighteen ex-guest editors in the photo. Why so much silence from the survivors of that broken star? I'd like to ask them if it's true that nothing succeeds like success.

*　　　*　　　*

"I didn't want my picture taken because I was going to cry."

By plane and train, from coastal cities and dusty inland towns, we crossed the Rockies, the Mason-Dixon, and the Mississippi. Twenty—count 'em, twenty—from urban universities and the towers of academia and many a Babbittville campus thick with the rotting lilacs of that fruitful May. Eisenhower-era innocents transported (Broadway! Times Square!) to the "real-life workaday world" of Madison Avenue. Half-century girls, strangers, we assembled in the Editor's office, hugging ourselves as if to contain the private ecstasy of winning: Grace, Eileen, Carol, Sylvia . . . others . . . the one at the bottom . . . (Would the Magazine be proud? Why doesn't it care what happens to its readers when they age?)

We were to use our talents to help create the August College issue and there would be fringe benefits (a wand appeared in the Editor's hand) prizes, luncheons, interviews in fashion, communications, the arts. . . .

> (. . . pretty parfaits produced by our hostess, an aging queen of Cosmetics. I sat, spooning manna, as Madame held off a photographer until she could slash a crimson lipstick across her cheeks and chinline. "Photographs better, dear," she sighed.)
> "But I grow old and I forget your name. . . ."

We marched twenty abreast from the hotel for women on glamorous Lexington to the office on glamorous Madison. We whispered in awesome places atop pastel carpets thick as cream cheese, our palms and upper lips sodden: each too self-immobilized to involve herself in the others' worlds, yet eager to submerge identity by joining the group. I must have joined. I looked everywhere, but I seemed to be missing, marching with the chosen.

"You and Sylvia are our writers," said the Editor, "I expect great things. . . ." (Would I like them to publish my humorous pastiche on college men? I would? Consider it done and done and June at times will never end.)

Sylvia asked why I hid my literary attempts, submitting only humorous bits and pieces, and I told her I needed time to develop style, sophistication. Rural roots, I explained, were a handicap in coping with The Wasteland.

By 1973, the pages long buried in desk drawers turn yellow when exposed to light.

"For now," said the Editor in caps and italics, "let's put all our sparkle, shall we?, into our fashion copy."

Sylvia and I passed each other, smiling, in hallways. I knew that she would be a great poetess someday. Sylvia knew that I would be a journalist (novelist? essayist? what? each? all?).

We billowed about the steaming summer-festival streets, trying to keep cool in below-calf cotton skirts. Much of the time I thought about Beauty. If only the Editor could have the wand, I wrote in my diary, and make me look like Sylvia!

She had a long rather flat body, a longish face, not pretty but alert and full of feeling, with a lively mouth and fine brown eyes. Her brownish hair was scraped severely into a bun . . .

                                                                —Alvarez

I longed to be tanned with a swinging American champagne-colored pageboy—like Sylvia's. But I had no choice; in her opinion, humorists ("look at Benchley and Dorothy Parker") must have dark hair and pallid flesh. I remember vowing to make a study of wan, dark-haired humorists, but of course I never did that, either. We passed each other in hallways, Sylvia and I, our teeth white against the magenta lipstick of 1953.

One afternoon we were curried and carted like horses in a van to Central Park to participate in the human-star photo. We posed in 94° sunshine in identical woolen tartans and 40-inch bust-producing longsleeved button-down boy-shirts (note the copywriting influence beginning to cross swords with Chekhovian dogma), our arms flung wide, while a mad photographer aimed at us from a footbridge and tried to evoke stylish delight from our general mood of prolonged humiliation. Would I have been more cooperative if I'd known that someday in a supermarket I would feel such a throb of . . . adulthood, at the sight of myself?

Instead, I squinted, shirt wet against the small of my back, and gritted through my cheshire-cat grin—I wished I'd remembered to dab some lipstick on my chin—and Sylvia to the rear gave a small yip of amusement.

Finally, near the end of that month that was not going to end, Sylvia and I talked until the wee hours—a marathon of shared impressions, confessions of mutual ambitions and future plans. We drank a great deal of a bottle of warm white wine, which had been smuggled into my room by a boy I knew before he was kicked out of our women-only residence by someone—maybe me. In 1953 it was called a "bullsession."

We examined our girls'-schooled-feminist liberal-arts' backgrounds. We pondered self-tragedies of regional origin. Sylvia thought Iowa was mysterious, and lamented my parents' thoughtlessness for raising me in a town, instead of on a farm. I told her how I used to imagine that my town was an island in the sea—cornfields surrounded my town on all sides—and I told her about trips to the Bohnsacks' farm ("Bohnsack!" Sylvia cried) for corn and cucumbers and pumpkins in autumn. And she told me about growing up near water . . . and it sounded much the same. . . .

We discussed books and writing and careers, and how I had mismanaged by chance to be a star of stage and screen. (This was in reference to the fact that the Magazine had granted all twenty of us a chance to ladder-climb and interview any celebrity we chose in New York.) Sylvia, choosing from a list that included Plimpton of the *Paris Review* ("But I've met him, anyway . . .") had interviewed Elizabeth Bowen. I had chosen Richard Rodgers, the composer. I had intended to break into song, once alone with him, at which he'd scream, "A star is born." I didn't. Nor did he.

"You could've at least hummed a bit," Sylvia said.

Rodgers had even conducted the interview seated at a piano. ("I think better this way," he said.) I rose to the opportunity by mumbling my questions over his music, neglecting to mention I'd sung with a band during college. . . . The guest editors had been unmerciful . . .

Which is why only one other guest editor knew that I had demolished a second chance at stardom shortly after the Rodgers fiasco. According to my diary, I told Sylvia about it that night. Maybe it was the white wine . . .

I had learned of the liaison between our friend (*The Bell Jar*'s "Doreen") and a disk jockey. "Doreen" arranged everything. I'd gone to the man's apartment; he'd directed me to sing *a cappella* into a tape recorder. I obeyed. My voice quavered as I sang—possibly because my host was wearing only a small towel. Then, he sat beside me on the couch, listening to my voice, and said, "A star is born. All you have to do is (slight pressure on my knee) put yourself in my hands . . ."

"I fled," I told Sylvia.

Her response was: "Should I, after tea and cakes and ices, have the strength to force the moment to its crisis?" I was impressed with her wit; years later, I discovered the line was Prufrock, not Plath, and cringed at my ignorance . . .

"I don't think you want to be a singer," she added. "Maybe you'd better stick to writing."

We agreed that night we would not rush into marriage, if at all; we were never to "end up in suburban boxes" . . . Nothing more exists of that night, except for one last thought recorded in my diary (purchased at an Iowa Woolworth's, it has held up uncommonly well over the years): "Re-read *Tempest*. S. thinks Ariel male—animal power, fiery depths. I said air, heaven, female. . . ."

*   *   *

Some of the guest editors were startled to tears when June ended, but most of us were too tired to protest. We dispersed in different directions to have our letdowns alone. I remember Sylvia's wide painted mouth and her June Allyson pageboy. "Write to me," she said. There seemed only light in the fiery depths; there was no "brownish bun" about S.

I never wrote to her. I forgot her, and the others. (Are they even now at their typewriters?) I did not return to Iowa, but became a film critic in New York—or, if we bow to John Simon, a "movie reviewer." Fade out.

Until, years and marriage and Chicago and pregnancies later, I opened a national magazine and found a poem by Sylvia. Oh, I was publishing book reviews and articles in the Chicago newspapers, but now there was *The Colossus!* How annoying of her to haunt me from (glamorous) England, even as I sat reading her poems, my apartment overflowing with diapers and unfulfilled literary dreams. I planned to write to her, and didn't.

February, 1962. How could I know that Sylvia would present the world with an *Ariel?* I was creating my own, my way: feminine. As Sylvia arose, the same morning John Glenn stepped into space, in her "local manor—a few miles north of Exeter," I heaved myself from the

TV set to the delivery room. "Ought to name her John or Glenn," the doctor said.

"No," I decided, "Ariel."

("What a coincidence," said the bookstore clerk in 1966.)

"Are you crying," asked my husband as I read *Ariel*, "because she is famous, or because she is gone, or because her poems affect you that way?"

"Yes," I said, watching my golden-haired Ariel, dangling fearlessly, typically, from the top rung of the jungle gym in the yard, "and you can add Robert Lowell's foreword to that list . . ."

Ariel summons up Shakespeare's lively . . . spirit, but the truth is that this Ariel is the author's horse.

I left Lowell to pipe his song until the cave swallowed the townspeople's children forevermore, and went to unearth my 1953 diary. Why had we discussed *The Tempest?* Had Sylvia ever recalled our evanescent conversation?

"I think I made you up inside my head."

The Bell Jar: newly published. I drove, haunted, through cliffs of gray spring snow to the bookstore in my small suburban outpost and bought the book I never could have written.

The children were sick with spring flu, and I tore upstairs and down, bearing trays, reading nonstop in free moments, trembling first in fear that I would not be mentioned, later in fear that I would be. But Sylvia had zeroed in on "Doreen"—pre-Bunny, platinum-blond "Doreen." Here was Sylvia's disk jockey incident. (But, where was mine?) Here was Married Girl—we'd been so sorry for her—and here was Nice Girl. (Was "Betsy" me? No.) Nor the Towering Hayseed, lean and beige as a wheat stalk, who'd been transformed—the wand again—into a fashion model; and hadn't we all thought that a joy, and a blessing, and a miracle?

Twenty girls into a fictional ten and no me in sight. The children went back to school without lunch boxes, beds went unmade and dust gathered. When I finished the book, I read it again, looking for me, as I savored "Esther's" June and despised her July.

("If you only knew how the veils were killing my days. To you they are only transparencies, clear air." Blind! A toast, then, in remembrance, to Lady Lazarus from Tiresias in his female decade!)

I wrote to Lois Ames, Sylvia's biographer, of unmarshaled forces and dormant dreams; I was beginning to need to communicate my reaction to being haunted. Lois shared my letter with Anne Sexton, and both responded. "Write," they wrote. They had faith in me, they said. I was alive, they reminded me.

*   *   *

1972. I fly from home—still haunted, thanks to posthumous post-scripts from never-never land—to a writers' conference, where poets talk of Plath's "sense of oppressed womanhood."

"She was one of us," brays a large lump of a girl. She is imperious and her poems reek of omens and pitfalls.

"She was pretty," I mutter. The girl edges away to escape inanity. But I win first prize in the short story workshop, and others smile: "You must buckle down and produce . . ." and "you must try very hard and then, maybe. . . ."

*   *   *

I have begun to write again.

I can see her sunshine smile: "Just try to make it to the top of the star." She hovers; watches me try to keep the words from growing old and yellow on the page.

Through the glass, out in the world of awakening trees, and tea and cakes and ices, my children play. Ariel flies from the rungs of the jungle gym. . . .

I raise lax, too long aberrant fingers from the typewriter's keys, and lower them. Only the agony is fresh and young.

(The sunshine smile: "The bees are flying. They taste the Spring.")

You are laughing, aren't you, Sylvia?

DOROTHEA KROOK

As I was reading the poem "Daddy" for the first time, I suddenly recalled my earliest impression of Sylvia Plath, before I knew who she was. It was at the opening lecture of my course on Henry James, at the beginning of the Michaelmas Term, 1955, Sylvia's first year at Cambridge. I had walked into the Mill Lane lecture room a few minutes early, and was gazing idly at my new audience, observing that it was small and probably wondering whether it was also choice. As I gazed, I noticed a conspicuously tall girl standing in one of the aisles, facing toward me, and staring at me intently. I was struck by the concentrated intensity of her scrutiny, which gave her face an ugly, almost coarse, expression, accentuated by the extreme redness of her heavily painted mouth and its downward turn at the corners. I distinctly remember wondering whether she was Jewish. This was a thought that could not have occurred to me more than half a dozen times in all my thirteen years at Cambridge; one somehow never wondered whether people were or were not Jewish, unless presumably the Jewish marks were especially prominent. The tall girl with the face distorted by the intensity of her interest, curiosity, whatever it was, must have seemed to me to show the marks in this way, or I cannot imagine why the thought should have crossed my mind. I have remembered it often since, with the strangest emotions, as more and more has come to be known about her passionate feeling for Jews and her sense of belonging with them.

I never again, literally never, saw that expression on Sylvia's face in all the time I knew her at Cambridge. Only when at the time of her death the London *Observer* published a picture of her, along with Alvarez's moving notice, I seemed to catch a glimpse of it again, in the wildly, feverishly staring eyes of that dreadful unfamiliar face, the desperate-defiant look in the eye somehow intensified by the distaff of unkept hair hanging about her shoulders.

There was nothing wild, feverish or defiant, and nothing unkept, about the Sylvia Plath who came to me for supervision on the English Moralists from the second or third term of that year 1955/56. I see her clearly at this moment before my mind's eye, sitting on the sofa in my small sitting-room at 111 Grantchester Meadows: always neat and fresh, wearing charming, girlish clothes, the kind of clothes that made you look at the girl, not the garments; hair down to the shoulders still, but ever so neatly brushed and combed, and held back in place by a broad bandeau on the crown. I remember the bandeau because I think I never saw her without it; my first irrelevant thought as I stared, stupefied, at the picture in the *Observer* was "Where is the bandeau? It *can't* be her—she's not wearing her bandeau." This charming American neatness and freshness is what I chiefly recall about her physical person, even more than her beauty; though she was of course beautiful, as Wendy Campbell says, as we must have said to each other often enough. She seemed also, I remember, less tall than she was, because she did not hold herself in a tall girl's way: always straight and graceful, but somehow humble at the same time, which had the effect of diminishing her physical height.

This effect was produced even more by the typical expression of her face. Eager and mobile, tranquil and serene, all at once: I never saw her face express anything else in the many long supervision hours we spent together. I did not think of her as one of my most "brilliant" pupils (I shall return to this point); I thought of her rather as one of the most deeply, movingly, responsive pupils I had ever had. I felt the things I said, we said, her authors said, mattered to her in an intimate way, answering to intense personal needs, reaching to depths of her spirit to which I had no direct access (and didn't mind not having, being satisfied with the visible effects).

As every teacher knows, there is no greater inspiration to letting oneself go intellectually than is this rare kind of receptiveness in a pupil. I did let myself go with Sylvia, as I have done I think with no more than five or six others in a teaching career of nearly thirty years. It was a matter of spreading one's wings to the argument, as Plato says, letting it lead whither it will. Plato was indeed the central figure in our discussions; we seemed to linger on and on over Plato, doubtless at the expense of the other Moralists; but this was something that often happened with my best pupils, usually with no regrets afterward. Some time during the period Sylvia was coming to me for supervision, Miss Mary Ellen Chase of Smith College, Sylvia's special sponsor and friend, came on a visit to Cambridge, and reported amusingly on Sylvia's enthusiasm about her Plato studies. "She talks about *nothing* else," said Miss Chase, with much pretended exasperation, "Plato and Mrs. Krook, Mrs. Krook and Plato, Mrs. Krook on Plato, Plato on Mrs. Krook . . . It's hard to know *which* she's talking about, whether it's Plato or Mrs. Krook she admires most. . . ." I remember how we laughed about this at the dinner party at the Garden House Hotel, and how touched and flattered I was by this confirmation of my own feeling that Sylvia was greatly enjoying our Plato sessions.

I have racked my memory to recall what were some of the particular things I said to Sylvia or she to me about Plato and the rest. But I can remember nothing: not a single utterance. All that comes back to me is a general vision, clear and pure like the golden light of the Platonic world we had appropriated, of an extraordinarily happy freedom of communication. Love and beauty in the *Symposium,* justice in the *Republic,* the pleasant and the good in the *Gorgias,* knowledge and opinion in the *Meno,* the contemplative intelligence, the practical intelligence, the Platonic rationalism, the Platonic mysticism: these must have been some of the great topics we entered into and lost ourselves in. I remember that I pursued them with her further than I had done with any other student, drawing out implications, soaring into generalizations, reviewing my personal life's experience for illustration or proof, in a way I usually reserved only for my soul's most secret conversation with itself. The light of participation in Sylvia's eyes, shining so it seemed to me with understanding and delight, is one of the sweetest, most imperishable memories of my teaching life.

She wrote for me, almost every week, an excellent paper: long, full, cogently argued, carefully written—everything that goes to make an *alpha* paper. She got her alphas, and I praised the papers as they deserved; yet somewhere in the subconscious depths of my mind there was a reservation. I think I would have expressed it at the time (if I had attempted to express it, which I didn't) as a sense of their somehow, nevertheless, not penetrating all the way: neither to the depths of the subject, nor (more important) to the depths of her own experience. It seems this did happen in our oral communications, our joint explorations; it did not happen, in quite the same way, in her own independent grapplings with her authors; and it never occurred to me what the reason might be, that "criticism" was not for her the most natural, congenial mode of self-articulation. What I registered was only a sense of her seeming to hold off a little from her subject, not wholly surrendering herself to it; and of holding back something, perhaps a great deal, of herself. All unconsciously, of course; her conscious aim, clearly, was to put all she knew, give all she had, to her weekly academic exercises. Indeed (I remember this, too, as a distinct impression, though barely expressed at the time), I felt in her a certain strain or tension about these essays: arising from an anxiety (I supposed) to "do them well," to excel, to distinguish herself; and not just now and then, but consistently, without lapse. Of course I applauded this fine noncompetitive ambition; what teacher in his senses would not? But it contributed to the reservation which made me think of her as an excellent, not a brilliant, student; though I am sure I must have spoken of her as "brilliant" often enough, in the loose way one does in speaking of one's best students when one is in no mood for fine distinctions.

In this connection, I recall that the only hint I ever had about a more flamboyant "past" in Sylvia's life was something I heard about her first two terms at Cambridge, before she started coming to me for supervision. I don't think it was from Sylvia herself that I had it; it may have been from Wendy, or from someone else. What I heard gave me a vague picture of Sylvia during that time leading an intensely social life, writing or contributing to a woman's page in the undergraduate magazine *Granta*, involved in stage activities (Cambridge was a great place for amateur theatre), and being very popular and sought after. By the end of her second term, she had decided that all this was a "waste of time" (I seem to remember my informant using this phrase), that she must put it aside to concentrate on her studies, lead a serious, responsible life without frivolous distractions, and so on. I remember being amused at the fervor of the renunciation. She was not after all the first person who had succumbed to the glamour of Cambridge in her first few terms; I had had the experience myself in a mild form in my first year at Cambridge, when scarcely older than Sylvia I had come to Newnham as a research student; and I had learnt since that newcomers from outside (America, South Africa, or wherever) were particularly susceptible. I also felt, in a dim way, that her uneasy conscience about her first "wasted" terms, her self-reforming zeal, her desire to live down, live away, these passages in her recent past had something to do with the strenuous note I seemed to detect in her seriousness about her studies and her weekly essays. I didn't know anything about her life as a student in America; and I knew nothing, of course, about *The Bell Jar*.

Reviewing these remembered impressions or intuitions in the light of later knowledge, I have come to see in them meanings of which I had no inkling at the time. When after her death I read the poems in the *Arial* volume, and more recently *Winter Trees*, I thought I could see why I had felt that those long, full, excellent essays on the English Moralists did not reach down to her innermost being. And since the apppearance of *The Bell Jar* and Alvarez's account of her death, I have seemed to recognize in her whole academic effort at Cambridge a great, perhaps even a titanic, struggle for "normalcy" against the forces of disintegration within her. I knew nothing about these forces; but she, poor doomed girl, did; and I now believe that she may well have resolved, consciously and deliberately, to defeat them once and for all and save herself from destruction by the path Cambridge had opened up to her. To be a successful teacher of English Literature at Smith College (she might have argued to herself) is one obvious way of being "normal"; therefore, she must bend all her efforts to qualify herself for this saving normality; therefore, she must write excellent, the best possible, essays for me, get a First in the Tripos, and so on. I don't mean, of course, that her passionate interest in her studies was not genuine; I only mean that her secret fight against disintegration was a powerful additional motive for the interest and the passion.

In all this time, Sylvia never showed me a single one of her poems, and I never asked to see any, though I knew she wrote poetry. In this I was observing a private rule I had made for myself long since, tacitly to discourage those of my students who "wrote poetry" from bringing their productions to me for "criticism." I recognized this (and do still) as in some ways a harsh and selfish proscription, and was willing to believe that I might be the loser by it. But (I used to tell myself) I had my work cut out to cope with their academic productions, which I took very seriously—too seriously, some of my less gifted pupils used to intimate; and as at least half of my students wrote poetry and there would be no end to the poems I would be reading and criticizing if once I encouraged the authors to bring them to me, I felt I must in primitive self-defense be firm about this, bearing my theoretical losses for the practical gain of a few hours I could call my own. Whether Sylvia actually wanted to show me her poems I don't know. Very likely she didn't: because she supposed me not "interested," or because at that time she lacked confidence in her poetry, or perhaps both. If she did want to show them, perhaps she didn't because she guessed at my private rule and accepted it—so far I could judge, without resentment. At any rate, I never read a single poem of hers until after her death; a circumstance I have felt to be odd enough to require an explanation, in view of the intimacy of our intellectual relationship.

This relationship, it will already be clear, was mainly impersonal, or nonpersonal: the teacher-pupil relationship, full of the warmth, affection, appreciation that its blessed communications so often breed, particularly in the Cambridge setting and atmosphere with its magical power of encouraging the growth of intellectual intimacies. Ours were indeed almost exclusively intellectual; and though the mutual impact of personalities was an inseparable part of them, and the teacher's upon the pupil's was bound to be stronger than the other way about (the teacher having always the unfair advantage of a more developed personality to make the impact), I was never conscious of its intruding upon the sacred ground on which our minds met. Sylvia was extraordinarily modest, self-effacing, unassuming, unspoilt; never inviting attention to herself, seeming to want only the selfless intellectual relationship. I remember noting and appreciating it at the time; I think of it now—now that I know the full extent of the personality that refused to claim attention—with the utmost tenderness and admiration.

The more personal side of our friendship developed, I seem to recall, from the time of her marriage to Ted Hughes. I became involved in this for reasons serious enough for Sylvia at the start, though in the end amusing as well. At the beginning of the Michaelmas term 1956, her second year at Cambridge, Sylvia appeared, extremely agitated, to tell me that she had "secretly" married Ted during the long vacation, that they had had a marvelous summer in Spain, ecstatically happy, wonderfully productive—happy, obviously, because they adored each other, productive because (she said) they had both managed to write a great deal. But now the hour of reckoning had come: she had got married without tutorial permission, and had up to now kept it from tutorial knowledge (this is what she had meant by saying she had done it "secretly," which I had at first not understood), she was afraid now that her outraged college would recommend that her Fulbright scholarship be taken away, in which case she would have to leave Cambridge and come away without a degree, and please *what* was she to do?

I was a little taken aback, I remember, by the intensity of her fear and agitation, and, even more perhaps, by what I sensed to be a strong suppressed resentment: presumably, at Cambridge rules and practices, Cambridge dons and their demands, the Cambridge set-up as a whole perhaps. It was the first and the only time I glimpsed in Sylvia (without, of course, at the time knowing it for what it was) a small touch of the passionate *rage* which has since come to be recognized as a dominating emotion of her poetry, especially her last poems.

The problem of the illicit marriage was soon resolved. To mollify her resentment, I said some soothing things about the idiocy of Cambridge rules, and that the only way to live with them was not to take their idiocy too much to heart. I suggested that she go to her tutor, make a full confession of her crime, express a decent (though not abject) regret about not having asked permission, and plead love, passion, the marriage of true minds, and so on, as the irresistible cause. She was not however (I urged) to "criticize" the immortal rules or moralize about their iniquity. I knew her tutor to be a warm-hearted, rather romantic person, who I felt was likely to take a kindly view of Sylvia's lapse. And so in the event it turned out. Within a day or two Sylvia came back, happy and beaming. Her tutor had been completely charming, kind, understanding; she would not have her Fulbright award taken away; and she could now go and live with her legally recognized husband in any convenient place in Cambridge.[1]

Soon after this, she and Ted moved into a small flat in Eltisley Avenue, just round the corner from my own place in Grantchester Meadows. She was passionately, brilliantly, happy: incandescent with happiness, as Wendy Campbell has beautifully said. She spoke about it from time to time; and I remember at least once experiencing a thrill of fear at the idyllic pitch and intensity of her happiness. What would happen (I said, or half-said, to myself) if something should ever *go wrong* with this marriage of true minds? Nothing of course would, nothing *could*, go wrong: I was sublimely sure of this. Yet if, inconceivably, it should, she would suffer terribly; I held my breath to think how she would suffer. That was as far as my momentary fear carried my imagination; nor was it possible it should go further, in the face of her serenity, her tranquillity, her confidence, and (most of all) her marvelous vitality, which seemed a guarantee of limitless powers of resistance.

Sylvia mentioned during that winter that the flat in Eltisley Avenue was bitterly cold. She hated cold, she said; it reduced and diminished her, made her feel humiliated, degraded. I had a Fyrside oil-heater to spare, and offered to lend it to her for the winter. She accepted it with a gratitude quite in excess of the service, though obviously not of her need; and throughout the winter she kept on mentioning it, saying what a difference it made to their lives. I remembered the Fyrside (I should never have done so otherwise) when I read Alvarez's description of the icy London flat in which she killed herself. It tore at my heart to think how her anguish of spirit in those last months of her life must have been cruelly, intolerably, exacerbated by the cold she hated.

Though Sylvia repeatedly asked me to come and see them in the flat in Eltisley Avenue, I never did, so far as I can recall. Indeed I am sure I didn't, because I remember one of the rare moments of a more personal confidence from my side to have been connected with this. So I think Wendy Campbell must be mistaken when she refers in her memoir "Remembering Sylvia" to a dinner party at their flat to which we both came. She may be confusing it with the farewell dinner party at her own house in Harvey Road just before Sylvia and Ted were due to leave Cambridge, to which I did come and remember very distinctly: Sylvia sitting on the floor and talking, talking with enchanting animation; Ted, also on the floor, completely silent but evidently enjoying Sylvia's talk. This was the last time I saw her.

I felt very bad about saying no each time Sylvia asked me to come; so bad, that once, when she had asked me again and I had again to say I couldn't, I said to her: "You do understand, don't you, Sylvia? What the claims of my life are; how they leave no room for, let's call it, the pleasures of society . . . When I've the time I haven't the strength, when I have the strength I haven't the time . . . If I took time off, I wouldn't be able to do the things you've been so kind and generous about: the lectures, the pupils, the research and writing, the kind of thinking, living, that has to go into them to make them worth anything . . . And *life* going on all the time, you understand—never stopping for a moment, to give a breathing space for art . . . I simply can't fit in anything more just now, unless I tear myself to pieces . . . You do understand, don't you, the price one has to pay?" I don't suppose I used these exact words, but I did speak these thoughts, or something like them, just this once. She answered, "Yes, yes, I do understand—" with a kind of vehemence and a shiny light in her eyes which persuaded me she really did. The remembrance of her understanding has been a comfort I have clung to in the years since her death, when I have often been haunted by the thought that I was perhaps another of the people she loved who abandoned her, and by abandoning her betrayed her love and trust.

During the time she and Ted were in America she wrote to me a few times. I came on a brief visit to America in the autumn of 1957, and stayed more than a fortnight with relations in Cambridge, Mass. I tried to get in touch with her, in the hope that we could meet. But my letters were slow in reaching her, and in the end we only succeeded in having one telephone talk, on a very bad line. She was excited and moved, and so was I. I can't remember anything we said; I only remember it was the last time I heard her voice.

Presently she wrote to tell me that she and Ted were coming back to England. I remember the gist of that letter exactly: teaching at Smith was fine (she didn't say what has since become known, that she had taught brilliantly during that year); but it was a deadly distraction from writing, and she felt she must give it up, now or never, if she was to continue writing poetry. Ted felt the same, she said; and as he was not altogether happy in America, though he had made heroic efforts to acclimatize, they had decided to come back to England. I don't remember whether I wrote to her saying how much I applauded and blessed her decision, or just thought these things and never wrote. At any rate, I had a chance to say them to Miss Mary Ellen Chase, when soon after I had had Sylvia's letter she came on another visit to Cambridge. This time there were no drolleries about Sylvia and Plato and Mrs. Krook; she looked grim and angry when I mentioned Sylvia, and solemnly, tragically, in a low voice, let me know how disappointed, "deeply disappointed," she was about the defection of her favorite protégé. I remember feeling irritated by her solemnity; what on earth had she *expected* Sylvia to do if the teaching-and-writing plan did not work out? And was it such a new thing under the sun that a serious writer

should find it impossible to combine creative work with gainful employ-
ments—of any kind, let alone the particularly taxing demands of university teaching? I must have said something like this, though (I hope) less
roughly; and I came away with the impression that she liked me less
than she had done before, that she thought of me as wantonly aiding
and abetting Sylvia in her defection.

Reviewing this little episode in my mind now as I write these notes,
I am inclined to think that Miss Chase's extreme displeasure about Sylvia's
crucial decision to be a poet and nothing else may have been deeply
disturbing to her, in spite of the brave show she made, to herself and
all the world, of rejoicing and exulting in her act. If I am right in sur-
mising, guessing, that she wanted a successful academic career as a
symptom and proof of having attained the "normality" she yearned for,
her abandonment of this harbor of safety, so soon after she had entered
it, may have been a secret, or half-secret, disappointment to herself,
too: inducing temporarily at least, a sense of insecurity, loss of confidence, even perhaps a sense of failure. These self-doubts and misgivings
would have been exacerbated by Miss Chase's implacable disapproval,
which Sylvia was likely to have seen as an act of betrayal by someone
she had loved and trusted. In that case, it would have been a fresh provo-
cation to the rage, outrage, resentment, she was so fatally prone to, and
might have contributed its mite to the building up of the tragic state
of mind which within a few years led her to total breakdown.

The year (1959) in which Sylvia and Ted came back to England happened to be the year in which I was preparing to leave England, to
settle in Israel. For reasons connected with this momentous decision
(none of which seemed good enough afterward), I did not get in touch
with them; and I left for Israel at the end of 1960 without having seen
Sylvia again.

When three years later in Jerusalem I read of her death in the *Observer* notice, my horror, grief, incredulity, were the same as Wendy
Campbell's. I didn't, however, even for one wild moment, fancy she
had been murdered, as Wendy says she did. I could imagine only one
possible cause. Something *had* after all gone wrong with the idyllic
marriage of true minds. She had been, or felt herself to have been, now
as never before, betrayed and abandoned; her anguish of loss, outraged
pride, fury, resentment, despair—all mixed up, in what proportions one

would never know—had unhinged her mind, and in her madness she had killed herself. I still knew nothing about *The Bell Jar;* and when a little later I learnt that my intuition about the marriage had been approximately correct, I felt her own kind of passionate, bitter rage: against the beautiful, impossible illusion itself, against the shattering, and the shatterer, of the illusion. I couldn't bring myself to write to Ted; I only heard in my head, over and over again, like a drum-beat, Othello's piercing words:

> But there, where I have garner'd up my heart,
> Where either I must live or bear no life,
> The fountain from the which my current runs
> Or else dries up; to be discarded thence!
> Or keep it as a cistern for foul toads
> To knot and gender in . . .

To be discarded thence, discarded, discarded; I seemed to see the word burning her heart to ashes in her last days in the freezing London flat.

Then, presently, I came to know about *The Bell Jar.* Nothing had been more inconceivable to me. She had seemed to me, as I have said, a creature breathing only spiritual health, vitality, and resilience; to discover that there was also a pathological element to take account of taxed my imagination beyond its resources. Like everyone who loved her, I have brooded a great deal about this dark, death-enchanted side of her, trying to understand it, failing each time I tried. I have recognized its presence in her poetry, and have felt a fresh wonder and admiration at the transmuting power of art. But the experience itself remains impenetrable to me, and in the end I have fallen back on a passage in Thomas Mann's *Buddenbrooks,* read long ago, which to my mind succeeds better than any other account I have seen in communicating its final baffling mystery. Mann is talking about the mystery of human resistance and surrender to death in mortal bodily sickness, but what he says might be true also of a human creature caught in a mortal sickness of soul:

> Cases of typhoid fever take the following course: When the fever is at its height, life calls to the patient . . . The harsh, imperious call reaches the spirit on that remote path that leads into the shadows, the coolness and peace. He hears the call of life, the clear, fresh, mocking summons to return to that distant scene which he had already left so far behind him, and already forgotten. And there may well up in him something

like a feeling of shame for a neglected duty; a sense of renewed energy, courage, and hope; he may recognize a bond existing still between him and that stirring, colourful, callous existence which he thought he had left so far behind. Then, no matter how far he may have wandered on his distant path, he will turn back—and live. But if he shudders when he hears life's voice, if the memory of that vanished scene and the sound of that lusty summons make him shake his head, make him put out his hand to ward it off as he flies forward in the way of escape that has opened to him—then it is clear that the patient will die.

(Part XI, chapter 3)

By a strange poignant coincidence, she chose to die on my birthday, 11th February. It could not have been anything but coincidence, and I am not a superstitious person; but it has haunted and oppressed me ever since I have known. Following a traditional Jewish custom, I have each year since her death burnt a candle in her memory on that day: the tallest, handsomest I could find, of a brilliant jewel color if possible. The custom is simple and beautiful, and would I think have appealed to her imagination. You light the candle in the morning, and it burns quietly all day, letting you forget it most of the time as you go about your usual tasks; but each time you notice it, it meets your eyes, steadily, silently, a true *memento mori*. Though I hate and fear death, I am glad I am prevented from forgetting hers. My birthday, her deathday, a last sad, precious bond.

I have written these notes with much hesitation, feeling that I didn't have enough to say to justify the cost in the violation of privacy, or in relived anguish for myself. I feel I didn't know Sylvia in the least as well as other people knew her: Ted, or Wendy, or Alvarez, or almost any of the friends and admirers who have written about her. I didn't know *The Bell Jar* side of her at all; I didn't dream there was a part of her that was a kind of Catherine of *Wuthering Heights*, fighting (paradoxically, absurdly, for a Catherine nature) a hopeless battle to be an English don, a poet, a wife, a mother, and a charming woman all in one. I only knew her, really, as a beautiful, sensitive mind, ardently enjoying the exhilarations of the life of the intellect, living intensely, joyously, in the calm sunshine of the mind, as Hume calls it. I saw her only, or almost only, in the radiance of this light, and what I saw was I think a real, inextinguishable part of her, though not the whole of her.

6   "Gone, Very Gone Youth": Sylvia Plath at Cambridge, 1955-1957

Jane Baltzell Kopp

Sylvia Plath was twenty-three and twenty-four years old during the time when we knew each other; I was three years younger. We knew each other well for slightly less than two years, during which we were both American graduate students at Newnham College in Cambridge. We met at once in Cambridge, and were immediately thrown together in a variety of intimate ways, because we both had rooms in Whitstead, a small converted private residence on the far margin of the Newnham College grounds. Fewer than a dozen of us lived there, all graduate students and all from Commonwealth or foreign countries. The College dining arrangements were such that breakfast was served to us in intimate family style in the little Whitstead dining room, but dinner in the evening was available only in the formal Hall of Newnham College proper. Those of us who lived in Whitstead had to walk to Hall and back each night, a ten-minute trek either way over the College grounds. Most of my early acquaintance with Sylvia grew out of these homely routines.

Before ever arriving in Cambridge I knew of her, however, because I had seen something by or about her in *Mademoiselle*. All the same, I was taken by surprise when we actually met. Whatever I had expected, it was not what in fact she seemed to be. She did not present herself as high-strung, morose, sensitive, brilliant, introverted, or in any other way difficult or "artistic." I had the impression, primarily, of someone very *capable*. I sensed a certain habitual wry humor and a stubborn, even stolid capacity for perseverance. When I read it years later, the scene in *The Bell Jar* when Esther, fleeing the necking scene between Doreen and Lenny, walks "forty-three blocks by five blocks" back to her hotel, laconically informing the reader, "walking has never fazed me," [1] brought back sharply for me the flavor of this quality in Sylvia.

I have no recollection of our introduction. I remember that one evening during the very first week we conspired to avoid the evening meal in Newnham Hall and to ride into town instead on our bicycles, to find a restaurant. I don't remember where we ate or what we talked about during the meal. My vivid memory from that night is of my embarrassment when Sylvia rode up to a Cambridge bobby and asked him in a Massachusetts accent to suggest "somewhere really picturesque and collegiate" where we might eat. In those days I was self-conscious about the kind of thing the British found ridiculous in Americans. Sylvia absolutely was not, and she managed in the course of her first few weeks in Cambridge to run through most of the classic varieties—sublimely oblivious, I think, all the while.

Soon on in our friendship I sensed that Sylvia was driven by an array of formidable ambitions. And she said so herself. Of these, the hopes that she had for her writing seemed the most obsessive. I was struck by the fact that unlike all the other young "writers" I knew, Sylvia did not so much talk and seem to think about literature and writers, about "art," in short, as she did about the business side of things. The names and editorial leanings of magazines made up a large part of what she had to say whenever she talked about modern poetry, which really, for that matter, was not often. When she remarked to me one day that she "would rather have a poem published in *The New Yorker* than anything else in the world," I understood her to mean it fairly literally: that neither marriage nor motherhood, and certainly not academic concerns, could ever compete in her conscious mind with a record of success in established publications.

But in fact she was ambitious in many directions, and she rarely did anything without striving (I choose the word with care) to excel. During the first year I knew her she variously pursued horseback riding, sketching, and amateur dramatics, as well as, always, poetry. Every one of these things she did *hard*, not so much giving herself pleasure as somehow trying (so it seemed) to satisfy someone very difficult to please. The variety of the things she concerned herself with meant that her activity tended to be disintegral; yet when I think back now, it was as though her momentum was somehow along a vector into space, as though she was frantically trying to "get somewhere" in an almost literal sense. One vivid memory I have, a sight I must have seen a thousand times, is of Sylvia riding a bicycle. She was "goal oriented," to say the least, and would peddle vehemently, head and shoulders straining forward, as though pure will power rather than her legs propelled her. She rode, say, like a passionate little girl.

We had not been in Cambridge a month before certain of Sylvia's Americanisms acquired the status of bywords. She owned, for instance, a full set of Samsonite luggage in white and gold. On weekends when she would be glimpsed surrounded by all of this on Cambridge or London station platforms (its creamy whiteness made all the more conspicuous by the sooty backdrops of British Railways), she was the inspiration of much amazement, incredulity, and humor among the British. She had some habitual, very American mannerisms of speech also. She had a special attachment to the verb "enjoy" and used it constantly, sometimes in ways that the British found very odd. In her room in Whitstead, for example, she had a favorite piece of furniture, a coffee table, as she called it (using a term that, in itself, was bemusing to all but fellow Americans). She apparently would often remark on how much she "enjoyed that table," thereby unconsciously regaling her English visitors, for I heard the anecdote more than once.

(Her little attic room at the top of Whitstead was arranged very distinctively, with an almost professional sense of interior design. I recall a general impression of warmth and style, produced by a daring use of color and by very careful deployment of the few things she had to work with. For example, she owned many large costly art books; these were stacked, propped, and opened in interesting ways. There was also a full tea set of solid black pottery that somehow was always displayed so as to convey taste and luxury at the same time as hospitality. Some version of England's ubiquitous small, inadequate gas heater was necessarily the focal point of everyone's room; Sylvia made very much the best of hers, drawing up close and opposite to it a studio couch which also served as her bed, and furnishing the couch itself with bright pillows. The effect was almost of a sofa facing a fireplace. Overall, her room suggested intelligence, imagination, and some care spent on welcoming and impressing callers. In the mornings, especially, the large dormer windows let in a gorgeous flood of sunshine.)

I have referred to a tendency on the part of the British to ridicule

"Americanisms." Such ridicule was usually gentle and even affectionate; it could sting, nevertheless, if one was susceptible. Sylvia, as I have already mentioned, seemed generally oblivious of (or indifferent to?) such mockery, but of all things, she did learn British table manners— that is, keeping the knife in the right hand and the fork in the left, tines down, throughout a meal. For a time she would practice this technique, commenting and exclaiming at her own expense the while. Perhaps it was precisely *because* she had chosen to commit some ego to such matters that I once saw her, very untypically, display a kind of devastating vulgar wit. (It is a quality that appears everywhere in *Ariel*, but that Sylvia rarely if ever showed in public during the years I knew her at Cambridge.) The circumstances were as follows.

Included among the dozen residents of Whitstead were not surprisingly some high-strung, difficult temperaments; some of these were hardly at their best during the morning hours. The routine for breakfast in Whitstead, honored a little irritably by the old Scottish housekeeper, was that we as individuals could straggle into the little dining room of a morning at times of our own choosing. Breakfast service went on for hours, and on some days almost all of us would be at the table at once, but sometimes only two or three would happen to be. We came in dressing gowns if we liked, or dressed every which way, and we would read the newspapers or our mail, or converse if we wanted to, but generally it was understood that we would mind our own business.

One morning, as chance would have it, the table was rather full with most of us present, when suddenly one of us, an aristocratic South African who looked like Virginia Woolf, shrilled out hysterically, addressing Sylvia: "*Must* you cut up your eggs like that?" We all then woke up to what before we had registered only subliminally, namely, that Sylvia had noisily been employing her fork *and* knife to slice up her fried eggs. (There they lay on her plate, fantastically carved into squares, trapezoids, rhomboids, et cetera.) Sylvia and the girl eyed each other, the South African beside herself, Sylvia cool and unruffled, somehow *pleased* (I never again saw her that way). There was a pause and then Sylvia said, "Yes, I'm afraid I really must. What do you do with your eggs? SWALLOW THEM WHOLE?"

People always wonder and ask how Sylvia looked, how she *was*. My recollection is of a very active and vital presence. She was on the tall side of average height, slim without being thin, and though more good looking than not, she was not someone people would ever call pretty or beautiful in the usual way. Her face was invariably lit by interest in or attention to something or someone. (I do not remember, ever, a "withdrawn" or "melancholy" expression.) Either she was talking, or listening animatedly (herself on the verge of speaking again), or she was silently reading something with eyes very alive and attentive (a book, say, or a personal letter at the breakfast table). Her complexion was a little strange in quality, something at the same time was translucent and opaque about it (I remember wondering if there were old, slight burn scars on her face). The overall effect was of a kind of sheen, even a radiance. This was in part a quality of the complexion, in part, of her personal force.

She dressed tastefully in fifties Ivy League College Girl fashion: jumpers, turtlenecks, skirts and pullovers, loafers. Quite simply, her clothes were a part of her and rarely noticeable, either by way of being conspicuously colorful, stylish, formal, informal, well-fitted, or not. She inclined (but living in England we all did) to wools and to dark and natural colors. I am told that earlier, in America, at Smith she had bleached her hair. I remember it during the Whitstead years as a rich mingle of dark and blonde strands, worn always in a shoulder-length pageboy until her marriage, always well kept in a casual sort of way, never "dressed" in any finicky or self-conscious fashion.

She used lipstick heavily (this was the fashion then). One of my memories is that I was always aware of the perfume of her lipstick. She had a way, unusual in a New Englander, of drawing quite close when she was walking beside you: she would "lean in" so near that the scent of her lipstick was quite noticeable. Her way was to talk very, very intensely, more or less losing herself in her subject even if it was as trivial a matter as the supper menu. Very often, as I have said, the two of us would walk back together on winter nights from Newnham Hall. As she walked and talked along beside me, she would unawares gradually drive in across my direct path, so that, whatever we were saying, I was always slightly preoccupied with resisting the diagonal pressure, so to speak, and with keeping us on course toward Whitstead, dim in the wintry distance.

One night she exasperated me. We were walking and talking along in moonless darkness when suddenly a very furious activity of some kind took place in some fallen leaves directly in our path. A small animal or animals it seemed, and I myself was startled. But quick as a flash Sylvia leaped behind and literally gave me a solid shove forward. I was a little sullen, she a little chagrined the rest of the way home that night.

In retrospect I suppose that her nerves could simply at times betray her. I did not know, none of us in Whitstead did, of the seriousness of her undergraduate "breakdown," and she never exhibited any signs of anxiety or depression or the like. (Ironically enough, one or two others in Whitstead did, repeatedly, and were under psychiatric treatment.) But she had a great deal of physical restlessness. I remember two mannerisms, usually carried out in concert. One foot (I think the right, its leg crossed rather aristocratically over the left) was always kept swinging impatiently and the fingers of her two hands were always actively interacting—the fingers themselves interweaving, locking and unlocking, the two thumbs rather hostilely opposing each other, stabbing each other with their nails. Owing to this habit of hers, it happened that I paid unusual attention to the appearance of her hands. I remember them as slender through the palm. Her fingers were long with vaulted nails, which she generally kept polished with colorless nail polish.

I got to know her gradually as time went on. As might be expected, we kept together to begin with and talked about our American impressions of Cambridge and of the British. This topic was exhausted when both of us began to acquire British friends, and we gradually talked more about our studies (we were doing several papers in common). Ultimately we moved onto more intimate conversational ground.

Out of all this, my memory keeps chiefly now only the atmosphere of those night walks and my various perceptions of Sylvia. Two or three specific conversations I do recall, mostly because they puzzled or intrigued or disturbed me. One night, for example, talking in some connection or other about herself, Sylvia went on at great length about how a professor at Smith had once charged her with being "factitious." "Factitious, factitious," she said. "When he said that, I had no idea what it meant. I went home and looked it up, and I was devastated. Factitious. At first I thought it meant I was obsessed with facts." She told this story humorously, but she drew it out to a strange length. I did not really comprehend what it meant to her, but when later I heard her mention the same incident two or three other times, I realized that it went very deep.

Another time she overheard me and a British friend, also a Whitstead resident, talking during dinner about the array of distinguished figures at high table. Our talk had been on an idiotic, adolescent level, spun out of nothing but boredom, and it consisted of comparing the appearance of certain of these internationally famous women scholars to assorted household objects. One, an eminent historian, had a rather colorless complexion, a narrow skull, and stainless gray hair, which was pulled straight back. I remember that I asked my British friend if she had noticed how much this woman resembled a needle. On the way back to Whitstead Sylvia rather hotly announced that she did not appreciate that kind of talk. My feeling at the time was surprise (that she had not understood the spirit of our talk, which was pure silliness), but I also felt, given her reaction, clumsy and guilty. The skirmish ended amicably. My other friend and I tried to explain, lamely of course and feeling fools, and Sylvia allowed herself to be mollified. I remained at a loss, however, as to the exact cause of her anger, for she was not clear about it. Was it morality? Was it pique at not being included? Years later, reading her final poems, I was startled to see the devastating art of caricature that at times takes over there. I then remembered this whole episode, and wondered if she was frightened by our seemingly cold objectifying of other people because it was something she tried for a time to resist in herself.

Only once in our whole Cambridge acquaintance do I remember hearing in Sylvia's conversation the kind of image for which, among other things, her poems are now famous. Again it was a walk over the hockey fields and back gardens, and somehow we were on the subject of childbirth. Sylvia was describing a delivery she had witnessed (presumably the basis of Chapter Six of *The Bell Jar*). The whole drama of the birth seemed to have impressed her primarily by its grotesqueness. She did not seem frightened by it (she said nothing, for instance, about "never wanting to go through that" or anything of the kind), but she seemed fascinated and at the same time repelled. She said nothing about the laboring woman's pain or about the implicit human experience and emotion, but she seemed fixated on the spectacle of the *emergence*: "a watermelon through a keyhole."

That first autumn and winter in England, before she met Ted Hughes, her encounters with the men at Cambridge seemed not to go very deep. The ratio of men to women at the university was then something like twenty to one, and any presentable girl who was halfway interested could have as many invitations—to tea, to parties, to films, to dinners, to plays, to madrigal sings, to walks over the fields to Grantchester, to this or that—as she could possibly want or manage. Sylvia saw a number of men, and in her inimitable way would rave about each one. But there was something about the way she spoke about every one of her conquests up to Ted that gave the rest of us (though perhaps not Sylvia herself at the time) to suspect that they were of no real importance to her. A recreation of the style of her commentary about such minor involvements would go something like this: "I've just met this wonderful, wonderful English Jewish boy who does these fabulous, fantastic little wire sculptures. I really enjoy that boy. I can't help it, I just really do enjoy him no end. He's just this big, ruddy-faced bear."

Still during the autumn months of 1955 and long before she met Ted Hughes, she once astonished and discomfitted me (again on one of those walks of ours to and fro Newnham Hall from Whitstead for dinner) by suddenly saying, "Jane, I have just been thinking that what all these English boys need is a little of our good old sensible American attitude toward sex. I mean, I've just been thinking that what they all need is to go to bed with someone. I can't help it, I just do think that, and I was just wondering if you agree." What made me uncomfortable was my own sense, naïve as that was, that there was no such thing as a "good old sensible" attitude toward sex, American or otherwise, and that if there was, no one would want to have it. I mean, I sensed that she was putting up a bluff, for whatever reason. I thought that no one who had really had profound sexual experience would relegate it to the realm of "good, old, sensible" matters. I thought that she was somehow deceiving herself, and I felt afraid for her. I did not know how to reply to her question and I have no idea how I did reply.

One other remark that she made in the days of our early acquaintance also lodged in my memory, and it was to come up again later in more highly charged contexts. One night we were returning to Whitstead after dinner as usual and talking animatedly. Sylvia was perhaps unusually stimulated. Whatever it was we were talking about, she said something, and then I said something, and then suddenly she said, "You know, you often say things that I am just on the verge of saying. I feel as though you read the thoughts in my mind. Sometimes I think you are my "döppelganger." She went on to point out various things that we had in common (German ancestry, similar height and coloring, general facial resemblance, the fact of being Americans, Ivy League backgrounds, a common interest in writing, mutual friends, et cetera). "Cambridge isn't big enough for both of us," she concluded, speaking half-humorously but with a certain intensity that reached and disturbed me. In spite of the things she listed, I did not think we were really similar, and I did not think that other people thought so. Somehow I understood the whole conversation to mean "don't get in my way." I shrank a bit, and resolved indeed to keep out of her way, if that was how she wanted it.

Michaelmas term ended at last. Overseas students, epsecially, made at once for the Continent. I myself was bound for Italy, by way of a few days in London and Paris first. I knew that Sylvia was southbound, too, although we had not arranged to travel together. As it turned out, we did make a large part of the journey in each other's company. The result was that our friendship, which had generally been growing in spite of the döppelganger business, received a temporary setback. What happened was not without comedy. Nevertheless it was all very awkward and difficult to repair.

After leaving Cambridge for London on separate days, Sylvia and I first re-encountered each other in a shabby London air terminal waiting room. This belonged to a small, newly organized, almost literally "fly by night" airline company offering an air fare to the Continent that was fully competitive with Channel boat rates. One learned about it from the inevitable undergraduate tipsters. Obviously Sylvia and I had both got the word, for there we both were.

There we remained, too, for two or three hours during which the aforementioned shady airline proved, that day at least, unable to come up with even one plane certain to be safe off the ground. Finally they substituted ferry boat passages for our plane tickets and produced a dilapidated red bus to deliver us to the ferry docks (we wondered if this had been their game all along). After our two- or three-hour wait at the terminal, we had well over an hour's ride to the coast.

There followed a difficult, windy, mid-winter Channel crossing, the sea very choppy and a general cold, gray drizzle falling. People were sick all over the boat. Sylvia and I stayed on deck, tented together under my Burberry raincoat, which we used as a tarpaulin. Both of us kept our stomachs, despite the fact that pans of vomit repeatedly clanged down the deck nearby where we were huddling, wind-ripped away from their users and flinging out their contents as they flew along.

When we landed on the French coast exhausted, it was already after dark; but a final stage of travel, the train ride to Paris, remained. By the time we actually saw Paris it was ten or eleven at night. Sylvia had reservations in a little student hotel on the Left Bank. (The friend whom she was going to meet had arranged everything in advance.) I had no place to go, having expected to arrive in Paris nearer to noon than, as it was, to midnight. When Sylvia insisted that I share her hotel room for the night, I was in no mood to argue.

Soon we were actually setting down our bags in a Paris hotel room (third floor walk-up, amorphous feather mattress, the usual). In spite of bone weariness, I was very nearly as excited as Sylvia. We talked along can-you-believe-we're-actually-in-Paris lines. (It was the first time for both of us.) I was incredulous, however, at what Sylvia next proposed: that we "go right out and explore Paris." I said that Paris or no Paris I had to get some sleep, and I tried to persuade her to wait till morning, too. She was not to be talked out of it; she was bent on hurrying straight out into the night. We agreed that she would knock to be let in when she got back, and I locked the door behind her. By then it must have been 1:00 A.M.

My exhaustion was real and I did not wake up the next morning until, say, 8:30 or 9:00. Sylvia was not in the room. Not a little alarmed, I lay in the bed and studied the scene for a moment or two, hoping to detect signs that she had come and gone again already. It occurred to me also that she might have found her friend and stayed the night at his place. Then suddenly a knock. I opened the door and there, in dudgeon, stood Sylvia. "Jane, how COULD you?" she said. Of course I was baffled, but it came out that she had returned to our room only a little more than an hour after leaving, yet had been *unable* to rouse me by knocking. (Only one other time in my life, also after a long European journey, have I been known to sleep with such stupor.) She had frantically appealed to the concierge, who indeed had another key, but his key could not be used because I had left mine in place, and turned, in the lock. Sylvia had ended up being allowed, grudgingly, to sleep on the rug in his office.

Rarely have I felt more hopelessly embarrassed. My fault was the more grievous, of course, in that she had been doing me a kindness. At the same time, I found the peculiar intensity of her anger inappropriate. I had not, after all, locked her out on purpose; but she was angry just as though I had. She somehow conveyed as much, alluding to her döppelganger theory. (Not that she was irrational; what she said was to the effect that the incident was hard for her to take because of what she felt anyway.) We were both still not really rested. Our talk was wretched and muddled. I felt certain nightmare sensations that I had not felt since childhood. We patched up some sort of peace and I said that I would go out and find another place to stay (which had been our agreement in the beginning) and that I would be back later for my bags.

When I returned several hours later I knocked and got no answer, but the door opened when I tried it. Both there in the bed, and until my intrusion asleep, were Sylvia and her friend. They were fully clothed, and the situation was not compromising, but of course my timing seemed (if only in my own mind) to compound my offense of the night before. With minimal farewells I collected my belongings and fled.

Things were to get worse before they got better.

At the end of the Michaelmas terms and before we left for Christmas, Sylvia had loaned me several books. We were both reading for the Tragedy paper, and several dozens of other students in Cambridge were, too. I was not in a position to buy many books, and sometimes it was impossible to get what was needed from the Library. I had grumbled in Sylvia's hearing about the problem, assuming that she shared it. But it seemed that she owned nearly all the collections that we needed. (Marvel of efficiency, she had asked—months in advance and from America—for a booklist, and had bought what was needed out of her Fulbright book allowance.) She insisted on sharing with me, and of course I accepted.

Later on when I was using the books, I was a little surprised to see that Sylvia had underlined everywhere in them with black ink. Emboldened by this (I don't claim I should have been), I ventured a few pencil marks to facilitate my note taking. (I planned to erase these before returning the books.)

Unfortunately I had forgotten that very important step when, after the Paris hotel contretemps, I wanted to lose no time in returning her books. That first morning back in Whitstead I took them up to her room, Sylvia if anything made a point of being cordial. She seemed to have forgotten her indignation. We were probably still a little on guard with respect to each other; but I think that each of us believed that the other truly wanted peace.

My shock was great, therefore, when I answered a knock on my door a few hours later and again found a Sylvia incandescent with anger. Exactly as in Paris her first words were, "Jane, how COULD you?" With the other occasion to build on, my feelings instantly became those of the childhood nightmare. "What? What?" I said, and actually, I think, backed away. In a very vehement and dreadful way, then, she protested my marks in her books. I have never seen rage like it. More directly than in the hotel incident she put it to me that I had acted *maliciously*.

In spite of the fact that this threatened to arouse my own temper, I somehow felt a great desire to communicate with her, once and for all. I began by saying something very exigent—"In God's name, Sylvia" or something like it. Maybe this, or maybe just my own distress and lack of hostility, seemed to calm her. Of course, I immediately volunteered to clean up the pencil marks, and did so. We then had a long general talk. She returned very urgently to her döppelganger theory and said that she thought that, owing to what she saw as our inevitable rivalries, we could not ever be friends. (But she was by now speaking in a friendly way.) She seemed to want me to share this conclusion with her. In truth I didn't find us to be in the competition that she did, but I felt that it would be a mistake to argue with her.

After this strange afternoon we had far fewer contacts with each other, and yet without a doubt we were better friends. It was not long after that she met Ted Hughes and began to spend almost all her time with him, but even if that had not happened I suspect that she and I would thereafter have talked less. However, when we did talk now it was on a new basis of affection. It was as though all the emotion and nuance that normally go into years of a friendship had been packed into an hour or so.

Owing to a rather complicated set of relationships, I happened to be present at the party where Sylvia and Ted Hughes met.

(My own acquaintance with him was slight—we had been to a few of the same social gatherings; but I had a more intimate perspective than this would suggest, because we had close mutual acquaintances. I knew a young Southerner from Tennessee, perhaps Hughes's closest friend, and this American was friends also, and had been from childhood, with another Tennessean whom I knew very well. My own immediate friend had heard many anecdotes about Ted Hughes from his friend and he had passed them on to me. Hughes was story material.)

The pretext for a party that day was the publication of *St. Botolph's Review*, a publication of thirty-odd pages containing poems by Ted Hughes himself,[2] our mutual friend the Tennessean, and four or five others—the printing paid for, I think, by the contributors. My memory has it that it was a day in late winter, say, February. A unique thing about the party was that it happened (or at least began) at noon, on, I think, a Friday or a Saturday. It was a day of fine skies and sunshine. At the same time the party was an occasion of wet feet and mud tracked into the room. These details are vivid in my mind. I think it must have been a major thaw, perhaps the end of that winter, for spring did come early that year, and was exquisite. We all felt—end of the week, end of a difficult winter—stimulated and euphoric. The party took place in some fairly cramped private lodgings in Botolph's Lane, where some of the principals of the publication lived (hence its name). People were crowded into the large, bare kitchen drinking wine and ale. There was not much seating; we perched on stools, lounged against counters, stood about. It was informal and better than that: a rare case in genteel, sherry-drinking Cambridge of something proletarian in atmosphere and down to earth. As an American, I felt at home.

I had seen *St. Botolph's Review* before the party took place and had not been much impressed by most of its contents. I was, however, taken aback by the three poems by Ted Hughes, which were excellent. Nothing of the mannered, bloodless, facile style of the other undergraduate poets. These were savage poems, powerful and contemporary in content; they came very near to carrying off the audacity of the almost-Renaissance rhetoric in which they were written. One of my own motives in taking up an invitation to this particular party was to take a further measure of Ted Hughes (whose writing I had never seen before). Sylvia Plath, I am told, after seeing *St. Botolph's Review* went for the same reason. Some said she came uninvited.

Hughes was in a misanthropic mood, and sat brooding against one wall. He was large and alarmingly powerful, both physically and in psychological presence. Any mood of his was apt to impose itself on his associates; and on this day (weather and general high spirits notwithstanding) his dyspepsia, or whatever, was indeed beginning to depress the company. Because of what I sensed to be his frame of mind, and also because I had come with other people, I put aside the notion of getting to know him and began to talk to other people.

Sylvia arrived alone and still wearing her black student gown; she evidently came straight from a lecture or "supervision" or from the Library. (We were required to wear our short, knee-length gowns on all such occasions and also at any and all times after dark.) She came into the room tentatively, looking young and uncertain, which was not characteristic. I remember being surprised at this look on her face and surprised to see her there at all, because I had not known that she knew any of the *St. Botolph's* group. A few people came forward at once to greet her, and that is the last I remember of her on that occasion.

She saw Ted Hughes more or less daily all that spring, which was a gorgeous season, perfect in every day of its unfolding. As I have said, Sylvia spoke very little about Ted and said nothing at all about her own feelings; but for the first time since I had known her she seemed truly happy. Meanwhile we bystanders wondered at it all, and at least once Whitstead was treated to a first-hand display of Ted Hughes's eccentric (and violent) temperament.

He and his friend the Tennesseean had spent the afternoon sitting on a haystack in a field near Cambridge. They had drunk a great deal of wine and talked for hours about various literary Utopias. (This part of the story I got at second hand.) When they went on to elaborate Utopian societies of their own, Ted became so excited that he hurried back to Whitstead to tell Sylvia about them. He brought with him yet another bottle of wine, but one that was unopened. When he discovered that Sylvia had no corkscrew in her room, he plunged down the stairs to knock on other doors. As fate would have it, the door he chose first belonged to the resident Senior Member of Whitstead, a teetotaling Methodist. (Most of us at heart had learned to like and respect this woman, but that did not save us from being terrified of her. To ask her for a corkscrew, even to be overheard by her asking someone else for a corkscrew, was inconceivable.)

Her door opened; her face, framed in tight braids of dark hair, peered out; Ted Hughes asked her if she had a corkscrew that he could borrow. She began, disapprovingly, to say that most certainly she had not; but here Hughes—having no idea who or what she was, and suddenly overcome by impatience—struck the neck of the bottle off on her doorknob. He then bolted back upstairs, the problem solved in his own mind. (It is a testimony of some kind to Ted that, whatever she made of this whole affair, the Senior Member never tried to understand any more about it. She did not call after or pursue him at the time, she did not later inquire as to whose visitor he was, or in any other way protest. In short, she let the matter drop, perhaps preferring to believe it had not really happened.)

But this incident was unique. As the spring went on, it was clear that Ted and Sylvia were absorbed in each other. Their relationship seemed calm, quiet, and sure. Whereas about the other men in her life Sylvia had babbled and gushed almost inanely, about Ted she was secretive. His impact on her life and thoughts was unmistakable, but not so, owing to anything that she herself said. We saw him come and go from Whitstead over a fortnight or a month, the two of them steadily coming and going together, and over that very short while Sylvia became a different person. Before, she had been gushing and a little silly, restless, self-divided, always striving in several directions to "achieve": centrifugal, in short; but at a stroke she became private, serious, and seemingly centered. They were married, unbeknownst to all of us, early that summer, during the Long Vacation.

I do not recall any memorable encounters with Sylvia early during the following Michaelmas term when she and I—and all of us—returned to Whitstead from our various summer travels. Sylvia and Ted were plainly still close and seeing each other regularly. It was not until about a month had passed that the fact that they were long since married became known. After a day or two of "legal" skirmishes with the College, which fortunately ended happily, Sylvia suddenly moved out of Whitstead and set up housekeeping with Ted in a little flat in Eltisley Avenue near Newnham. I.V. Morris, then Sylvia's College Tutor and mine, recently provided some poignant background narrative to these events:

> The episode relating to her marriage is . . . evidence of her respect and even awe or "fear" of authority. At that time it was still more or less unheard of for undergraduates to marry and there was the College rule that "An undergraduate who marries may continue her course only if she has been given permission to do so by the Council". This rule was frequently interpreted as a bar on marriage by the College and gave credence to the belief that a student who married would be sent down. Sylvia was married in London in the Summer of 1956 after she had been at Cambridge for one year, and it was about half way through the following Michaelmas term that she rang me up from Whitstead. I cannot remember her exact words, but the gist of her message was that she had committed some great offence and wanted to see me to make this terrible confession. I did not know what to expect. It was therefore with relief that I heard Sylvia's confession—i.e., that she had got married—and could reassure her that she would not be sent down and that she had no need to worry. At that she threw her arms around my neck and hugged me saying I was the dearest, most understanding Tutor. Needless to say I was not accustomed to such demonstrative behaviour. Her marriage,

as I learnt later, had been discovered by the arrival of letters addressed
to her in her married name. Asked to explain this and reminded of the
College Regulations by the resident Senior Member, for at that time
each Hall or separate building was deemed to need "someone in charge",
she had obviously taken fright. She then told me of her meeting Ted
Hughes (he was at Pembroke College) the previous year at some literary
meeting: her life had been transformed since then, they had the same
interests and she was so immensely happy; they had got married when
her mother was over on a visit that Summer: it had seemed the most
natural thing to do with them all there together in London. In November 1956 the College Council was informed of her marriage and she was
given permission to continue her course.[3]

The marriage itelf, as might be expected, inspired various less official
reactions. The Tennesseean, who did not yet know Sylvia very well, and
who was initially dismayed by her Samsonite luggage and coffee table
propensities, once talked a little about his own misgivings. Shaking his
head, he said, "I never, never thought that Ted would marry an *American*
girl." I gathered from something Sylvia told me that the Hughes family,
or some member or members of it, had made her feel less than welcome.
In something of her old style, she enthused about the *picturesqueness* of
Ted's native landscape, and described vividly the darkness and coldness
of the family house she had visited in, meaning only the architecture; but
I saw that her eyes darkened as she talked, and I took it that her visit to
the new relatives had been troubling to her.

On Sylvia, the effect of marriage and happy commitment of herself to
Ted seemed to be an impressive new self-assurance and a new range of
emotional honesty. After the fact of their secret marriage became known,
she once said to me, "Jane, you can't imagine what a relief it is to be free
of that dreadful social pressure." This was said in so earnest a way that
I was struck by it; she seemed exceptionally present. I understood that
she referred to the pressure to "date," to pretend this and that, to seek to
marry, etc. She did not mean that the "dreadful social pressure" was *why*
she had married Hughes, but that the relief from all of that was a very
blessed thing for her. I believe that in saying what she did to me she
also meant to allude tacitly to the naïveté of all her earlier babbling about
men and sex. Such things are sometimes conveyed quite precisely, without words. From my point of view, it was one of the closest conversations we ever had.

I have been asked whether or not she presented herself at Cambridge as a poet. The answer is both yes and no. As I have said, she made no secret of her ambitions to be a writer, and all of us Americans, at least, knew that she had published here and there, had had the *Mademoiselle* guest editorship, etc. It was common knowledge in Whitstead that when Sylvia worked furiously, as she did very early in the morning, it was usually on her poetry. (We would hear her typewriter jingling and clattering at a terrific rate, as early as 6 A.M. every day.) But the truth was that up until then Sylvia had not published anything that was truly extraordinary. She was becoming, but was not, even the poet of *The Colossus*. That she could or would write the poems of *Crossing the Water, Ariel,* and *Winter Trees* was not to be guessed, not even, I dare say, by Sylvia herself. The poetry of hers that one saw in 1955-1957 was always good, very well crafted and so on, but (as someone at the time said) none of it had to be written. Cambridge was full of poetry by young and old, and while hers was with the best, nothing about it then inspired awe.

Miss I. V. Morris, our Newnham Tutor in 1955-1957, touches on this in the same personal recollection of Sylvia that I have quoted earlier.

> There were ten or eleven rooms in Whitstead and Sylvia had one of the smaller ones at the top of the house: rather pretty and picturesque with a slanting roof, dormer window and window seat and a fine view over the Whitstead garden and the broad expanse of the College grounds. She expressed her delight in the room and particularly in the window seat where she would sit and write poems she told me; I was a bit surprised and touched at the intensity of her delight. I asked about her poems and writing, but I did not register the fact particularly: so many students write poems and want to be writers, and Sylvia seemed to be so youthfully and touchingly enthusiastic.

In any case, while she was known to "write," Sylvia also did so many other things. Often one or another of these would seem prominent in its own right in her life. (For instance, she once got the part of the whore in Ben Jonson's *Bartholomew Fair* and she was busy with that for weeks, cycling to and from rehearsals, exclaiming about her costuming, and so forth. For some reason it hugely delighted and amused her to have this particular part; she would always bring out the word "whore" with gusto.) In short, Sylvia presented herself as an energetic, many-aptituded young woman. It was possible to imagine that she would become a "little magazine" writer of distinguished poetry, but not that she would become great; and it was equally possible to foresee that she would go into journalism, or (in spite of what she said about her ambitions) that she would simply marry and have children.

An academic career was another possibility, and of course this is what Sylvia actually began on immediately after Cambridge. My belief is, however, that her heart was never fully in that. Had it not been, in fact, for the example of Dorothea Krook, one of her supervisors at Cambridge and a woman for whom Sylvia had the highest affection and regard, I seriously doubt that she would ever even have tried teaching. She and Ted Hughes were obliged, after Cambridge, to earn money somehow. The ready and waiting job at Smith (and the one for Ted, later, at the University of Massachusetts) were simply too good to turn down. But I knew from many conversations with her that she somewhat desperately feared the role of "lady professor." It was not, of course, that she could not handle it intellectually, or that the interaction with students would prove a problem. It was simply a dread (based upon the example of the women teachers she had known at Smith and Cambridge) that the role would be defeminizing and, too, a threat to the particular kind of psychical organization or "set" that she thought she needed as a writer. (Specifically, she thought that the obligation which a teacher faces to be generally rational and analytical was incompatible with an artist's need to be impressionistic, emotional, and even irrational.) The example of Dorothea Krook, whose intellect Sylvia very much admired, but whose womanliness, as Sylvia saw it, impressed her if anything even more, seemed to do a great deal to comfort Sylvia with respect to these worries. But they lingered in her mind, and as the time drew near for her return to America and to Smith, she worried also, actively, about the possible temptation to "regress" that might be facing her. In England she had matured in various ways that she cherished, rightly so. Her marriage was the most important of these to her and she feared being treated again as a schoolgirl by old professors and acquaintances at Smith. She feared, as she said, "being diminished and closed in upon."

At a cocktail party given late in May, just before the English Tripos (our round of final examinations) began, and at which, as I recall, very stiff brandy stingers were the only drink provided, Sylvia and I stood and talked at length about these fears of hers, some of which I shared. It was the last significant private conversation we ever had.

(I was in a position to know that at least some of her feelings were well founded. I myself had recently had tea with two Smith "lady professors" who were visiting in England, and I had been in my own right a little incredulous, a little chilled by the proprietary way in which they spoke of Sylvia in her absence. Striking and unforgettable in appearance, one of those women is no less memorable to me for the vehemence of her opinions. She was convinced of Sylvia's genius and thought that marriage in her case was inappropriate: "a blunder." "I have nothing against Ted Hughes personally," she said, "nor against the institution of marriage, but I think that for a woman of Sylvia Plath's stature this is simply a disaster of the first water." Sylvia was already married at the time, as this woman knew, and she was happy in her marriage. I had never heard such talk and I was repelled by it. I understood very well Sylvia's apprehensions about re-entering the valence of people with such thoughts about her, people who were all the more difficult for her to "handle," in that they were sponsors and benefactors to whom she owed much.)

We sensed it dimly if at all, talking at random over potent brandy stingers on that afternoon, but that cocktail party in May was really the end of our knowing each other and of the Cambridge experience for us both. The next morning the English Tripos began, many days in a row of grueling examinations, and after that came the unreal whirl of too many May Balls. Then one day all of us were packed and gone—forever.

Yet our two years in Cambridge seemed to have lasted much longer than that. There was a peculiar endlessness about time there: Sylvia and I discussed this sensation several times and agreed about it. Back in America we found that our lives accelerated disagreeably. In February of 1958 I had a letter from her, written on pink Smith College memorandum paper.

It asked if I had become used to "the academic grove" and stressed how odd she felt returning to Smith campus, like "a rather antique and fallen angel." It seemed tinged with rue and suggested that she found it difficult to write while buried under academic chores, although there was also a sense of coming of age and a genuine delight in teaching "very intelligent" and "eager" girls, especially in such an ideal setting. But her mind was made up: she did not intend to remain at Smith and looked forward to a free year devoted to nothing but poetry, her own poetry.

The regret found articulation in nostalgia for Cambridge, which, she said, bloomed "like a green Eden" in her mind and about which she yearned to write and make legends. In particular, she remembered the ancient university as "one of those primitively mystic places" that seemed drenched in the past. Even the gray, sodden weather no longer ruined the lush landscape of memory, though she was not blind to the confusion, misery, and weariness of those days as well. At the end, she invited me to visit her if I ever came East to my home in Rhode Island, asking me to write to her.

I did write back, and promptly. But there were many moves and changes of address for us both; we both were soon living under many kinds of demanding and stressful obligations. We failed to write regularly, and in the end we lost touch.

A day or two ago in the course of writing this I had memories of Sylvia very much in my mind when I glimpsed on the street a young woman of her height and build and generally of her appearance. She was just slipping behind the wheel of a car. For an instant, I took her for Sylvia. The force and quality of the leap of affection I felt then—mingled, I will add, with a certain bracing of myself—reminded me of how I always felt about her.

Devon. Sylvia told me that it was entirely Ted's idea. He, she said, wanted to escape literary cocktail parties and the invasion of television cameras, which were assaulting his privacy and muse. Nevertheless, she threw herself into the role of country woman and farmer's wife, contending with Wellington boots, woolies, the ever-lasting mackintosh, chillblains, and jam jars.

In the early spring of 1962 Sylvia began imploring Paul and me to visit them in Devon. She was obviously feeling isolated and beginning to feel oppressed as well. (She was writing *The Bell Jar* then.) But we did not go. As the months went by, spring came in properly, with daffodils, apple blossoms, and hints that life might again be tolerable. Sylvia's mother came to England that summer, and she was a godsend, for a holocaust was brewing at Court Green.

Fortunately, we still have a few of Sylvia's letters from that period. In October she wrote to inform us of an impending divorce, claiming that Ted had, in effect, "deserted" her and the children. She also claimed that he had told her that he had not wanted to have any children and blamed him for having dragged her away from the London life she had loved. Other bitter accusations included the charge that Ted and his family did not want to support her and the children. But her main complaint dealt with the unbearable loneliness she was enduring, a loneliness made sharper by a recent bout of flu and the continued absence of friends and relatives, particularly social-minded intellectual friends from the city. She more or less pleaded for Paul and me to pay a visit and mentioned that she planned to go to Ireland near Galway for a rest before tackling another novel in December.

I did go. It was icy and foggy everywhere, and it took forever to travel from the bottom of Kent to London to Exeter—and heaven knows where else—to North Tawton. No one but me and my five-week-old baby got off the train, and no one was at the station but Sylvia. I can still see her there in the rain, the November night so dark that it scarcely shadowed her form, with a great city-gent's umbrella shored up with both hands. As I climbed down from the platform, she hugged me and said over and over, "You've saved my life." I thought it merely an expression.

Sylvia drove me to Court Green and the torrent of words began. We talked through four days and much of the nights. I think she suddenly felt very near to me. We were fairly old friends, but I suspect I was a kind of anchor. We were tied by Smith (which was always extremely important to her) and our myths were the same. We were Americans, contemporaries, and both of us had married poets, whose genius we had once thought we could sacrifice anything for and now were not so sure. We were mothers of small, dependent things and treading the water of sleepless nights, "nappies," near-poverty, spilled porridge, hills of laundry, loneliness, and the cold. And we were both willful about our love for England, despite the sometimes insupportable obstacles of daily life and the lack of family and old friends. Sylvia never even mentioned the possibility of giving it all up and going home to the United States—not to me at any rate.

It was natural enough that Sylvia should talk a great deal about Ted. She was divorcing him and the wounds were raw. The strong, passionate, sensitive Heathcliff had turned round and now appeared to her as a massive, crude, oafish peasant, who could not protect her from herself nor from the consequences of having grasped at womanhood. She cursed and mocked him for his weakness, and she called him a traitor.

Ted, however, had grown up in austere, dour Yorkshire—during the war—where his father kept a tobacco shop and his family was a fixed part of an age-old community. There, in those days, one didn't look to the glossies for an identity or for a scheme of values. One took life as it came, and "jolly well" made the best of it. I do not know, of course, but I would wager that Ted had little sympathy with Sylvia's midnight tears of sheer frustration that life wasn't as she had planned it.

And, too, I have wondered if the inventive Sylvia did not mastermind the Ted Hughes who was her husband, if she did not create him, like some sumptuous dessert to satiate her sensuous appetite for affection, poetry, acclaim, and life itself. I have wondered if Sylvia did not find just the right ingredients in Ted, a poet of passion and power, an Englishman of physical strength and intellectual ardor, and will them into a romantic being who was to be her perfect counterpart. Nature had long since molded this "giant of a man and a poet" before Sylvia unearthed him in Cambridge, however, and I dare say he was not prepared to be recast.

Whatever the reasons, life together was impossible. Ted had been spending more and more time in London, Leaving her in that cold, autumnal place on the verge of the moor and within the purlieus of Dartmoor prison. Sylvia gathered the apple harvest and plaited the onions, weeded the cobbles and pruned the roses, and she, the city girl, immersed herself in the land and in Devon lore. But how was it possible to cope with a large house, two small children, several acres of meadow and garden, crumbling outbuildings, shopping, cooking, and cleaning? And all in the middle of nowhere, without a friend in sight, without moral or physical support, hollowed of family, exhausted, lonely, and hounded mad—like Io—by the gadfly of poetry! Spies were peering into the blackened windows, the cold nipping at her ankles and "leering neighbors" were gossiping about her. Court Green was hell, and she was living in it. Ted had deserted her and the babes. He was enjoying the fleshpots of money and fame and was having affairs. Sylvia was angry, and the very walls must have trembled with her rage, her venom, her fear.

I am sure Sylvia brooded on suicide that fall, but two things distracted her. A kind, sensible, educated woman came for some weeks as a nurse. I suppose she initially was engaged for the children, but Sylvia spoke of her with such affection and admiration that she must have nursed her confused heart, revived her with friendship. The second distraction was a much more sinister preoccupation: Ted's treachery had to be dealt with.

Only once did I go into Ted's study at Court Green. Sylvia, with a sort of decisive flourish, opened the door to reveal a room with an oddly Edwardian atmosphere. There was about it an air of finality, as if there should have been a black ribbon above the lintel. It was as if the room had stopped at an instant of death. Some days before, Sylvia told me, when the moon was at a certain stage, she had skimmed from his desk "Ted's scum," microscopic bits of fingernail parings, dandruff, dead skin, hair, and then, with a random handful of papers collected from the desk and wastebasket, she had made a sort of pyre in the garden and around this she drew a circle. She stepped back to a prescribed point, lit the fire with a long stick of a torch and paced around, incanting some hocus-pocus or another. Flames shot up toward the moon, and smoke sketched weird shapes in the mist. Then fragments of letters and manuscripts fluttered like moths, hovered and, after the heat abated, floated to the ground. One charred piece settled at Sylvia's feet. It had been reduced to an ash save for a corner. She picked it up and by the light of the moon read "A_____," the name of a friend. Sylvia now knew the woman with whom Ted was having an affair.

When she died, I shuddered to imagine what curses she had hurled at Ted, and what maelstroms of sorcery she had conjured up on those winter nights alone by the moors, and, worse still, I had a horrifying vision of the first scenes having been played by this New England Medea.

Sylvia was a superb raconteur, and she told the tales of her witchcraft with racy humor and relish. She was delighted to discover she was so successful a sorceress. She knew what she was meddling with all right, and she was fiendishly serious, but I do not think for a moment that she was indivisibly resolute. Sylvia was exacting revenge, but she was also exorcising herself from Ted. Before she could move on to the next phase, she had to free herself from her demon-lover. And she was a pathetic supplicant, begging help from any source, ghoulish or not.

Though Sylvia really adored Court Green, she thought of it as a dungeon where Ted had buried her away. It was essential to escape, at least for part of the year, and she organized a retreat to London. But again she had to have help. Instead of invoking the devil, she turned this time to her beloved Yeats. (There is another strange, mystical story concerning Sylvia and Yeats at his tower in Ireland which I cannot remember.) Sylvia drew the curtains in the sitting-room at Court Green, turned out the lights, and lit a candle. She then picked up *The Complete Yeats*, set it on her lap, concentrated, closed her eyes, aimlessly opened the book and ran her finger down the page. After a moment's pause, she opened her eyes and read something to this affect: "Take up your things and come with me." I once scoured the plays of Yeats, as I am fairly sure she said the passage came from one of them, but never recognized the line. Whatever the precise words, the message directed her to him.

She left the children with the nurse then staying with her and set off for London. Now, Sylvia knew London reasonably well, but Hampstead was her most familiar haunt, so that is where she headed. From Waterloo Station she took the tube north and arbitrarily disembarked at the Chalk Farm stop. Outside most tube stations, as anyone who has been to London will know, are cards of advertisements: requests for things like lost dogs and small bicycles and usually notices of rooms or flats to rent. Quite naturally, Sylvia stopped to read these. Her attention was seized by one in particular, which looked too good to be true. It was just the perfect size, nearby, and available for occupancy within weeks. She was sure it would already be gone, but still rushed to the address given on the card. And when she stood at the edge of the road and saw the advertised house, Sylvia shook all over. There was a blue plaque on the wall with the legend, "W. B. Yeats lived here." So did Sylvia Plath, for a while.

Except for the finishing touches, the dots and commas, *The Bell Jar* was over and done. I suspect that Sylvia intended this book to symbolize the end of her affair with death. Yeats had sent this amazing omen of resurrection and poetry, and she felt sure that she was about to begin *writing*, that she had been given starter's orders and nothing could stop her now. While I was with her in Devon, the astonishing output of poems was underway. Sheets of paper flew from her typewriter like tickets from a machine gone wrong, and they lay uncollected on the otherwise tidy floor. Sylvia was inspired. She just needed some help.

During the time I knew her, this plea for support cropped up again and again. It is nearly a cliché to say that Sylvia Plath should have had a Leonard Woolf to indulge, nurture, and protect her. Nevertheless, it remains obviously true. Sylvia and I talked about Virginia Woolf and the paradox of their situations. There was a discrepancy of half a century in their youths, and yet Virginia Woolf had possessed an inherent independence Sylvia lacked. She had been hesitant of ever marrying, but Sylvia had regarded it as an absolute priority. Virginia had married in response to Leonard's quiet, deliberated, kind persuasions, while Sylvia married in a flourish of egotistical and poetical infatuation. Sylvia was as much an intellectual; and as sensitsive, as intolerant, as imaginative, as single-minded as Virginia Woolf, but she was naïvely romantic, and probably had never seriously entertained the idea of life unhusbanded. The women's magazines and the popular literature of the fifties, obsessed with "the man in your life," intensified the gnawing vacuum her father had left in her own existence.

When Virginia Woolf was young there was no dirth of intrepid spinsters who, if unemancipated, hadn't hesitated in charging into deepest Africa, confronting savages with umbrellas unfurled. In 1900 an unattached and determined woman, if educated, could enjoy a satisfactory, amiable, even exotic existence. It was our mothers and our generations, frightened by the necrology of two male-slaughtering wars, who whispered the agony of old maid. The pathetic, unwanted soul who hadn't "got a man" was like a clock without a spring. When she was twenty, twenty-one, twenty-two, Sylvia did not know there were alternatives, she said, nor could she have embraced a dullard like Leonard Woolf.

If Sylvia genuinely wanted more children, as she said, it is a bit of a puzzle. Nevertheless, she professed to desiring a good-sized brood—but without the manacle of a husband. We dreamed up a scheme. I knew a rather splendid man of about fifty who, as vice-president of something or other of one of the world's biggest companies, was naturally quite rich.

He traveled widely in his job and could easily drop in to Court Farm from time to time to father babies. He had no children by his wife, and he surely would welcome this opportunity. And, best of all, he was Polish. I know now it isn't true, but Sylvia told me her father was a Pole. (She was wildly proud to possess the red blood of those courageous, virile, passionate people, whose spirit could be halted or maimed by anyone.) Sylvia would add some lovely little Poles to her clutch, and this brave ex-cavalry officer would finance all her children, her writing, Yeats's house in London, a nanny, holidays in the sun—heaven knows what else we had this Daddy Long Legs providing!

The two children already created were darling. Small though they were, both gave the impression of astuteness and cleverness. Neither appeared to miss a note, an innuendo. They observed . . . I remember that well. And they were so quiet. Sylvia's little boy watched and listened and appeared to absorb every movement and sound, but made almost none himself. The bright eyes of her compact, charming two-year-old daughter noted every minutia, and she seemed to tip-toe through the day. She was intrigued with the brand-new infant I had with me and silently attached herself to us. There is a curious incident I recall when she was looking through our things. Sylvia told her she must not. I replied that I didn't mind in the least, that all children loved to prowl in guests' belongings—it was a way of identifying and smelling them out. But Sylvia insisted that I might have something dangerous and then began scooping into my bags. She hauled out a bottle of iron pills and hid them atop a very tall cupboard, saying that they could have been sleeping pills. She was clearly upset.

I was fascinated by the Hughes' children because they were so different from any small things I had ever lived with, who chattered, and pestered, as if the very act of mother-torment would turn tiny shapes into real living creatures. These strangely independent children seemed to sense Sylvia's preoccupation and detachment, as well as the futility of demanding her attention or overt affection, yet they seemed sure enough of her love. Sylvia talked incessantly about her children, but I cannot remember her hugging or fondling her *bunnies*—as she always called them. In the same house together, it was as if they were already severed.

In her witty conversation Sylvia instilled an extra dimension into the most ancient art of procreation, and she had wonderful tales of her lyings-in. I cannot remember any of the colorful details. But the actual bearing of children was important to her; almost more real, it seemed to me, than the resulting children. She talked a lot about midwives. I think she liked the sound of the word and the connotations of primordial efficiency, deftness, simple deliverance. Again, the need of help preyed upon her. I thought it odd at the time that Sylvia should refer to the good woman sent round by the National Health as "my midwife." Doctors, nurses, midwives, these words peppered her conversation and letters. My doctor, my nurse, my midwife; intimate yet impersonal; recruited from the newspapers, nanny-finding agencies, National Health clinics; they took the place of nonexistent family and friends.

Rather like those millions of women who go to a hairdresser to be administered to and fondled, Sylvia longed for undivided attention. And often enough she needed more consideration than an ordinary person could provide or understand. Her own metaphors, undefined illnesses, fevers, chillblains, flu, all various weaknesses that nagged the tall, strong New Englander, demanded alleviation and assistance. When she cheered her freedom from the fiendish Ted, she was weeping aloud the loss of love, her counterpart, and she longed for her loneliness, her fear to be doctored. Her children—her precious bunnies—were her regeneration, womanhood, the life force itself, but without a nanny they siphoned off fancy and left dried petals of an isolated harridan. Without help her farmhouse was a ghost, her adored English home her jail. Sylvia intoxicated herself with midnight revelations of Ted's nefarious family, yet once she had expected their interest and care. It was her mother who nursed her through the impossible summer of 1962 and restored order in her life, perhaps restored life itself. Nurses and doctors and midwives were her prescriptions for living—if only Sylvia could be delivered from chaos, the Poet could evolve.

Most of us who knew Sylvia knew a different Sylvia Plath. This is partly because she was secretive and devious and selective, but I think, too, it was because aspects of her character were dispersed. In a curious way she seemed uncompleted. Like fragments of mercury racing and quivering toward a center to settle in a self-contained mass, the myriad ramifications of her personality sought a focal point. At various stages Sylvia had tried to center her existence on school, on love, on children, even on market gardening, but always her creative genius was the core which drew everything to it but could not muster control. It seemed as if every thought, passion, regret, delight, terror, experience, vision, bruise, contempt—anything and everything—darted straight to a sort of honeycomb (bypassing tangibles), where it was trapped, zealously horded by her greedy genius, which forbade her simple, uncomplicated reactions or feelings, and where it cruelly barred her from ordinary living. The only way to govern this confusion of incarcerated emotion was to regiment it in magnificent, tidy lines of metaphor, meter, meaning, and beauty on shiny, virginal bits of paper.

Whatever efforts she made, however she worked at fabricating a life for herself, the demon Poetry—creator of artifice, simulator, spectator—took over. She had to be a woman and she had to be a poet with equal intensity. Liveliness in the fullest sense pinioned poetry, and poetry trammeled humanity. Poor Sylvia was a kind of prisoner, even if self-imprisoned, and she was a perpetual supplicant for rescue and release.

Though Sylvia was most artful and carefully spoke in riddles, there was many a clue thrown out. It was as if she had been saying, "If you were half as clever as I, or if you cared, you'd see through the cross-talk and help me." I did partially understand this, and so did others. We thought of helping her in whatever manner we could. Her mother buoyed her morale with affectionate letters and what money she could spare. Friends sympathized and wished her well. But what none of us could properly comprehend was Sylvia's soul-shredding, relentless drive to write. Somehow one forgot about the mysterious shadow that chased her from sleep and hounded her into dark corners at dawn, forcing her to spew onto paper the quintessential Sylvia.

When *The Observer* announced her death in February, I was so stupefied that I was convinced they mistook her for another. A dead Sylvia didn't make sense. There was something almost powerful about her physical presence. Dead! With that great lusty laugh and original flair for life? There was no palely loistering poetess about her. She was positive, almost to the point of aggression. She was skillful, creative, alive. There was nothing ethereal about Sylvia.

She had always remained a warm, affectionate, talented, amusing person, self-centered but excellent company, a vivacious friend. And yet, after all these years, I wonder if it was the shock of her death that left a certain imprint on my memory or if it was the force of her personality that has clung to me in stray vignettes. And too, I wonder if Sylvia's suicide caused me to remember bits and pieces I now regard as portents and clues, or if she was so coated with death and destruction that that had been as much a part of her character as her intelligence and wit. Also, what Sylvia would I remember if she had wandered into the road and been run over by a bus? Whatever the answers, I know I cannot think of her without thinking of death. Sylvia made a study of it, and, infuriatingly, she makes me study it too. I have mulled over dozens of ideas and always come back to the conclusion that her suicide was a twist of fate. The Sunday newspapers did not make a mistake, Sylvia did.

I have a recurring image of Sylvia lying on her back, indulging her nasty habit of smoking an opium pipe of death—like some white-suited Cantonese in a white-walled den, drifting into a hazy sanctuary. She had picked up this habit when she was far too young and, rather than shake it off, she had conscientiously hooked herself further, boastfully calling herself a connoisseur of death. It and her father were almost one and the same, and if she were to keep alive the one she must cling to the other. Stark deadness was an aphrodisiac to her senses. The thought of it excited her, intensified living, concentrated the mind wonderfully. Rather arrogantly, Sylvia liked keeping death beside her, flirting and teasing it with a thrill of mastery. Once she described to me her suicide attempt in farcical detail and several times emphasized the miracle of her survival. It was her iron will to live, she said, that saved her, and she displayed the scars to prove her prowess. When she was as good as dead, some gigantic, bellicose spirit inside refused to be extinguished and literally pulled her to her feet and cried out from the tomb! Death himself knocked her down and the cold concrete of her grave clawed her face, but she won the day and was there—alive, valiant, triumphant. I shall never forget her eloquence or her pride.

Sylvia had a Renaissance fascination for the finite body, for death's corrupting, corroding guises of misshapen bones, spilt blood and entrails, worm-infested organs. Like the ruffed statesmen of finite worldly power who modeled their own effigies and death masks and kept a skeleton beside the privy seal to remind themselves that one day all would turn to dust, Sylvia courted death to stimulate life. She fancied herself the temptress, not the tempted. Death might play the tune, but she was the librettist—and in control.

I went to see Sylvia in London when she moved to Yeats's house. It was England's famous winter of frozen canals and frozen oaks. The trains were more or less mummified, and people skidded about, mystified by the ice. At her door the snow was deep and unindented—pure New England morning whiteness. Sylvia came down to let me in in her dressing gown. She was ill with flu. She showed me her part of the house and the preparations being made for the *au pair* girl, who was due to arrive within the month. The flat was really too full of modern conveniences to be reminiscent of black-cloaked Yeats. The sitting room was biggish, its furniture neither here nor there in style, but it was spruce and trim. There was a large electric fire on the wall, high enough away from small fingers, and wonderfully warming to us when we sat in front of it. The kitchen was very smart. I had been living in England long enough to be amazed by all her gadgetry.

The whole flat was efficient. Sylvia had spent a good deal of thought in organizing her new existence. Not only was she making curtains but she was making plans for her writing and for her new life. She had twenty pounds a week from Ted (a large sum in those days), and an aunt was sending her some money every month. She told me she had just the right sort of sick humor to turn out stories for *The New Yorker*. That would pay well. She could discipline herself, she said, to produce them quickly and leave plenty of time for poetry. When the *au pair* girl came everything woud sort itself out. With help all would go well.

I would not want to give the impression that Sylvia was living in the land of milk and honey. It is, however, a gross exaggeration to assume that she was oppressed by poverty the last weeks of her life. Even for an American she was living reasonably well. Certainly she was no martyr to the muse, huddled in a garret with newspapers wrapped around her feet or pathetically singing lullabies instead of writing them. Yeats made her most comfortable. Ted, her family, her pen, all provided her with sufficient income. As soon as the "help" arrived, she could write and live.

The Bell Jar was in proofs then. Sylvia used a pseudonym so that her mother would not read the book and be hurt, she said. If she told others that she was ashamed of having written a mere novel, she did not tell me. In fact, I remember a plot for another she had mapped out. It had to do with a nice, simple girl with nice, simple, generations-old values who is made fun of for being straightforward and decent by a worldly roommate in college. The artful roommate corrupted the innocent by mockery, and when she packed her bags for the summer holi-days she left a confused, hardened cynic behind.

Sylvia was writing poetry at a tremendous rate. She wrote possessed, as if the poem she was driven to create was herself. Before dawn she was at her desk, furiously scribbling out the life force, as she called it. Of course this left her exhausted. And she was already drained and weary by the move from Devon, by fear of the future alone, and by a pernicious attack of the flu.

Outwardly, she seemed to have things under control. There were no heaps of dirty dishes, no piles of unwashed linen. The children were clean and dressed. The rooms were tidy. Even the beds were made—the astounding orderliness of a real hausfrau. The kitchen was so neat that I suspected she hadn't used it, and I made her and the children a meal of pork chops and tinned corn. Even in a state that would be chaotic to anyone else, she had daily menus arranged and the ingredi-ents laid out. Sylvia devoured this so ravenously that I was suspicious, and, sure enough, she confessed eventually that she had not been eating the meals she so carefully planned. In fact, I think she was ill enough to muddle the days and nights. Sylvia then went to bed for a time and slept until my husband arrived with my other two children. When she came down there was no apparent trace of her feeling awful. She was a past master at disguising any state.

We talked about the literary world of London. She was scathing about the "worthies." Typical of Sylvia, she laughed at the sycophants who courted her and Ted. She told how they had got a pass to the court trial of *Lady Chatterly's Lover*—by bullying a famous poet. The best way to get on in the world, she said, was by bullying, especially in the literary world where the nature of the beast is weak. She was malicious and dishonest, too. But, somehow, when Sylvia talked, she was so animated and amusing there was no sense of the negative, the distor-tion. She said she had done book reviews not because the money was good but because she got free books. She would be sent a bunch, read and review one or two, and keep the lot. If her name was seen in print, she would be thought important, like a roadside sign. She laughed and laughed at the toadies, yet I know she was proud to be accepted as a poet by these very people, honored to be published alongside them.

Sylvia and I shared a curious alliance in my sister, whom Sylvia had never met. This sister had, like her, mesmerized teachers and other students by sheer brilliance, charm, and talent. She was an American Dream Girl, brandishing an all-A record in school (on the "Queen's Court"), invariably given leading roles in the plays, and so on. This sister of mine whirled through the College Board exams and would have been given a full scholarship to Smith except that my father was thought to be able to pay. She went off to Smith with a fanfare of trumpets, but she had not been there more than a few months when she ran away out of loathing and contempt for the place. My father took her back and was about to reinstate her when he discovered that she was supposed to be "studying" a William Penn Warren book in freshman English. So he too decided Smith was lousy . . . "of all the superb books in the English language—to peruse a third-rate Book of the Month Club novel!" My sister was set free. The tale fascinated Sylvia. She cross-examined me over and over about her, and she pumped me for information to such an extent that I suspected one day my sister would reappear in a Sylvia Plath story.

It was not until years after she died that I learned of Sylvia's emotional ties to and deep love for Smith. With me she lampooned the whole Smith scene and all those teachers and pupils who took it seriously. I naïvely believed Sylvia and never guessed that she had flogged herself to that summit and that acceptance into Smith was so terribly important to her—a huge ambition fulfilled. But the pose Sylvia took with me over the Smith business was in its own way genuine. She had a way of courting, conquering, and then scorning. She was inclined to belittle and cast aside any achievements she had pursued and trounced, like a rakish libertine who dismisses the virgin he has seduced.

The day I had gone to visit Sylvia I had taken the two smaller children with me. Paul had turned up with the older two, so our progeny seemed to be all over the place. Sylvia emphatically decided that he was the perfect father (rather to his annoyance). Paul was a fellow poet, but she chose to ignore this triviality. He was a father and that was that. I can actually see her flashing dark eyes fixing him with a kind of awe.

When we left Sylvia the night had come. She promised to get back to bed immediately. We returned to Kent. Sylvia was to come down and stay with us if the *au pair* didn't arrive within a few days, as she hoped she would.

I knew Sylvia was weak, and I knew she wasn't eating properly. And I knew it was as difficult to go out shopping in London as it had been in Devon. But she assured us that she had friends who could see her through until the nanny arrived. If she found herself alone, without help, she promised to join us in Kent. We had a spare room at the top of the house waiting. I had so many children anyway that looking after two more would not create much of a difficulty. We would keep in touch. I went off with the proofs of *The Bell Jar*.

The winter of 1963 was like the one Virginia Woolf described in *Orlando*, when Russian ships were frozen in harbor, and one could skate for miles along the canals, as in an animated Brueghel painting. I worried about Sylvia. I wrote her. (I think her telephone had not been connected.) I returned the proofs. But I did not press her to come to us. The only heating we had was a coal stove in the kitchen and a portable kerosene burner. The coal merchants refused to supply us because they said we hadn't paid a bill. Whether that was so or not, I do not know, I just know we were damn cold. The toilet and the bath were solid chunks of ice, absolutely useless. Six of us huddled by the gas oven and, with the rest of England, waited for the thaw. Sylvia's flu —perhaps it was pneumonia—had become worse. Her children were ill and running scalding fevers too. In her last letter: "I am writing from bed where the doctor has put me . . ." and "My very wise and kind doctor got me a private day-nurse for 10 days or I don't know what I would have done." The long-awaited *au pair* was to move in with her and the children, at Yeats's house, at the end of the week. Obviously, she was better off there than with us in Kent.

Sylvia wrote on and on in a crescendo of poesy. The doctor came and went, never suspecting what miracles he was to perform. Her secret affair—the dizzying fever her mind and imagination whirled about in— she hoped could be pried from her moribund heart by a thermometer, clean white sheets, and ministers of mercy, as if all the pain and evil of the human spirit could be cauterized by a wise and kind man with a black bag.

Then Sylvia was dead. I still don't know the details. They don't matter. She had lost the long-standing game of Russian roulette. Dazed, stunned by blackouts and near comas, staggering beneath the pounding of relentless words, her foul, habitual consort won the day. Her desperate, perpetual efforts to rub out the tattoo of death she wore most of her life—that very act of writing to stay alive, as if speaking of and to death could keep him at bay—exhausted her. Her mind and body checkmated each other. Sylvia lost control. The temptress was tempted.

8   For Sylvia at 4:30 A.M.

PAULA ROTHHOLZ

Flung into consciousness
to impact steel despair
doll-lids click-up

light years of energy
surge through her
and cannot be dispelled

relentless inner forces
leave her grape-peeled
her own S.S.

The chimneys would be welcome

Her red shoes
will not stop
cannot be undone

against her irresistible
forces are no
immovable objects

not even babies.

Brain washer agitates
present, future, past
too heavy a burden

for the döppelganger
crone who never
leaves her

murmuring unceasingly
of the engulfing loneliness
of the endless coming

Galaxies smash
in her brain
friction sparks
                    demons
                    poetry
                    fiction

Coronas flare
showing her universe
without shadows

razor sharp detail
slashes her into
irredeemable bits

of blinding clarity

Time is her relative

Sandman cometh not;
eyes glitter refuse
to grain

"I am going insane

(word is father to the deed)

Indeed father,
I have lost my mind
and don't know
where to find
it
If I leave it alone
will it come home
entailing me
behind
it?"

They will return
to torture me
with electrocutions

for sins of elocutions
I never knew
I committed

I will not allow them
to make me
impotent

I will not let them
rejoice at how the
I Mighty has fallen.

                The oven waits.

Watch me
all you murdering
daddy-o's—

The gas too
has a cock
            sucker!

Sylvia in Devon: 1962

ELIZABETH SIGMUND

I first met Sylvia Plath almost exactly a year before her death; her daughter Frieda was nearly two and Nick was a month old. She and Ted had bought Court Green, a beautiful, eleventh-century thatched house in North Tawton, a tiny mill town in mid-Devon.

My first impression of Sylvia was of a tall, slim, vividly alive young woman, with waist-length brown hair. She wore a long skirt and dark stockings, which were unusual for those days, and I admit to being enchanted and overwhelmed by her and Ted and their beautiful house.

As they were in the process of furnishing Court Green, we sat and had tea in the playroom on deckchairs near a long trestle table, which Sylvia had painted white and decorated with little, enamelled flowers. The room had a black-and-white tiled floor, like a Flemish painting, and looked out onto a lawn with a laburnum tree, and beyond lay the orchard and the village church and its graveyard. One wall of the room was all shelves, full of children's books, many of which Sylvia had reviewed for the American press, and there was a piano in the room, which Sylvia admitted to "trying to play, but I have no ear."

Ted and my (then) husband David, who was also a writer, at once began writer's talk about agents and publishers, and our small son James set up a watchful parallel play with the three-year-old Frieda.

Sylvia's approach to me was all questions—children, home interests, and politics. When I admitted to being a member of the Liberal Party, she jumped up and almost shouted, "Thank God, a committed woman!" —which made me smile as it wasn't totally true, but pleasing. We discussed national policies on armaments, and she told me with bitter anger of the involvement of American big business with weaponry. She obviously cared deeply about her country.

Baby Nick was asleep in his pram under the laburnum tree, and Sylvia kept running out to see if he was warm and sleeping well. She told me of the vegetables she was growing and the plans they had for the house—"We shall have five children, the boys will sleep here and the girls there. This is Ted's writing room. Here is where Nick was born." All plans, all life.

She had painted brilliant little hearts and flowers on her sewing machine, a doll's cradle, and even the door sills; later, she told me she had decorated her beehives too. "Now bees land on *my* flowers."

So much energy, such intensity of experience and expression, but with an underlying pulse of pressure which was disturbing. I felt then a sense of urgency in her to do everything, and to do it now, a pressure *on* her and *in* her toward excellence, which was both stimulating and daunting, but made me afraid for her.

I told her of our remote North Devon mill house, with well water, no electricity, which delighted her; she was a purist and hated smoking and phony foods. Frieda had dates and nuts instead of sweets, and Sylvia made delicious banana bread with whole flour which we ate for tea—and it has been a family favorite of ours ever since.

At this stage I didn't know of her literary talent; I knew that she was a writer, but of what and with what success I had no idea. Neither she nor Ted gave any indication of this, all Sylvia's literary talk with me concerned Ted's brilliance and successes, and her grave pride in him was most moving.

When we were leaving we made plans for them to visit us, and she spoke of Devon as the first place she had really felt at home, providing the ancient roots which she had so desperately desired and never found in America. Her "wall of dead," which she loved like history, was true, they were really there, forming a boundary to her orchard, and their dust gave her peace.

At the time, I was the wife of a poor and hard-working author with very little time for discovering myself or my own potential. Bringing up three children in a primitive remote cottage on a tiny and fluctuating income took all my energy and mental strength. Therefore, Sylvia conceived a picture of me which was very incomplete and in some ways unreal. I think one of her faults was a tendency to see what she wanted in people, rather than what was there.

My concentration on homemaking and child-rearing in such an out-of-date and rural setting made me something of an Earth Mother figure for Sylvia, and she had a need to see me as such. She once said, "You must never leave here. I see you with your little twinkly lights always round you." (She meant our smoky oil lamps.) Later, she said that we were destined to appear in her second novel, about North Tawton, as saints. So pitifully far from the truth!

When Sylvia and Ted came to visit us I felt the impact of their stature, and their unassailable closeness, a "keep out" sign which one respected totally, their shared reactions to life which needed no words between them. I have a picture of them together leaning over an ancient stone bridge, gazing down into the peat-brown Devon trout stream below our house, entranced and silent, with a quality of utter concentration usual only in children, but also like visitors from another planet who *had* to understand and were communicating completely without words.

I first learnt of Sylvia's work from Ted some weeks later when I asked, "Does Sylvia write poetry, too?"

Ted answered "No, she *is* a poet," which put it all clear for me at last.

On my thirty-fourth birthday she and Ted arrived unexpectedly in the evening. He brought a bottle of wine, and she carried a glorious iced cake wrapped in her beautiful shawl. She had baked and iced the cake and put thirty-five candles on it. "One for you to grow on," she said.

No one gave Sylvia one candle to grow on. Seven months later she would be dead.

We saw a lot of Sylvia and the children that spring, though Ted was usually working or in London. We became very close, though she never talked to me about her work. She wanted to be known and loved by us as herself, apart from her achievements, and was intensely excited by her home and her children and all the potential she was finding in herself for homemaking, which had so far been unrealized. I met Nancy Axworthy, who cleaned house for Sylvia, a wonderful, strong, kind woman, whose calmness and gentle common sense meant so much to Sylvia. Nancy has told me of Sylvia's diffident approach when interviewing her for the job, until Frieda peeped round the door and, in a few moments, was sitting on Nancy's knee with both arms around her neck. Sylvia walked over and said, "Please come. We'd love to have you." From then on, Nancy was "My Nancy" to Frieda, who trotted around each day "helping" with her tiny brush and dustpan.

Nancy's love for Sylvia is unchanged, and her sadness and bewilderment at the things she has read about Sylvia since her death are heartbreaking.

In the summer I also met Aurelia, Sylvia's mother. I knew that the relationship was a close but difficult one for Sylvia. Not having read *The Bell Jar*, I didn't know much, but I felt in Mrs. Plath a brittle anxiety, an anxious pride, which I could see stretched Sylvia and made her nervous. I could see that Mrs. Plath wanted to help, particularly with the children, but that to Sylvia this was trespassing, and I understood the tensions very well. On this visit Sylvia also told me a little of Ted's family, though she didn't seem to understand the North Country bluntness and diffidence which I know so well, having come from Lancashire myself. When Sylvia went to stay in Yorkshire she felt totally alien. She feared the dark brooding country, as seen in her poem "Wuthering Heights." She felt it forbidding, and the close Hughes family shut to her. When Ted's mother, Edith, refused to allow her to help in the kitchen, it was from respect for and awe of Sylvia's education and class, though Sylvia as an American could only see it as a rejection. I knew Edith, and know that she was a deep, intelligent, and sensitive woman; she suffered greatly from Sylvia's death, and was never well again after. If only she and Sylvia could have overcome, or at least recognized, the barriers between them, Edith could have been a source of comfort and strength to Sylvia beyond any other. Edith had an inborn sense of poetry and beauty and a deep understanding of the mysteries of the world, but balanced always by the practical sense of a working woman, who had been forced to survive in a rough world.

The most difficult person in Ted's family was his sister Olwyn, who feared and resented Sylvia's talent and beauty, as well as her relationship with Ted. Sylvia felt this terrible jealousy deeply, and recognized an insurmountable anger. She often told me that Olwyn hated her, resented her position as another daughter in the family. When I met Olwyn after Sylvia's death, I felt that she had understated Olwyn's attitude; it was one which I found hard to tolerate even at second hand. Unfortunately, most of the censorship and angling of material available to people wishing to write of Sylvia comes from this source, and must therefore be regarded as somewhat suspect.

I tried to explain to Sylvia the terrible, crushing class system in this country, and how people like the Hugheses suffered from it in ways which would be hard for an American college girl to understand. I asked her if she didn't think that, somewhere, Ted had a feeling of inferiority. Her answer was a bitterly scornful laugh. "Ted has lunched with the Duke of Edinburgh," she said, which of course was no answer at all.

Over these months as I got to know Sylvia better, I recognized a basic timidity and fearfulness, which she often cloaked with defensive acerbity. I saw her being extremely entertaining and humorous with friends from whom she felt no threat, and I learnt of her love for riding and the joy she garnered from gathering wood and lighting incense-smelling fires. We made plans for family picnics to North Devon beaches, and always talked as if we should all know each other for years.

Then suddenly, late one evening, Sylvia arrived with Nick in his carry cot, and the change in her was appalling. She kept saying "My milk has dried up, I can't feed Nick. My milk has gone."

At last she told me that Ted was in love with another woman, that she knew Assia and was terrified of her. She wept and wept and held onto my hands, saying, "Help me!"

What could I do? I have never felt so inadequate in my life. She claimed, "Ted lies to me, he lies all the time, he has become a *little* man." But the most frightening thing she said was, "When you give someone your whole heart and he doesn't want it, you cannot take it back. It's gone forever."

I knew that this was the truth, I had seen it in her. Having watched them together so often, sensing the minute and powerful filaments of perception and understanding between them, I knew that to break these would be the greatest agony imaginable.

Brought up, as she had been, in a male-oriented society, with its Freudian extrovert emphasis, conditioned to develop the competitive, striving, intellectual side of her nature, this life with Ted here in Devon —with all its sane roots in history and the natural cycles of planting and harvesting, birth and death—had allowed her to begin to recognize and feel her female self at last. With this flowering, however, came also the terrible vulnerability of all dependent creatures.

The poet's genius, which must be rooted in opening eyes to everything, without the possibility of self-protection—as Emily Brontë says —had come to Sylvia. Thus, her brilliant last poems.

She stayed that night with us, refusing to take our bed and sleeping on the sofa. First thing next morning, I came down to find her bending over a box containing a cat and her new kittens. I can see her now, wearing a pink, woolly dressing gown with a long, brown plait of hair falling into the box, turning her head and saying, "I never saw anything so small and new and vulnerable. They are blind."

What could I do to protect and help this amazing person?

She came often after this, now smoking cigarettes, becoming thinner and more desperate. She told me the terrible incident of the telephone call, which caused Ted finally to leave her. The poem "The Fearful" is about this. Assia apparently rang Court Green to speak to Ted, but when Sylvia answered Assia pretended to be a man. Sylvia said she knew who it was, but Assia kept up the charade, asking to speak to Ted. Sylvia did finally fetch him to the phone, but when the conversation was done, pulled the wires from the wall. Ted left.

One night she and I drove to a Bach concert in a nearby town, and it was obvious that she was ill. She later wrote to me about "Fever 103°," saying, "I have been getting up at five in the morning to write dawn poems in blood."

At this stage she was composing all the brilliant last poems. It was the most desperate time, and she was trying with all her strength and intellect to face the unbearable. The therapeutic value of writing *The Bell Jar* to assimilate and exorcise the terrors of her adolescent breakdown had been obvious; and I believe that she was attempting the same catharsis during the early autumn.

She was fortunate in having found Susan—the daughter of a couple who lived in Belstone—as a nanny for the children. Susan's father is a writer, and her mother a sensitive and charming woman. They live on the edge of Dartmoor in a lovely old house, and knew and loved Sylvia. They told me about Ariel, the horse Sylvia rode on the moor. It is a sad little story as Ariel was old and rather reluctant to move fast, but extremely safe to ride. The impression from the poem called "Ariel" is of a young, fiery steed galloping recklessly over brambly moorland. The truth gives a deep insight into this girl's underlying fear of life, and her parallel wish to be daring in the eyes of others.

Susan was a nurse, and a godsend to Sylvia, giving her peace of mind about the children and the time to rest and write, which she so urgently needed.

Sylvia then told me that Ted had asked her to take the children to Ireland with him to stay with a friend. She obviously thought that this was to be an attempt at reconciliation, but, in fact, he only settled her into the cottage and left immediately again for London. It was obvious that things were now even worse; and though she came to see us, bringing home-grown honey, apples, potatoes, and onions, she was being torn apart. Only finishing the work on her dawn poems was keeping her together.

She had friends to stay who didn't help. They lost Frieda's doll's pram and struck her as selfish and insensitive—her poem "Lesbos" is about her brief stay later with them in Cornwall.

When she decided to go and remain in London for the winter, I felt most apprehensive. But at least, I thought, she had friends there, and having found Yeats's house seemed of great significance. She wrote several times, and I believed that, despite her illness, things were improving and that she was growing a skin over the wound. She wrote, "Bringing up two children alone leaves one feeling quite black and empty inside. Ted comes to see the children sometimes, but I keep sighing for lost Edens." She asked if she might dedicate *The Bell Jar* to us, and mentioned again her work on the new novel about North Tawton "in which you appear briefly as angels." She said that she *never* wanted these novels to appear in her own name, as they would hurt too many people.

Her last letter to me was all plans, dated February 7, 1963. She was coming back to Devon ("Thank God you are there"), was to appear on "The Critics" (a BBC radio arts program), and was to complete a poetry reading. *Punch* had also asked for some articles, and she had got Frieda into a small baby school for a while. She wrote to Nancy by the same post, saying much the same things, and asking her to have the two cats, Tiger and Skunky, doctored, claiming, "I don't want to come home to a house full of kittens." She then wrote, "I long to see my home, and will be back soon."

Four days later she was dead.

It was unbelievable. It couldn't be. I remember walking in the dark country lanes, and saying over and over to myself, "Where is she?" There were tracks of a fox in the snow, wandering this way and that, sniffing for answers to its own secret questions. I bent over the prints, tears making holes in the snow. She would have understood.

Since then I have had to endure reading and hearing descriptions of Sylvia and her life which are unrecognizable. To die once is bad enough, but to be repeatedly crucified in this way by people who never knew her is unforgivable. Amateur psychologists have analyzed her poetry, people who never met her have pontificated on her depressive, schizophrenic personality that could not form relationships. Many times it has been stated that she "rejected her marriage."

When a writer from America wrote to ask if I could see her to talk about Sylvia, I went and asked Ted what he felt. His answer was: "The time to tell the truth about Sylvia is when you are dying." I reckon that—with Robert Louis Stevenson—we are dying every day that we live.

In Sylvia's own words, in a funny little private poem I found at Court Green—"Magna est Veritas et Prevaelabit"—which roughly means, "Truth is mighty, and will prevail. In a bit."

II

SYLVIA PLATH:

THE WORK

10   Architectonics: Sylvia Plath's Colossus

PAMELA SMITH

When Sylvia Plath and Anne Sexton met in 1958-1959, while both were auditing one of Robert Lowell's classes at Boston University, they made a weekly ritual of going to the Ritz cocktail lounge, in the company of George Starbuck, to drink martini after martini and to reminisce again and again about their attempted suicides. Poetry stayed in the never-never-land of Robert Lowell's spectacles and the B.U. classroom; suicide belonged in the posh, alcoholic dreamland of expensive stemware and the Ritz bar. Sexton has attempted to explain: "Poems left behind were technique—lasting, but, actually, over. We talked death and this was life for us, lasting in spite of us, or better, because of us. . . ." [1] But despite all the talking, all the taunting death, Sylvia Plath in the coldly sober hours of the years while she was building *The Colossus* [2] chose to concentrate on the "technique" of writing poetry rather than the expectant "life" of dying, fixed on the how, not the what to do.

Anne Sexton has joined the mainstream of Plath criticism by saying that in those days of the late fifties, when the first book of poems was still a work-in-progress, Sylvia Plath was constrained by "her preoccupation with form." Of the works which Plath submitted to Lowell, Sexton says, "Those early poems were all in a cage (and not even her own cage at that). I felt she hadn't found a voice of her own, wasn't, in truth, free to be herself." [3] This notion has become a convention of commentary on *The Colossus*. Reviewers including A. Alvarez, Peter Davison, A. E. Dyson, Marjorie Perloff, and Eleanor Ross Taylor have propounded the idea that Plath was not sure of herself, was not mature as an artist, until she could declare to "Daddy" in *Ariel*,[4] "Daddy, daddy, you bastard, I'm through," and warn as "Lady Lazarus":

Herr God, Herr Lucifer,
Beware
Beware.
Out of the ash
I rise with my red hair
And I eat men like air.

A reader excited by *Ariel* would not be much encouraged to look back to *The Colossus* by the rather scornful dismissals of the volume, even by those who raved about *Ariel*. Richard Howard simply pronounces the poems "well-behaved, shapely"; Peter Davison terms them "advanced exercises." The judgment of Alvarez seems typical: "Throughout *The Colossus* she is using her art to keep the disturbance, out of which she made her verse, at a distance. It is as though she had not yet come to grips with her subject as an artist. She has Style, but not properly her own style." [5] A portrait of the young poet takes shape from such review sketches: poor Sylvia hammers out her spondees, iambs, and trochees to keep from going crazy or killing herself.

What results from the generally distorted commentary on Sylvia Plath is an exaggerated division, an oversimplified, schizoid picture of Plath in her two books: we have in *The Colossus* the monolithic, formal, self-conscious Sylvia Bound (but alive and well); in *Ariel*, the demonic, fearlessly casual, fiercely candid Sylvia Unbound (but psychoneurotic and suicidal). Fortunately a few men have been incisive enough to resist the tendency to superimpose divisions and have been sensitive enough to perceive the continuity in her work.

Foremost among these more perceptive critics is John Frederick Nims, a considerably talented poet himself, who recommends *The Colossus* as a model of a well-served poetic apprenticeship. But, even while he is pointing out the fact that the first book is structural and stylistic groundwork for the second, he hedges by remarking, "Without the drudgery of *The Colossus*, the triumph of *Ariel* is unthinkable." [6] Denoting the work as "drudgery" is quite likely too severe. If the poems are merely prosodic warmups for the virtuoso performance of *Ariel*, then they might fairly be termed "drudgery." Some of the poems, the failures of the first book, are unquestionably just that. "Aftermath," for example, is a poem which makes cynical observations of a crowd of sensation-seekers gathered at the site of a fire. Sickly fascinated, the mob watches the pathetic behavior of a lady who has lost everything in the blaze. The technical problem is that there is absolutely no reason for the poem to be a sonnet: the poem is narrative rather than lyric, dispassionate rather than involved. "Aftermath" as a sonnet is almost as ludicrous and inappropriate as Karl Shapiro's "Auto Wreck" would be were it a triolet.

Although Nims does not mention them, a reader would be likely to notice that at least two of the syllabic poems in *The Colossus* similarly appear to be mere technical exercises, interesting only as shows of skill. "Departure" is constructed of a stanzaic pattern of 11-9-7-5 syllables in each quatrain—presumably intending to reinforce by a numerical arrangement the idea of leavetaking in the poem, with the five-syllable line at the end of the stanza a tense, difficult, but determined goodbye: "The money's run out." But, even with that going for it, the poem does not really work. Another poem which depends on technical trickery is "The Companionable Ills," an eight-line poem on the subject of how nice it is to learn to live with one's idiosyncracies, "the old imperfections." The poem, though it is suitably short for its small subject (an offhand bit of folk wisdom), is too reliant on its cleverness of form. The rhyme scheme of each quatrain is abba; the syllabic pattern is 12-10-9-6 then 6-9-10-12— in we go, out we go. The poem, if typed as shape, would take the form of George Herbert's "Easter Wings" or Dylan Thomas's Part 2 selections in "Vision and Prayer." All this, yes, is cleverness, but it does not redeem the metaphoric confusions of the poem in which a nose twitch and facial moles inexplicably become horses (described as some sort of fallen Houyhnhnms) which go to their barn stalls as "Bedfellows of the spirit's debauch, fond masters." If all the poems of *The Colossus* were only mathematical displays, then they would indeed be drudgery. But if some of the poems combine Plath's mastery of metrics, syllabics, rhyme, sound, puns, and metaphor with fitting subjects—and I submit that most of the poems in the collection do—then *The Colossus* emerges as something more significant than a poet's workbook, more than some literary equivalent of the Hanon exercises of piano.

Despite the misleading remark about "drudgery," Nims has been the only one so far to discuss at any length Plath's excellence at the craft of poetry. That excellence deserves some scrutiny before one can fully sense how the charges were set for the explosion of *Ariel*. One thing that is certainly obvious from *The Colossus* is that Sylvia Plath spent a great deal of time experimenting with metrics and syllabics, trying to make those forms belong to her, trying to make them suit her poetry. Nims observes, "In *The Colossus* there are ten poems that read themselves naturally, if freely, in the folk line." [7] By the "folk line" he means the four-stress line characteristic of Anglo-Saxon alliterative verse, complete with its mid-line caesura. Citing "Suicide Off Egg Rock" and "Blue Moles" as prime examples, Nims ignores her most meaningful and inspired use of the rhythms of Beowulf and Grendel in "Faun," a poem in which a lusty drunk looping through the woods transfigures into a wood-troll.

Nims further notes that up to two-thirds of the poems are loosely iambic and that eight of the poems are in iambic pentameter "in the organic, not the metronomic sense." (The iambic pentameter is so organic and so nonmetronomic that scanning the lines is exasperating; Plath more often than not turns iambs into spondees, trochees, anapests, and dactyls.) His discovery (dubious as it sometimes is) prompts Nims to praise Plath for her use of the English meter for its mimicry of the human heartbeat and breath rate. But Nims's observation unfortunately illuminates very little about Plath's poetry except to note that Plath knew how to write iambic pentameter and that, by the time she published *The Colossus*, she knew that she had to disarrange and derange it to express herself.

Plath likely shared Nims's conviction that "iambic is the lub-dubb of the heartbeat, perhaps the first sensation that we, months before our birth, are aware of." [8] She, however, uses the iambic foot with deliberate irony— a point which utterly escapes Nims. The Man at Egg Rock gets ready to walk into the water, "his blood beating the old tattoo / I am, I am, I am," making his existential declaration (lub-dubb: I am) as he resolutely sets forth to drown himself. That suicidal "I am"/iamb holds the key to Plath's use of iambics. The lub-dubb of the heartbeat becomes the "I am" of a man realizing his own death.

With similar irony the iambic "Two Views of a Cadaver Room" is Plath's *memento mori.* In the first section of the poem, a girl visits her boyfriend, a medical student, in the laboratory where he is dissecting a cadaver. As if that setting for lovers were not grisly enough, Plath turns the affair inside out by its lovers' keepsake: "He hands her the cut-out heart like a cracked heirloom." (A less grotesque account of the same incident is given at the beginning of Chapter Six in Plath's autobiographical novel, *The Bell Jar.*) [9] In the second part of the poem, she describes a detail from the lower right-hand corner of Brueghel's "The Triumph of Death." The two lovers in the corner sing together, totally oblivious to the plague-wasted men, the hanged men, the mortifiers of the flesh, and the death-dancers all around them in a scene as hair-raising as that of the frenzied penitents at plague time in Bergman's film *The Seventh Seal.* Plath concludes, in a perfect line of iambic pentameter, that, like the coed and the medical student, "These Flemish lovers flourish; not for long." In another iambic poem, "Water-color of Grantchester Meadows," the Cantabrigians are likewise unaware of the terror, the doom, immanent in their surroundings. They see innocently that "spring lambs jam the sheepfold," but, amid all the pretty peace of a spring day, they miss the Darwinian activity of nature red in fang and claw:

> Droll, vegetarian, the water rat
> Saws down a reed and swims from his lumber grove,
> While the students stroll or sit,
> Hands laced, in a moony indolence of love—
> Black-gowned, but unaware
> How in such mild air
> The owl shall stoop from his turret, the rat cry out.

In both poems the "I am" that the students apparently need to learn is that survival is murderous and that learning life is really learning death.

"The Beekeeper's Daughter," an iambic poem which fluctuates between pentameter and hexameter, darkens the "I am"/iamb. The poem, obsessed with the death of Plath's father, implies the Electra complex displayed in her contemporaneous (but uncollected) poem, "Electra on Azalea Path," in which the daughter makes her retreat into beehives on the day of her father's death and, blaming herself, tries to commit suicide: "It was my love that did us both to death." [10] With that primitive taboo coursing through auricles and ventricles, the daughter offers herself, "My heart under your foot, sister of a stone," to her father, the beekeeper. Into the dark fertility and all the happy fecundity of pollen ("The anthers nod their heads, potent as kings / To father dynasties") and the sweetness of honey-making, death intrudes. A flower brings forth poison, "A fruit that's death to taste: dark flesh, dark parings." The lub-dubb of this iambic poem is, once again but more profoundly, a vision of death-in-life and life-in-death, replete with poison flowers, sacrificial drones giving their all to the queen bee, an incestuous daughter, and a death-fixation with its implicit wish to join the father in death.

> Father, bridegroom, in this Easter egg
> Under the coronal of sugar roses
> The queen bee marries the winter of your year.

Sylvia Plath's use of iambic pentameter, however moribund it may be, is not left merely to declaring the "I am" of the dark and death-bound. It is also associated with a sense of impossible other-worldliness and with the ends of things. "The Ghost's Leavetaking," a highly irregular poem, is a sleeper's work, a lament for the loss of dream and nightmare, a driven longing (without the glad comfort of "intimations of immortality") to comprehend and find some way back forever to "A world we lose by merely waking up." "Snakecharmer" is a sad chronicle of a yogi's piping which turns into a multipoem about the futility of day-to-day life, about the fatigue of the artist, about Creation giving way to millennium, about a tired-out God:

> And snakes there were, are, will be—till yawns
> Consume this piper and he tires of music
> And pipes the world back to the simple fabric
> Of snake-warp, snake-weft. . . .

Then there is the whole "I am"/iamb of universal guilt. "The Thin People" is a poem about the "persistence of memory," a poem in which the eyes of the emaciated millions of Jewish scapegoats stare their accusations:

> They persist in the sunlit room: the wallpaper
> Frieze of cabbage-roses and cornflowers pales
> Under their thin-lipped smiles,
> Their withering kinship.

The memory is there, in the spare stanzas, the jarred couplets, insisting on itself as unforgettably as the limp watches and the beached embryo on a Dali shore.

Only two more-or-less iambic pentameter poems, "Moonrise" and "Flute Notes from a Reedy Pond," express anything like hope. And in "Moonrise" the hope, addressed to the moon by a chanting lunatic, is that "The white stomach may ripen yet," based on the belief that living and dying (like the lilies of the field and the birds of the air) is "Vocation enough: opening, shutting / White petals, white fantails, ten white fingers." In the poem, the hope, the wish, seems to be to join company with the mulberries that redden, then purple, then bleed, to feed on death as the ant eggs and grubs do, to trail along after hoary, tired Father Time, knowing that "Death may whiten in sun or out of it. / Death whitens in the egg and out of it." The urge is to taste and see ("The white stomach may ripen yet") until satiation; therefore the iambic lub-dubb of this poem (fibrillating now and then) is not the heartbeat continuous and life-promising, but the lub-dubb of the heart wanting fulfillment so its valves can slam shut at last. "Flute Notes from a Reedy Pond" is similar to "Moonrise" in its visual movement from the underworld underground, where plant and animal encase themselves for winter, up to the sky, the air, the heavens above. But this poem is a statement, so unlikely in Plath, of faith in the life cycle. In a rare moment, she envisions the Blakean ideal: "To see a World in a Grain of Sand / And a Heaven in a Wild Flower" (in "Auguries of Innocence"). As the "Caddis worms drowse in their silk cases" and the "Puppets, loosed from the strings of the puppet-master / Wear masks of horn to bed," she foresees fruition, dehiscence, seed-dispersal:

> This is not death, it is something safer.
> The wingy myths won't tug at us any more:
> The molts are tongueless that sang from above the water
> Of golgotha at the tip of a reed,
> And how a god flimsy as a baby's finger
> Shall unhusk himself and steer into the air.

The "I am"/iamb of that unhusking is the only real life-hope Plath ever seems to have.

Sylvia Plath's use of syllabic count for lines of poetry is quite another thing, neither ironic nor obviously symbolic. Yet the syllabic count is more than a simple mathematical exercise. As noted before, she intends the syllabics of "Departure" and "The Companionable Ills" to be diagrammatic of meaning. Nims says, "Writing in syllabics can be a salutary exercise in countering the sing-song—and this is the importance of the syllabics in *The Colossus*. They tend to be the colder poems: objective, intellectual, descriptive." [11] This is probably true of "Departure," "The Companionable Ills," "Frog Autumn," and "Mussel Hunter at Rock Harbor." But for a quartet of poems, poems also written in Plath's modified terza rima, there is also an intrinsic, organic cause for her use of syllabics, a reason much more complex and meaningful than Nims's notion of "countering the sing-song," a reason only vaguely associated with the seasonal swing of Oriental syllabic verse forms like haiku and tanka. In this quartet there is a deliberate, purposeful meaning for Plath's syllabics: she wants to make each breath, each syllable, count.

"Medallion," "Man in Black," "The Fathom Five," and "Lorelei" are

all poems breathing their last. Their terza rima, interlocking though somewhat askew (where moon-sun, wood-dead-crooked, jaw-arrow-eye are
rhymes), seems to signify the entanglement of death, life's entanglement
in death, man's entanglement in his own mortality. The snake in the garden in "Medallion," sunstruck, afire with life, is caught in the violence
of survival and ensnared as he is surprised by his own death. In lines that
are enjambed, in stanzas that spill into one another (as guts spill from a
snake when a hurled brick hits), an onlooker recounts the scene:

> And I saw white maggots coil
> Thin as pins in the dark bruise
> Where his innards bulged as if
> He were digesting a mouse.
>
> Knifelike, he was chaste enough,
> Pure death's-metal. The yardman's
> Flung brick perfected his laugh.

"Man in Black," though vague and dreamy-nightmarish, is a poem
which brings death horrifically closer. In a poem which tries to be as
distant and uninvolved as a still life, the mortician-man, the devil-man (a
sinister Emperor of Ice Cream), rears up, proud, irresistible, to make a
black joke of the breakwater, the prisons, the henhouses, and cattle—all
man's silly attempts to preserve himself from the threats of the sea, crim-
inals, starvation. The "Man in Black" is death the conqueror, the eternal
seducer, drawing, overpowering his feeble victim:

> And you, across those white
> Stones, strode out in your dead
> Black coat, black shoes, and your
> Black hair till there you stood,
>
> Fixed vortex on the far
> Tip, riveting stones, air,
> All of it, together.

Everything is locked up in the formal (though disrupted) terza rima;
everything is run together, phrase after phrase, in this poem which is, in
its twenty-one lines, just one sentence long. The man in black, the
haunter, brings "All of it, together" into the only sentence there is, the
inescapable period of death.

"Full Fathom Five," like "Man in Black," is set at sea, comprised of tercets which are syllabically, as they rise and fall (7-9-5), the figure of "A dragnet, rising, falling as waves / Crest and trough." Again, the terza rima entraps (a dragnet) in undeniable but uncomfortable rhymes: seldom-foam, coming—far-flung—miles long, waves-sheaves—survives. Death is recognized but put off in "Medallion" and "Man in Black," represented in one as natural phenomenon or biological drama, abstracted in the other as a flat, faceless figure beckoning from the mist. In "Full Fathom Five," however, Plath brings the idea of death into proximity with herself. The "old man" addressed at the beginning of the poem is at once Alonso and Prospero of *The Tempest,* Neptune, Father Time, God, and her own "Daddy," the deceased Otto Plath. Here, as in "Lorelei," Sylvia Plath expresses the suicidal urge, the death wish, that inspires and racks *Ariel.* Fascinated by death, attracted to its dangers and its human figure, driven herself to put "All of it, together," to clarify as "vapors / Ravel to clearness on the dawn sea," she aspires: "Father, this thick air is murderous. / I would breathe water."

"Lorelei," the most anguished and suicidal of the poems in this quartet, appears to be based on two tales from the Rhineland, "St. Goar: Lorelei" and "Oberwesel: The Seven Maidens." [12] Both legends, significantly, are stories of fatherless siren-temptresses who frustrate and destroy the men they enrapture until the sirens themselves are punished by drowning. It is noteworthy that the concept of Germany (the native soil, the guilty fatherlands of *Ariel*) is presented in Plath's "Lorelei" in an orderly style, the intellectualized seven-syllable lines, the terza rima which is a figure for "a well-steered country / Under a balanced ruler." But the rhymes are also gone manic enough (insheen, lapsing-dropping-sleeping, fishnets-turrets-float, glass-face-ponderous, etc.) to be a representation of the insidious, satanic power (the *geist* of Hitler?) of the seven sisters of Schönberg castle and the siren of the Lorelei rock, "Deranging by harmony / Beyond the mundane order, / Your voices lay seige." "Lorelei," in its combination of two tales from Rhineland folklore, thus reiterates the longing for death expressed in "Full Fathom Five" as the poet here insists, "I would breathe water." But the poem moves closer to the spirit of *Ariel* by connecting the longing for death with fatherlessness, a contempt for men, a submerged impulse to incest, and an obsessive sense of national guilt. Like the German tales which are its prototypes, Plath's "Lorelei" is decidedly suicidal. Identifying with the siren who purposefully strides into the river (to join her "father dear" in the German tale) when captors threaten to throw her into the Rhine, envying the seven maidens who are taken unaware and drowned for their cruelty to suitors, Plath, as persona of the poem, invokes a river in a cold-blooded, determined, absolutely orderly way:

> O river, I see drifting
>
> Deep in your flux of silver
> Those great goddesses of peace.
> Stone, stone ferry me down there.

In this poem the syllabics are especially significant: each breath wants to be a last gasp.

Plath's syllabics are probably best understood by way of Dylan Thomas, who used syllabics more than anyone seems to have realized—and then almost always in his most death-conscious lyrics. In "Especially When the October Wind," a poem wholly composed of ten-syllable lines (shrewdly appropriate to October, the tenth month), Thomas says, "My busy heart who shudders as she talks / Sheds the syllabic flood and drains her words." [13] For Sylvia Plath, as for Dylan Thomas, syllabics are the slow drip, as unstoppable as the bleeding of a hemophiliac, of words expiring syllable by syllable—breathing out and dying.

Plath's structures, though possibly too contrived and practiced in *The Colossus*, are metaphorically important to her poems. Even in the midst of fixation on death (cosmically and personally) she was puzzling out her poems with meticulous, almost disinterested care. At the same time she was wildly aware of the things of this world, and her sensory perceptions, like her poetic structures, are vital to her meanings. Her visual sensations, her images, are incessantly vivid and exact, and, as a result, her poetry is particularly pictographic—as in the description of Brueghel's "Triumph of Death" in "Two Views of a Cadaver Room," in the verbal reproduction of a Rousseau painting in "Snakecharmer," in the pointillism (as infinitesimal as a Seurat) in "Watercolor of Grantchester Meadows," in scapes and landscapes. Ted Hughes has revealed the importance of art to her perpetual theme:

> In *The Disquieting Muses*, as in *Snakecharmer*, *The Ghost's Leavetaking* and several poems not collected, she shows how native she was to the world of the Primitive Painters. Her vision, particularly in its aspect—strong at this time—of the deathly paradise belongs with theirs perhaps more

readily than with anything in poetry, but these poems are, ultimately, about her world, not theirs, and it is not a world of merely visual effects.[14]

As vital as her vision is, the sensations of sound inform even more, both supportively and metaphorically, the substance of her poems. Her consciousness of sound—and her masterful, inspired use of sound effects—is likely something she learned while she was practicing and publishing throughout the fifties. The sound effects of Plath's poems are evidently indebted to Lowell and to Richard Wilbur (a contact she made through collegiate work with *Mademoiselle*). Plath's uses of sound, even if they are in principle imitative, are in practice original and brilliant. Nims remarks, "The sound of words—any page of Sylvia Plath shows her preoccupation with it. *The Colossus* shows a concern almost excessive. . . ." After commenting on some of her onomatopoeic effects in "Night Shift," Nims continues, "More interesting than such onomatopoeia are those words whose sound is an analogy for, a little charade of, their meaning: smudge is smudgy to say; globe is a roundness in the mouth; sling hisses and then lets go. The thousands of hours Sylvia Plath spent with her thesaurus must have considered words as embodiments." [15]

Her fascination with the poetry of words themselves is nowhere better seen than in her petrified (both frightened and turned to stone) "Hardcastle Crags." The opening of the poem with its clicking consonants ("racket," "tacking," "crooks," "black," "firework") sounds itself like flint and steel striking up a fire:

> Flintlike, her feet struck
> Such a racket of echoes from the steely street,
> Tacking in moon-blued crooks from the black
> Stone-built town, that she heard the quick air ignite
> Its tinder and shake
> A firework of echoes from wall
> To wall of the dark, dwarfed cottages.

Throughout the poem phrase after phrase sounds like itself: the irritating, restless "incessant seethe of grasses," the dull, underfoot sand-shuffling of "the sandman's dust / Lost luster under her footsoles," the hollowing out of "In the whorl of her ear, and like a scooped-out pumpkin crown / Her head cupped the babel," the snuffing of "Enough to stuff the quick / Of her small heat out," the grittiness of "mere quartz grit," and the end balking as the girl (runaway or potential suicide) makes her about-face: "She turned back."

"Point Shirley," a remembrance of her grandparents' seaside home which becomes a lament for the damage done in a hurricane and an elegy for her grandmother, fairly sums itself up in one despairing, antagonistic, stubbornly articulated phrase: "Such collusion of mulish elements." Sylvia Plath piles sound on sound as rapidly, passionately, and perhaps excessively as Hopkins heaps sight on sight and sound on sound in his ecstatic poetry; she makes her own "mulish elements" a "collusion" of substance and style. Again and again, she accomplishes what Richard Eberhart, lacking her supercharged sensitivity, implores: "If I could only live at the pitch that is near madness." [16]

Over and over, Plath's sounds almost become the things they are: the teat-pulling piglets in "Sow" who are "a litter of feat-foot ninnies / Shrilling her hulk / To halt for a swig at the pink teats"; the low-slung, filthily hungry goats of "Departure" which "shamble, morose, rank-haired, / To lick the sea salt"; the belly of the snake in "Medallion" where "white maggots coil / Thin as pins in the dark bruise / Where his innards bulged." Plath also has a handy ability of impersonating those infamous, clipped New England sentences. With all the plain small-mindedness of the man in Frost's "Mending Wall" who assures "Good fences make good neighbors," with all the terrifying terseness of the conversations in Ethan Frome or the chilling old saw in Shirley Jackson's "The Lottery"—"Lottery in June, corn by heavy soon"—Plath turns out her own witch-burning poem, "The Times Are Tidy." The last stanza recounts "The last crone got burnt up / More than eight decades back" and then, with a bewildered shake of the head, gives its brief, shrugging approbation of the witch-hunts: ". . . the children are better for it, / The cow milk's cream an inch thick." The line jerks out of a laconic Green Mountain throat to stick in the reader's craw.

While Plath uses sound effects to intensify her meanings, she puns, creates ambiguities (mostly of the third type, for Empson enthusiasts), to extend them. Although she prudishly avoids sexual puns (no doubly meant "dyings" here) she makes macabre ones reminiscent of Dylan Thomas's frequent play on "grave" (inherited, no doubt, from Shakespeare's Mercutio). Sylvia Plath's great favorite for word play in The Colossus is "stiff." Without abandoning the ordinary denotations of "stiff" as adjective, she double-plays it as the slang noun for "corpse." The doomed queen in "The Bull of Bendylaw" gazes from her mulberry bower "Stiff as a queen on a playing card"; the skeleton of the woman in the Cambridge Museum in "All the Dead Dears" is "Rigged poker-stiff on her back"; "The Thin People" intrude in "stiff battalions"; the dead "Blue Moles" lying on a roadside "stiffen in a family pose." Similarly, museum-goers are "deadlocked" before the skeletons of women, mouse, and shrew, and the frogs of "Frog Autumn" slowly "croak" as winter comes on.

More notable, however, than any of her displays of skill with rhyme, metrics, syllabics, or her facility with sound effects and puns is her gift for astounding but peculiarly apt metaphor. Nims has catalogued a number of her more striking metaphors:

> In *The Colossus* we find "The pears fatten like little buddhas"; a corpse is "black as burnt turkey"; "Sun struck the water like a damnation" and "Everything glittered like blank paper"; dead moles are "shapeless as flung gloves . . . blue suede" and they have "cork-screw noses"; a dead snake lies "inert as a shoelace" and the maggots are "thin as pins"; burnt wood has the "char of karakul." [17]

Aside from these obvious ones, it seems to me that Plath's most surprising metaphors are made of or for parts of the body. For the runaway in "Hardcastle Crags" who is confused in the wind, "like a scooped-out pumpkin crown / Her head cupped the babel"; at Plath's grandmother's house at "Point Shirley," "The sea in its cold gizzard" grinds away at shore stones; sheep sleep "in their tussocks of wool"; in the woods a drunkard is watched by "An arena of yellow eyes"; and in "The Colossus" the simple, workaday girl creeps around the giant ruins brushing "The bald, white tumuli of your eyes" and rests "in the cornucopia / Of your left ear . . ."

The metaphors of *The Colossus*, themselves as distinctively powerful as the whole poems, announce most of the themes that become the madness and the ecstasy of *Ariel*. The restrained anger over social abuses ("Night Shift," "Strumpet Song"), the sense of shared guilt in history's ugliness ("The Thin People"), the love-hatred for the father ("The Colossus," "The Beekeeper's Daughter"), resentment of the tyrannical baby ("I Want, I Want"—her own Frieda?), the discomfort of the alien body, the sense of terror in nature and the attractive-repulsive identification with animals, the fascination with illness and hospitals ("The Stones"), the inescapable presence of "These barnacle dead," and, repeatedly, the drawing toward death, the urge to suicide—all are themes abundantly evident in *The Colossus*. But in this early work the poems keep their distance all the while they are struggling to say something definite. Thus, perhaps through mortal dread, perhaps through inconclusion, the mad stuff of Sylvia Plath's poetry is, in *The Colossus*, controlled—straitjacketed, possibly—in learned, practiced method.

The obtrusive methodicalness of her poetry probably explains the recurrent uneasiness among her reviewers who, even when impressed by *The Colossus*, talk almost exclusively of Plath's expert craftsmanship. Judson Jerome, Guy Owen, Gilbert Philips, and John Simon are all somewhat too much struck by her "architecture," her "obsessive fiddling with certain forms and devices," and not enough arrested by what is lurking in and behind the poems. Roy Fuller best sums up the general reaction: "And though the themes of these poems are the traditional deep ones of poetry —time, death, and the curiousness of the physical world—the poet is always well in control. Possibly too well." [18] What Fuller implies is that Plath's impeccable workmanship is compulsive—as deliberate and tense as her habits of composition. "Writing poetry on a precise schedule," says Lois Ames, longtime friend of Sylvia's days at Smith College, "she sat with her back to whoever entered the room, as she circled words in the red leather Thesaurus which had belonged to Otto Plath." [19] She persisted in this practice, stiffly fixed on forms, calculating her words, writing "in her large, strange handwriting, like a mosaic, where every letter stands separate within the work, a hieroglyph to itself," [20] Ted Hughes attests, throughout the writing of these early poems.

So careful, so conscious as to be self-conscious, Sylvia Plath constructed *The Colossus* out of everything she knew: literary tradition and her chosen poetic masters (Thomas and Lowell, most often), visual art, the vivid, heightened sights and sounds of the natural world, the vast, eerie other-world of her imagination, and consummately skilled poetic craftsmanship. As E. Lucas Meyers has said of the first work, "There is not an imperfectly finished poem in Sylvia Plath's book." [21] But her formality, her obscurity, is sometimes artificial, often sedative. The manic and destructive imagination of Sylvia Plath which breaks out in *Ariel* is still too much what Sexton calls "technique" and too little "life." As of the writing of her first book, Sylvia Plath had yet to begin to "put together entirely" her life and her art and, as their end, her death. Which probably explains why, when an interviewer questioned her about *The Colossus* poems less than four months before her suicide, she responded, "They, in fact, quite privately, bore me." [22]

11 On the Road to *Ariel:* The "Transitional" Poetry of Sylvia Plath

MARJORIE G. PERLOFF

Sylvia Plath has become a true cult figure. A few years ago, the Savile Book Shop in Georgetown, D.C., had a huge window display in which copies of *The Colossus, The Bell Jar, Ariel,* and *Crossing the Water* encircled a large photograph of Sylvia Plath, which rested against a copy of A. Alvarez's *The Savage God: A Study of Suicide,* that ultimate tribute to Sylvia Plath as our Extremist Poet par excellence.

In the face of such publicity, the poems themselves become almost an irrelevancy in the search for the real Sylvia Plath, the Laingian heroine behind the mask of beautiful, brilliant, superefficient Smith girl, who married the most admired British poet of our time. Yet in the long run it is, of course, the poetry and not the life of the suicidal poet that matters, and I did not think that the cause of Sylvia Plath's poetry was particularly well served by the publication in 1971 of two volumes of previously uncollected poems: *Crossing the Water* and *Winter Trees.*[1] To read the *Ariel* poems in the context of these "new" volumes was somewhat like trying to concentrate on Renoir's great "La Source" of 1875 in the Barnes Foundation, where it hangs on a large wall full of third-rate Renoirs. In such a setting, the power of the major work of art may well be dissipated rather than enhanced.

To begin with, both of these volumes showed signs of very careless editing on the part of Ted Hughes. *Crossing the Water* is subtitled *Transitional Poems,* and according to the dust jacket, "The poems in this collection were written in the period between the publication of *The Colossus* (1960) and the posthumous book *Ariel* (published in England in 1965). As a group, they illuminate an extremely important period in Sylvia Plath's life; they also mark the point at which her work moved beyond great promise and competence and began to burn with genius." Reviewers, following this lead, began to speak of Sylvia Plath's transitional style. Thus Douglas Dunn wrote in *Encounter*: "Sustained poems of great quality are gathered in this . . . indispensable book" which is "much freer in style" than Plath's early work, and Lyman Andrews said in the *London Sunday Times*: "Assurance was sometimes lacking in her earlier poems, and in the last poems at times there was a loss of control, while these poems are an almost perfect marriage of strength and elegance." Ted Hughes himself, discussing the volume in a BBC broadcast, said: "This work from the interim is fascinating and much of it beautiful in a rich and easy way that we find neither in *The Colossus* nor *Ariel*." [2]

These are rather extravagant claims for, in fact, almost half the poems in *Crossing the Water* belong to the period of *The Colossus*! Of the thirty-eight poems in the volume, eleven were published before the end of 1960, and internal evidence suggests that an additional six were written in late 1959 or early 1960.[3] On the other hand, certain poems in *Crossing* are contemporaneous with certain *Ariel* poems. "In Plaster," for example, is the companion poem to "Tulips" (*Ariel*, p. 10); both were written in March, 1961, when Sylvia Plath was recovering from an appendectomy.[4] The confusion is further compounded by Hughes's prefatory note to *Winter Trees:* "The poems in this volume are all out of the batch from which the *Ariel* poems were more or less arbitrarily chosen and they were all composed in the last nine months of Sylvia Plath's life." But three of these eighteen "new" poems—"Lesbos," "The Swarm," and "Mary's Song"—are, it turns out, *Ariel* poems, for although they had not been included in the British edition of 1965, they did appear in the U.S. edition of 1966, which is the text of the current Harper paperback.

If a poem as well known as "Lesbos" is reprinted in *Winter Trees*, why are so many other poems, which appeared in leading periodicals both before and after Sylvia Plath's death, omitted from both new volumes? "Ouija," for example, originally appeared in the *Hudson Review* (Fall, 1960) together with "Electra on Azalea Path"; the first is included in *Crossing* (p. 44), the second omitted. No explanations are given. Yet "Electra," an earlier variant of the famous "Daddy," seems at least as relevant to a study of Plath's interim work as does "Ouija." Again, all the poems published in the March, 1962, issue of *Poetry*—"Widow,"

"Face Lift," "Heavy Women," and "Love Letter"—find their way into *Crossing*, with the exception of "Stars Over Dordogne." "Purdah," published posthumously in *Poetry* in August, 1963, appears in *Winter Trees*, but its companion poem, "Eavesdropper," an interesting analogue to "Lesbos," does not. And "The Jailor," published in *Encounter* in October, 1963, is not reprinted in *Winter Trees*, although "Thalidomide" and "Childless Woman," printed in the same issue, are.

In view of these discrepancies and errors, we will have to wait for a *Collected Poems*, originally scheduled for publication by Faber and Faber in 1973 (and hopefully more carefully edited!), before we can venture to assess Sylvia Plath's place in the history of modern poetry. What follows is, accordingly, in the nature of an interim report.

I

We may profitably begin our consideration of *Crossing the Water* by looking at a representative poem that really is "transitional": "Parliament Hill Fields" (p. 7), which first appeared in the *London Magazine* in August, 1961, and has as its subject the miscarriage Sylvia Plath suffered less than a year after her first child Frieda was born.[5]

In Plath's poetry, pregnancy is usually regarded as a temporary suspension of anxiety, for carrying a child gives the poet a sense of being, of having weight, of inhabiting her own body. In "Letter in November," for example, the speaker says:

> I am flushed and warm.
> I think I may be enormous,
> I am so stupidly happy,
> My Wellingtons
> Squelching and squelching through the beautiful red.
>
> (*Ariel*, p. 46)

Conversely, the termination of pregnancy is seen as a frightening state in which one feels weightless, empty, disembodied. So, in "Parliament Hill Fields," the poet mourns, not for the loss of her baby as a new human being whom she might have loved and cared for, but rather for the loss of a vital part of herself, without which she becomes a sheer vacuum, an empty vessel. Plath's use of nature imagery in this poem may be glossed by the following account of the childhood experience of a mental patient, which R. D. Laing cites in *The Divided Self* as an example of the schizophrenic's typical fear of engulfment, the fear that other selves threaten to absorb one's already fragile identity, and implosion, the terrible impingement of reality upon the empty self:

> I was about twelve, and had to walk to my father's shop through a large park, which was a long, dreary walk. I suppose, too, that I was rather scared. I didn't like it, especially when it was getting dark. I started to play a game to help pass the time. . . . It struck me that if I stared long enough at the environment that I would blend with it and disappear just as if the place was empty and I had disappeared. It is as if you get yourself to feel you don't know who you are or where you are. To blend into the scenery so to speak. Then you are scared of it because it begins to come on without encouragement. I would just be walking along and felt that I had blended with the landscape. Then I would get frightened and repeat my name over and over again to bring me back to life, so to speak.[6]

The tension described here between the desire to "blend into the scenery," thus becoming invisible and beyond attack, and the opposite urge to maintain one's autonomy as a person, is precisely the theme of "Parliament Hill Fields." Sylvia Plath's poem is above all a poem of absence, absence not only of others but of oneself. Witness the opening stanza:

> On this bald hill the new year hones its edge.
> Faceless and pale as china
> The round sky goes on minding its business.
> Your absence is inconspicuous;
> Nobody can tell what I lack.

As she strolls on Parliament Hill, the highest point of Hampstead Heath, which overlooks the city of London far below, the poet longs to blend with the "bald hill" and "faceless" sky, for if she can only disappear completely, "Nobody can tell what I lack." Gradually, "the city melts like sugar" and an "ashen smudge" covers Kentish Town, transforming the vista into "a snowfield or a cloudbank." The poet envies the "dark-boughed cypresses" that "Brood, rooted in their heaped losses" and longs to dissolve into the "spindling rivulets" that "Unspool and spend themselves" as "The day empties its images / Like a cup or a room."

But despite this longing for dissolution, a part of the self still struggles for autonomy. Surrounded by alien selves that seem to assert their own being remorselessly, the poet withdraws further and further into her own isolation. Thus the very gulls frighten her, "stirring like blown paper / Or the hands of an invalid." Next, "A crocodile of small girls / Knotting and stopping, ill-assorted, in blue uniforms, / Opens to swallow me." The poet can respond to this danger only by self-petri-faction: "I'm a stone, a stick." Having turned herself into a hard, frozen substance, she need no longer fear the "crocodile" of schoolgirls: "Their shrill, gravelly gossip's funneled off." But one threat gives way to an-other: the wind tries to stop her breath "like a bandage," and even the new moon seems to cut through her like a knife: "The moon's crook whitens, / Thin as the skin seaming a scar." As night falls and she re-members that she must return to her other baby, the one that did not die, who is asleep indoors, she suddenly imagines that the trivial little picture on the nursery wall has come ominously alive: "The blue night plants, the title pale blue hill / In your sister's birthday picture starts to glow" and "Each rabbit-eared / Blue shrub behind the glass / Exhales an indigo nimbus, / A sort of cellophane balloon." Reality thus be-comes increasingly oppressive, swallowing her up, depriving her of oxygen. Finally, however, just as Laing's patient repeats her name over and over again so as to bring herself back to life, the speaker of "Par-liament Hill Fields" forces herself to remember "The old dregs, the old difficulties," and enters "the lit house."

Thematically, "Parliament Hill Fields" is very much like the *Ariel* poems. "Little Fugue" (p. 70), for example, similarly explores the pre-cariousness of identity, the fear of being alive, the longing for dissolu-tion, and the imagery of absence so prominent in the earlier poem—"bald hill," "Faceless and pale as china," "wan / Sun," "ashen smudge," "snowfield," "cloudbank"—reappears in the "featurelessness" of the "cold clouds" which is one of the dominant motifs of "Little Fugue."

But "Parliament Hill Fields" is much more conventional than "Little Fugue" in terms of its tone and structure; it often substitutes contriv-ance for emotional coherence. Ostensibly, the poem records, in sequen-tial form, the process whereby the self becomes increasingly disembod-ied until the final effort to "snap out of it," to return to reality is made. But the voice of the middle stanzas is oddly knowing and explicit: it is difficult to believe in disembodiment in the case of an "I" that makes such statements as "You know me less constant, / Ghost of a leaf, ghost of a bird," or "Your cry fades like the cry of a gnat. / I lost sight of you on your blind journey." What we miss here is a rendition of the poet's mental processes themselves rather than such after-the-fact rationalizations of them.

The sound structure bears this out. Throughout the ten six-line free verse stanzas, with their short choppy phrases, enjambment, and strong caesurae, Sylvia Plath invents elaborate phonetic patterns, as in the penultimate line of the poem:

> Gulls stiffen to their chill vigil in the drafty half-light.

Surely this a virtuoso line: it contains alliteration of f's, l's, and t's, assonance of short i's and a's, two examples of internal rhyme ("chill" / "-gil" and "draf-"/"half"), and consonance ("gull"/"chill"/"-gil"). But no sound device can save this line from being pretentious. The gulls must turn cold and "stiffen" at this point for no better reason than that the poet needs to find an objective correlative for her fear. It is she, of course, who must "stiffen" to her "chill vigil" in the "half-light" which is euphoniously but all too conveniently "drafty."

"Little Fugue," I would argue, is a much more satisfying poem. The use of the fugue as structural principle is particularly effective here, for the whole poem is a polyphonic composition based on two basic themes which appear in the first two lines of the poem:

> The yew's black fingers wag;
> Cold clouds go over.

Both the black yew and the cold cloud symbolize suffering and death, but the former is active, the latter the passive death of annihilation. The poet says, "I like black statements," whereas she is terribly afraid of "The featurelessness of that cloud now! / White as an eye all over!"

The key words, "white," "black," "fingers," "ear," and "eye" are now submitted to elaborate contrapuntal treatment. The black yew, for example, is associated in the poet's mind with great passion—"The yew hedge of the *Grosse Fuge*"—and thus with the love she felt for her father: "Such a dark funnel, my father / I see your voice / Black and leafy, as in my childhood." But the memory is not happy; the father image is transformed into a "yew hedge of orders, / Gothic and barbarous, pure German." At this point, the suffering triggered by the memory becomes most intense; the yew is associated with Christ and then turned into a pun: "And you, during the Great War. . . ." Finally, the poet makes a specific connection between her father's death and the yew: "Death opened, like a black tree, blackly."

The image of the cold cloud undergoes similar metamorphoses. In rapid transformation, it becomes "the eye of the blind pianist / At my table on the ship," and in the fourth stanza, "Black yew, / White cloud" refer to the keys on which the pianist performs the *Grosse Fuge*. Then, after the sudden intrusion of her dead father's image, the poet returns to the first motif: "Now similar clouds / Are spreading their vacuous sheets." Finally, she sees them as "a marriage dress, of that pallor," the symbol of her impending marriage with death.

Because "Little Fugue" is primarily a composition in black and white, the introduction of bright color in stanza nine comes as a shock. It is important to note that the only color images in the poem refer to the dead father:

> And you, during the Great War
> In the California delicatessen
>
> Lopping the sausages!
> They color my sleep,
> Red, mottled, like cut necks.

The butcher knife seems to cut right through the poet. She sees her father not as a person but in terms of oddly distinct attributes: "You had one leg, and a Prussian mind . . . I remember a blue eye, / A briefcase of tangerines." The bright colors—red, blue, tangerine—associated with the father image are more than the speaker can bear. The image is expelled and she is left with the recognition of the black and white of death.

A second set of images developed contrapuntally in "Little Fugue" is that of eyes, ears, and fingers. The poem begins:

> The yew's black fingers wag;
> Cold clouds go over.
> So the deaf and dumb
> Signal the blind and are ignored.

The third and fourth lines are ambiguous. In one sense, the poet herself is "deaf and dumb," and it is her signal to the blind pianist that is ignored. But when we read these lines in the context of the whole poem, they have a further irony: the dead father, who is deaf and dumb, signals his daughter, who would like to be blind to his image but cannot ignore it. The daughter's terrible fate is that she can only see, not feel. Thus she envies the blind pianist whose "fingers had the noses of weasels" and who "could hear Beethoven." "I couldn't stop looking," she says. This fear of her own vision culminates in the climactic line, almost midway through the poem, "I see your voice." Note that the father says nothing (l. 43), and indeed his daughter calls herself "lame in memory." Because he is defined only in terms of loud color and distasteful action, never in terms of his words, his presence is all the more elusive and menacing. The last stanza is particularly poignant:

> I survive the while,
> Arranging my morning.
> These are my fingers, this my baby.
> The clouds are a marriage dress, of that pallor.

Here, as in "Parliament Hill Fields," the speaker tries to convince herself that despite her suffering she is alive, that she is a survivor. She must work at "Arranging" her morning; she must reassure herself that "These are my fingers, this my baby." But her fingers, unlike those of the pianist, which have "the noses of weasels," or the "black fingers" of the yew tree, are wholly lifeless. She has to remind herself what they are just as she seems to have forgotten that she has a baby.

This odd lapse of memory suggests that the title "Little Fugue" has a second meaning. A fugue, according to the *Random House Dictionary*, is a psychiatric term for "a period during which a patient suffers from loss of memory, often begins a new life, and upon recovery, remembers nothing of the amnesic period." In Plath's poem this meaning is neatly inverted. The poet cannot remember her real situation because the visual image of her dead father blocks her mind. The only way for her to forget him, to undergo a fugue leading to "recovery" and a "new life," is to die.

To see how carefully Sylvia Plath organizes her central images in "Little Fugue," a diagram might be helpful (see page 133).

In diagraming "Little Fugue" in this way, I wish to emphasize the poem's economy of statement. In "Parliament Hill Fields," Sylvia Plath introduces a whole string of images, all of which point to the same fear of engulfment: the crocodile of girls, the wind that stops the poet's breath "like a bandage," the "ashen smudge" that "Swaddles roof and tree," and so on. Lines—or, for that matter, whole stanzas—could be reversed without changing the poem appreciably. Occasionally, moreover, the tone of the poem is, as I argued earlier, too self-indulgent:

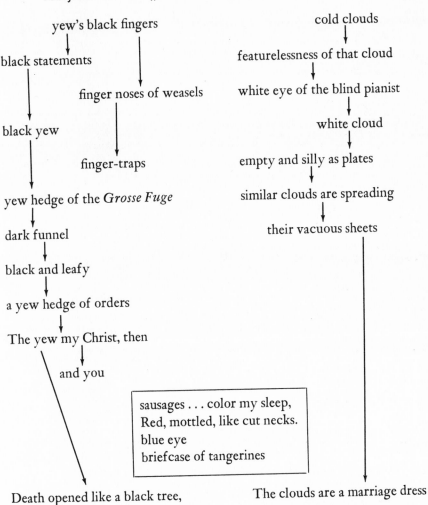

yew's black fingers

black statements

finger noses of weasels

black yew

finger-traps

yew hedge of the *Grosse Fuge*

dark funnel

black and leafy

a yew hedge of orders

The yew my Christ, then

and you

cold clouds

featurelessness of that cloud

white eye of the blind pianist

white cloud

empty and silly as plates

similar clouds are spreading

their vacuous sheets

sausages . . . color my sleep,
Red, mottled, like cut necks.
blue eye
briefcase of tangerines

Death opened like a black tree,

blackly.

The clouds are a marriage dress

of that pallor

"I suppose it's pointless to think of you at all," "I lose sight of you on your blind journey," and especially the line, "The old dregs, the old difficulties take me to wife."

In "Little Fugue," Sylvia Plath works the other way around. She uses a very limited number of carefully chosen images but gives them every possible sort of variation and resonance. The speaker does not tell us that she suffers; rather, we catch her in the very process of trying to blot out the image of her dead father. We see him through her eyes as a kind of nightmare figure, "Lopping the sausages" in the "California delicatessen." Furthermore, the speaker's intense suffering is objectified and distanced by the poem's syntax and sound. "Little Fugue" is made up of a series of simple declarative sentences, seemingly unrelated to one another: "The yew's black fingers wag," "Cold clouds go over," "I like black statements." It is as if the poet must grope, in fragmentary fashion, for some kind of connection between these disparate items. The short end-stopped three- and four-stress lines convey the rapid movement whereby images arise in the poet's mind only to be dispelled and transformed. The abrupt movement culminates in what is appropriately the longest line in the poem:

> the clouds/are a marriage/dress/of that/pallor

with its five heavy stresses, frequent breaks, and feminine endings.

If "Parliament Hill Fields" and "Little Fugue" are representative poems, it would seem that the so-called "transitional" mode of *Crossing the Water* is quite simply the mode of *Ariel* in its early, tentative, often prolix form. To talk of the "interim work" as if it were really a distinct phase in Plath's poetic development—like, say, Eliot's Sweeney period—is to make unnecessarily large claims for it. Let us see why this is so in the case of the volume as a whole.

II

The poems in *Crossing the Water* fall into roughly five thematic groups: (1) moralized landscapes in the vein of "Parliament Hill Fields" and many of the *Colossus* poems (e.g., "Wuthering Heights," "Finisterre," "Private Ground," "Sleep in the Mojave Desert," "Two Campers in Cloud Country," "Crossing the Water"); (2) hospital poems—that is, poems describing the pain or bizarre incongruities of life on the medical ward or in the mental hospital, usually from the point of view of the speaker as patient ("In Plaster," "Face Lift," "Insomniac," "The Surgeon at 2 A.M."); (3) poems about pregnancy, giving birth, or the relationship of mother to infant ("Heavy Women," "Magi," "Love Letter," "Candles," "Small Hours," "Metaphors"); (4) character sketches or surrealistic portrayals of personal relationships, expressing the poet's fear, suspicion, or hatred, especially of other women ("Leaving Early," "Widow," "Two Sisters of Persephone," "The Babysitters"); and (5) poems explicitly about death, the wish to lose consciousness, the longing to transcend the self ("Blackberrying," "I Am Vertical," "Last Words").

This is not, of course, a hard and fast classification. "Blackberrying," for example, could also be placed in the first group, "Parliament Hill Fields" in the third or the fifth. The very fact that there is a good deal of overlap shows that Sylvia Plath's thematic range is fairly small. On the other hand, the classification may be helpful in tracing Sylvia Plath's use of a particular genre, her drive to remold it to her own purposes.

Compare, for example, "Leaving Early" in *Crossing the Water* to "Lesbos" in *Ariel*. Both poems fall into the fourth category above, having as their subject matter the hostility between the "I" of the poet and another unnamed woman. In both poems, the furnishings of the other woman's house become emblematic of what the speaker senses to be her "friend's" aggressiveness, hypocrisy, and bad taste; in both cases, the reader recognizes that the friend is hated and reviled because the poet really hates herself, because her own sense of identity is so weak that she must fear the other woman's offer of friendship as a threatening intrusion. In "Leaving Early," the decor consists of a strange assortment of dead flowers, rotting in assorted vases, pots, and jugs among the red velvet sofa cushions, magenta sofa, and mirrored walls. In "Lesbos," the emphasis is on the vulgar modernity of a neighbor's "all Hollywood, windowless" kitchen, with its "flourescent light wincing on and off like a terrible migraine," "Coy paper strips for doors," and the pervasive "stink of fat and baby crap."

But "Leaving Early" lacks the dramatic tension of "Lesbos." Sylvia Plath spins a series of variations on the statement of the opening line: "Lady, your room is lousy with flowers." The red geraniums that "stink of armpits," the dead roses whose "yellow corsets were ready to split," and the crysanthemums "the size / of Holofernes' head" surrealistically loom larger and larger until the musty odor all but chokes the speaker:

> Lady, what am I doing
> With a lung full of dust and a tongue of wood,
> Knee-deep in the cold and swamped by flowers?

A sense of violent unease emanates from these lines, but what is behind the macabre Gothic trappings of "Leaving Early"? The poet succeeds in expressing her personal antipathy for the other woman, but it is difficult to relate her private hostility to a larger human situation. The writing of "Leaving Early" may well have been cathartic for Sylvia

Plath, but her irritation, sarcasm, and outrage are not sufficiently objectified.

"Lesbos" is a much more complex poem, contrasting two opposite female roles: that of the modern streamlined wife, who has "blown [her] tubes like a bad radio" and seeks ways of dominating others so as to fill the enormous void in her life, and that of the "I," neurotic, "doped and thick from my last sleeping pill," necessarily hypocritical in dealing with her neighbor when it comes to protecting her children, but insisting on her autonomy and freedom: "Even in your Zen heaven we shan't meet." The poet is victim, the other woman victimizer, "kleptomaniac," suburban Gorgon. "Lesbos" is like a miniature novel, a condensed statement about the false relationship between "enlightened" young mothers in the world of the modern apartment complex.

The sound structure of "Lesbos" is also much more effective than the rather flaccid blank verse of "Leaving Early," with its somewhat tiresome alliteration and assonance:

> Musky as a lovebed the morning after.
> My nostrils prickle with nostalgia.

Compare the following passage from "Lesbos," with its jagged line lengths and subtle rhyme:

> Your voice my ear-ring,
> Flapping and sucking, blood-loving bat.
> That is that. That is that.
> You peer from the door,
> Sad hag. "Every woman's a whore.
> I can't communicate."
>
> I see your cute decor
> Close on you like the fist of a baby. . . .

Here the ironic repetition of "That is that," rhyming with "bat," reminds one of the Michelangelo refrain of "Prufrock," as does the rhyme of "whore"/"decor," whose implication is that the latter is a reflection of the former. The language is wholly colloquial and yet the sound pattern is highly wrought, for example the repetition of the suffix "-ing," rhyming with "ring" or the consonance of "-cate"/"cute."

Just as "Leaving Early" is an earlier, slighter version of "Lesbos," so poems like "Face Lift" and "Insomniac" seem like early sketches for "Tulips" or "Fever 103°." "Face Lift" (p. 5) is a dramatic monologue, a genre that Sylvia Plath, with her intensely personal, oracular vision,[7] never really mastered. The poem splits into two parts: the voice of an "I" who reacts intensely to the world of operating rooms, and sounds precisely like Sylvia Plath herself (stanzas 1, 2, and 4), and the speech of the elderly lady who is having the face lift (stanza 3). Here is the first voice:

> When I was nine, a lime-green anesthetist
> Fed me banana gas through a frog-mask. The nauseous vault
> Boomed with bad dreams and the Jovian voices of surgeons.
> Then mother swam up, holding a tin basin.
> O I was sick.

These lines are reminiscent of many passages in *The Bell Jar* describing Sylvia Plath's own experience. The second voice is quite different:

> I grow backward. I'm twenty,
> Broody and in long skirts on my first husband's sofa, my fingers
> Buried in the lambswool of the dead poodle;
> I hadn't a cat yet.

It is difficult to believe that the "I" of these lines, the lady of sofas and poodles, would be capable of articulating the thoughts presented in the first two stanzas. In her later hospital poems, Sylvia Plath solved this problem by dropping all masks, by placing her own "I" squarely at the center of the poem as an object to be contemplated by the poem's inventor. "Fever 103°," for example, is a highly charged account of the poet's reaction to the delirium of high fever, a condition at once terrifying and thrilling, for it allows her to transcend her ordinary self and enter a pure deathless realm, a paradise where pain can no longer hurt:

> I think I am going up,
> I think I may rise—
> The beads of hot metal fly, and I, love, I
> Am a pure acetylene
> Virgin
> Attended by roses. . . .
> (My selves dissolving, old whore petticoats)—
> To Paradise.

In discussing *Crossing the Water*, critics have been particularly enthusiastic about Sylvia Plath's moralized landscapes (the first group in my classification), arguing that here the poet shows that she is capable of writing excellent descriptive poetry, at once less mannered than that of *The Colossus* and less strident than the hallucinatory lyrics of *Ariel*.

But despite Ted Hughes's suggestion that Sylvia Plath might have been another Elizabeth Bishop, had she chosen to stick to the descriptive mode,[8] I cannot help thinking that much of the descriptive detail in the landscape poems is gratuitous. In "Wuthering Heights," for example, the poet, crossing the moors toward her house, is obsessed by the frightening emptiness of the landscape. As in "Parliament Hill Fields," the landscape becomes the embodiment of her most deep-seated fears. The horizons "dissolve and dissolve," and the wind, which bends "Everything in one direction," is "trying / To funnel [her] heat away." To identify with this world of grass, pale sky, and wind is to die, and the speaker is both tempted to give in and yet fearful lest she do: "If I pay the roots of the heather / Too close attention, they will invite me / To whiten my bones among them." The poet merges with the world of nature and knows what it is to be subhuman: "The grass is beating its head distractedly. / It is too delicate / For a life in such company."

In these metaphors of animistic identification, the poet succeeds in drawing us into her circle of experience. But the intensity of the poem is diminished, at least for me, by certain passages in which the poet seems bent on being clever at all costs. Thus the sheep are described as "All wig curls and yellow teeth / And hard, marbly baas"—a description which may be accurate enough, but one wonders how the speaker, in her disembodied state, could notice that the sheep's teeth are yellow. Or again, consider the last three lines of the poem:

> Now, in valleys narrow
> And black as purses, the house lights
> Gleam like small change.

The comparison of narrow black valleys to change purses and of house lights seen in the distance to the small change one is happy to find at the bottom of the black purse may be ingenious, but the conceit does not provide effective closure. Unlike the reference to the "marriage dress, of that pallor" in the final line of "Little Fugue," which, as I argued earlier, has been anticipated by every image that precedes it, the black purse image, suddenly introduced at the end of "Wuthering Heights," breaks the spell of the preceding stanzas, calling attention to the poet's ability to make daring metaphors rather than to the intensity of her vision.

The same tendency to sacrifice intensity to ingeniousness spoils many of the other landscape poems. The title poem, for example, describes the sudden descent of night on the waters of a Canadian lake, a blackness so all-embracing that the poet, from the vantage point of her little rowboat, knows suddenly what death must be. One thinks of Hopkins's "Spelt from Sybil's Leaves" or Stevens's "Domination of Black" as possible models. The opening of the poem is intentionally low key:

> Black lake, black boat, two black cut-paper people.
> Where do the black trees go that drink here?

Rapidly, Sylvia Plath conveys the sense that the speaker is being absorbed into the blackness of the lake, that her urge is not so much to cross the water as to drown in it. To introduce the image of the snag "lifting a valedictory, pale hand" in line nine is therefore to overstate the case, to spell it out too neatly. Similarly, the final line reasserts rather flatly what we already know: that "This is the silence of astounded souls."

It is entirely possible, of course, that had Sylvia Plath lived to supervise the publication in book form of such poems as "Crossing the Water," she would have revised the lines in question. Nevertheless, it seems excessive to say, as does Peter Porter in the *New Statesman*, that *Crossing the Water* is "full of perfectly realised works." [9] The book's weaknessses—gratuitous description, overingenious metaphor, mannered sound patterning often unrelated to meaning, and occasional tonal and structural irresolution, as in the case of "Parliament Hill Fields"—are, I would argue, the very faults critics have noted in *The Colossus*. Some of the later poems in *The Colossus*, for that matter—"Mushrooms," "Blue Moles," "The Stones"—are more fully achieved works than any single poem in *Crossing*, with the possible exception of "I Am Vertical," that famous Roethkean poem describing the longing to become one with the flowers and trees. One cannot help wondering, then, if Sylvia Plath would have cared to publish many of the poems in *Crossing* in book form at all, or whether Ted Hughes's posthumous edition of these "transitional poems" is not a disservice to her best work.

III

Winter Trees raises rather different issues. Setting aside the radio play "Three Women," which had already been published in the appendix of Charles Newman's *The Art of Sylvia Plath*, and the three poems printed in the U.S. edition of *Ariel*, this slim volume contains only fifteen poems (twenty-three pages in all). True, the poems stem from Sylvia Plath's "great period"—the last nine months of her life—and could easily be included in an expanded edition of *Ariel* since they burn with the same central passion to destroy the old ego and create a new self, to undergo death and rebirth, to enter the lives of animals, plants, or inanimate objects so as to transcend one's humanity. The nagging question that troubles the reader of these supplementary *Ariel* poems, however, is whether Sylvia Plath's range is not perhaps too narrow, whether a major poet, as Plath has been called by Alvarez and others, should not be capable of greater depth and variety.

Thus, many of the poems in *Winter Trees* which are very striking when read singly, begin to take on an air of *déjà vu* when one is familiar with *Ariel*. The imagery of hooks and wires, for example, referring to the mechanization of human relationships, can become monotonous:

> Bright fish hooks, the smiles of women
> Gulp at my bulk. . . .   ("Gigolo")

> And we, too, had a relationship—
> Tight wires between us.
> Pegs too deep to uproot, and a mind like a ring
> Sliding shut on some quick thing,
> The constriction killing me also.   ("The Rabbit Catcher")

> The air is a mill of hooks . . . . .   ("Mystic")

> And my baby a nail
> Driven, driven in.   ("Brasilia")

Images of engulfment and constriction similarly become repetitive. The poet must always hide from a nameless threat:

> Pocket watch, I tick well.
> The streets are lizardy crevices
> Sheer-sided, with holes where to hide.
> It is best to meet in a cul-de-sac. . . .   ("Gigolo")

In "Purdah," the speaker must pose as a meek concubine, submissive to her lord:

> Jade—
> Stone of the side,
> The agonized

> Side of green Adam, I
> Smile, cross-legged,
> Enigmatical. . . .

But all the time that she hides behind veils and "silk / Screens, these rustling appurtenances," she is plotting the triumph of female over male, the death of the "bridegroom" who has oppressed her:

> And at his next step
> I shall unloose. . . .
> From the small jewelled
> Doll he guards like a heart—
>
> The lioness,
> The shriek in the bath,
> The cloak of holes.

This climactic ending with its allusion to the murder of Agamemnon, immediately recalls the brilliant conclusion of "Lady Lazarus":

> Out of the ash
> I rise with my red hair
> And I eat men like air.

One wonders how frequently a poet can use this type of dramatic Gothic twist without dissipating its force. I have the same reservations about those poems that deal with nursing one's baby. "By Candlelight" (*Winter Trees*, pp. 28-29), for example, is surely an impressive rendition of the mixture of love and fear the poet experiences while nursing her infant in the small hours, but Sylvia Plath has treated this theme so frequently, using candlelight imagery that is all but interchangeable from poem to poem, that one begins to question the need for yet another version of the same thing:

> These little globes of light are sweet as pears.
> Kindly with invalids and mawkish women,
> They mollify the bald moon . . .
> The eyes of the child I nurse are scarcely open.
> In twenty years I shall be retrograde
> As these drafty ephemerids.
>   ("Candles," *Crossing the Water*)
>
> The candle
> Gulps and recovers its small altitude,
> Its yellows hearten.
> O love, how did you get here?

O embryo . . .
The pain
You wake to is not yours.

　　　　　　　　　　("Nick and the Candlestick," *Ariel*)

At first the candle will not bloom at all—
It snuffs its bud
To almost nothing, to a dull blue dud.

I hold my breath until you creak to life,
Balled hedgehog,
Small and cross. The yellow knife
Grows tall.

　　　　　　　　　　("By Candlelight," *Winter Trees*)

Confronted by these candlelight poems, one begins to speculate that perhaps, in the case of Sylvia Plath's poetry, less is more. The lyric intensity of her vision somehow seems more impressive when one first meets it in the slim and rigorously selective *Ariel* than when it is placed in the perspective afforded by the publication of her uncollected poems. This is not to say that Sylvia Plath is not an important poet. The influence of her work on the diction, syntax, and imagery of younger writers—especially women—could hardly be greater today, and it shows no signs of abating. It was Sylvia Plath, after all, who took the poetic premises of Roethke, of Lawrence, or of Thomas to their logical conclusion, who showed contemporary poets that there was a viable alternative to the Projectivist mode on the one hand and the realist-confessional mode of Lowell and his followers on the other.

Nevertheless, a reading of *Crossing the Water* and *Winter Trees* suggests that Sylvia Plath's imaginative world is, despite its power and coherence, essentially a limited one. Alvarez has gone so far as to compare her to Keats,[10] but surely Sylvia Plath was the Christopher Smart rather than the Keats of the early sixties, a poet who will be remembered less for a major *oeuvre* than for a handful of astonishing and brilliant poems, a fascinating autobiographical novel,[11] and for the example of her life with its terrible tension between success and suffering—a tension peculiarly representative of her time and her place.

12   The Double in Sylvia Plath's *The Bell Jar*

Gordon Lameyer

Many poems by Sylvia Plath contain references to mirrors and to "doubles," psychological projections of some aspect of the speaker. "Strumpet Song" from *The Colossus* is such a poem, and "Mirror" and "In Plaster" are the most obvious "doubles" poems in *Crossing the Water*. I also believe that her notorious "Daddy" poem in *Ariel* is spoken by the author's evil double, resenting her father's death and consequent loss of love, which contributed to her truncated Electra complex.[1] But the place where Sylvia Plath explored the psychological double to the fullest was in her semiautobiographical novel, *The Bell Jar*.

Sylvia Plath's study of the double in two of Fyodor Dostoevsky's novels, as recorded by her as yet unpublished Smith College honor's thesis, *The Magic Mirror* (1955), provided her with insights for the structure of the doubles in her own novel. When she returned to Smith in the spring of 1954 to repeat the second half of her junior year, Sylvia became interested in Dostoevsky from a course on the Russian novel given by George Gibian, who became her senior honors' thesis advisor the following year. In dramatizing the projection of the schizophrenic's fears upon a double figure, Dostoevsky gave her a deeper understanding of her own nervous breakdown, attempted suicide, and recouperation than had her limited psychoanalysis at McLean, the mental hospital where she had spent four months.

Written in the fall of 1954, *The Magic Mirror* is a scholarly analysis of the dynamics of "the double," first, in Dostoevsky's early novella by that name about Golyadkin, a functionary who drives himself mad with the hallucination of his own projected double, and, second, in the great study of parricide, *The Brothers Karamazov*. In the latter, Ivan evolves two kinds of doubles. One is a hallucinatory figure, the Devil, and the other is his bastard brother, Smerdyakov. Perhaps the image of the bastard double suggested the final startling image for her later parricidal poem, "Daddy."

At the time of the writing of her thesis, Sylvia told me that she was terribly frustrated in not being able to understand German well enough to read the definitive study called *The Double* by the psychoanalyst Otto Rank. In the notes for her thesis she does refer to three of his articles, but unfortunately she did not read Rank's book. It was not until 1971 that an English translation was made of Rank's book by Harry Tucker, Jr., published by University of North Carolina Press. Had it been available, Rank's book would have provided her not only with additional background on the double in literature and anthropology but also with a vital insight, I think, into the connection between narcissism and the double. According to modern psychoanalytic theory, it is the narcissist's failure to fulfill love needs in childhood that causes the personality to split, projecting onto another the deepest guilts and destructive forces within the self.

As we shall see, *The Bell Jar* is full of "doubles," mirror images that polarize the attitudes of the heroine toward herself and toward others. Some of the "doubles" are positive and innocent, while others represent antipathies or the repressed, libidinal urges of the heroine. But the technique of structuring the conflict Sylvia derived from Dostoevsky. The analysis which she makes of the novella, *The Double*, in the first half of her thesis sheds light on the heroine Esther Greenwood all throughout her breakdown and the first part of her hospitalization. However, unlike Golyadkin, Esther does not go mad but rallies and gets well. In this sense she is like the heroine of the much more romantic *I Never Promised You a Rose Garden*, which, along with the writings of R. D. Laing, has gone a long way toward uncovering the anguish of a schizophrenic, but not with the poetic intensity of Sylvia Plath.

As distilled in the second half of her thesis, what Sylvia learned from the kind of reconciliation achieved by Ivan Karamazov with himself through his understanding of his guilt and his acceptance of responsibility gave Sylvia an insight into her own conflicts that caused her to see the world unconsciously in doubles. *The Brothers Karamazov* provided a way—but a very different way—to resolve the heroine's incipient madness in *The Bell Jar*. By killing off her own primary double, Sylvia Plath rearranged her own experience so that at the end her heroine could be free of her bell jar of "stifling distortions" and become psychically reborn.

It would be convenient to say that Sylvia's analysis of Dostoevsky's

The Double provided a key to the first half of *The Bell Jar* and *The Brothers Karamazov* to the second, but it is not so simple. Certainly the insights Sylvia gained from a close scrutiny of Ivan's two distinct doubles helped to suggest that a positive resolution to the problem of schizophrenia could be made. However, as I will suggest later, it is another Dostoevsky novel, *The Possessed*, that provided a clue for Sylvia's ending of her novel. It suggested a major alteration in her own experience at McLean which she felt artistically should be incorporated into her book.

A few pages into *The Bell Jar* we learn that the speaker is a few years older than the heroine, Esther Greenwood, who has the nervous breakdown; she is, in fact, a mother. Reminiscing on some of the souvenirs she received a few years earlier when she spent a month in New York City as a magazine editor, she says that "last week I cut the plastic starfish off the sun-glasses case for the baby to play with." There is no further mention of her baby, but we see in her novel from the many references to babies that Esther Greenwood was obsessed by them—the foeti in the bottles at the medical school, the babies of Dodo Conway, the similes for pureness with which she concludes some sections of the book, in the way Sylvia Plath did the poem, "Getting There," which ends with her stepping forth "Pure as a baby."

As reflected in her Victorian upbringing, Esther Greenwood's feeling about "purity" in the sense of being virginal is partly the cause for her neurosis. She is shocked to learn that Buddy Willard is not pure. Her anger at his hypocrisy, as she sees it, is really an anger at her own repressed feelings. Some readers of *The Bell Jar*, I think, miss this irony. It is not so much Buddy Willard's hypocrisy which is being criticized as it is Esther's "up-tight" attitude toward his seeming innocence with her, which was really quite genuine. The bell jar of myopic distortions makes Esther see Buddy's actions as malevolent. What Esther learned only later from Dr. Nolan was that she had repressed her natural desires, and so Esther goes forth near the end of the novel with Irwin to relieve herself, as she sees it, of the burden of her virginity and the fear of sex which has been hinted at throughout by her obsession with babies or, rather, with *not* having babies.

At the beginning of *The Bell Jar*, Esther Greenwood is depressed by the Rosenbergs' execution, the hot streets of New York City, and a cadaver she once saw with Buddy Willard. She feels like a numb trolley bus or "the eye of a tornado."

Esther is living in the Amazon (Barbizon) Hotel, where reside other girls whose wealthy parents "wanted to be sure their daughters would be living where men couldn't get at them and deceive them." Sex and money are Esther's two big "hang-ups," and in both these regards she feels inadequate and insecure among the twelve girls chosen for the magazine contest. As she herself claimed, she had always had trouble trying to imagine people together in bed, and her limited background makes this fling in the big city seem extravagant and sinful.

Esther's first double, like the projection of the prodigal personality in *The Three Faces of Eve*, is the sarcastic and flamboyant Doreen. She has bright white hair and comes from a society girl's college in the South. Esther is attracted to Doreen "like a magnet" because of the "elaborate decadence" attached to her background. But Doreen becomes associated with light and life, whereas Esther is content to fade into her shadow like the negative of a photograph. At the magazine Doreen can never make a "deadline."

Their boss at *Ladies' Day*, Jay Cee, is the first of a series of surrogate mothers or doubles for Esther's mother. As the heroine points out, "All the old ladies I ever knew wanted to teach me something."

If Doreen represents the vamp side of Esther's nature, then her friend Betsy certainly represents the side of purity and innocence. She can make producers cry, talking about male and female corn in Kansas, and with her cover girl beauty she tries to "save" Esther from Doreen, who sneeringly refers to Betsy as "Pollyanna Cowgirl."

Like Blake, whom Sylvia became interested in through Alfred Kazin's introduction to the Viking *Portable* edition of his works, she contrasts innocence with experience. Her heroine is attracted and repulsed by both types. As Sylvia observes in the introduction to her thesis, "This simultaneous attraction and repulsion arises from the inherently ambivalent nature of the Double, which may embody not only good, creative characteristics but also evil, destructive ones." The real conflict, however, is centered more on the contrast between the heroine and her destructive double. As Sylvia continued, "More often the Double assumes the evil or repressed characteristics of its master and becomes an ape or shadow which presages destruction and death."

Everything Doreen says seems to Esther to be like "a secret voice speaking straight out of my bones." Doreen, however, does not represent the bones or deathlike side of Esther's nature, but rather the daylight, extroverted side. When Doreen and Esther are picked up by Lenny and enter a dark bar, Doreen, who is said later to look like a bleached-blonde

Negress, was so white she looked "silver." By contrast, Esther, like Golyadkin, feels herself melting into the shadows "like the negative of a person I'd never seen before in my life." Esther's sense of unreality is also accentuated by the feeling that she is losing her tan, her skin beginning to yellow into a Chinaman's.

In the bar Esther orders a vodka, because once she had seen a vodka ad where a glass was standing in blue light in a snowdrift, looking "clear and pure." Here is the first time that the motif of pureness is linked with snow, which we will see later becomes ironically associated with Buddy Willard. In effect, the sophisticated disk jockey, Lenny Shepherd, is a double for Buddy Willard; Lenny later takes the girls to his apartment where he is figuratively split inside Esther's mind by the fact that his "ghost voice" booms from twenty-grand worth of recording equipment. And yet, what he sings reflects the Betsy side of Esther's nature:

> I was born in Kansas, I was bred in Kansas,
> And when I marry I'll be wed in Kansas . . .

Meanwhile, Esther is trying to fend off Lenny's friend, Frankie. She even assumes a kind of alter ego, a pseudonym, "Elly Higginbottom, from Chicago," which is her first attempt to escape her identity (as she sees it) as a Boston bluestocking. She is really, she feels unconsciously, like Betsy who is ironically "a true-blue gal . . . the sunflower of the Sunflower State."

Blonde Doreen spoons up hunks of fruit with a "silver" spoon, and at Lenny's the ice for their drinks comes from a "silver" ice-bucket. The drinking only makes Esther feel more depressed. She slumps to the floor and begins the first of several Alice-in-Wonderland transformations: "I felt myself shrinking to a small black dot against all those red and white rugs and that pine paneling. I felt like a hole in the ground." Like Golyadkin, she is beginning to retreat into herself, as well as into a life-less, schizophrenic state. Watching Doreen and Lenny dance, Esther feels like a fifth wheel.

When Esther returns to the Amazon, she sees in the mirror of the self-service elevator a "big smudgy-eyed Chinese woman," the first of a number of mirrored distortions or hallucinatory pictures of herself that will prevail throughout the novel. She becomes depressed by her own silence. The bedside telephone, "china-white," sits there like "a death's head." The warped mirror seems "much too silver," and her face is "like the reflection in a ball of dentist's mercury." The glass of the mercury-backed mirror even seems distorted. She has been trying to escape from the bright, blonde, and gaudy world of *Mademoiselle* into a dull, conservative, shadowy one, and the fact that her face seems like a mercury ball will become significant later at the mental hospital, when she hoards the pellets of mercury from the broken thermometers, symbolic of her own shattered identity. As Sylvia said of a similar experience in her thesis, "The reflection of Golyadkin's face in the looking-glass takes form as his Double, who steps from mirror person into Golyadkin's world with much the same facility expressed by Alice when she reversed the process and entered Looking-glass Land."

Esther decides to take a bath. In a kind of pagan baptism she lowers herself into the hot water of a coffin-shaped tub. She symbolically sinks down into death, the image of Doreen in her mind dissolving, until she finally is reborn again, purged of the dirt, "pure and sweet as a new baby." But before that, Esther thinks, "I never feel so much myself as when I'm in a hot bath." We find in Sylvia's thesis:

> Golyadkin is not merely fleeing his enemies, however; he is fleeing himself, that self which caused the scandal at Olsufy's, that self which he refuses to acknowledge. Golyadkin's central problem of identity has previously been referred to in an oblique way by his nervous attempts to prove that he is "quite himself, like everybody else" (483). The colloquial phrases "he was quite himself" and "he came to himself" now become a refrain which possesses a more meaningful content with every reiteration and evolves into a kind of word play on the questionable identity of Golyadkin's "real" self.

When Doreen returns drunk to the hotel, she knocks on Esther's door and, ironically, still calls her Elly, as if somehow, like Huck Finn taking on the role of Tom Sawyer, her identity had been transferred to her double. The hotel maid who helps Doreen reminds Esther of her Austrian grandmother, "stern and hardworking and moral," another parental double.

After Esther sees Doreen fall into the pool of her own vomit, which seems to Esther "like an ugly, concrete testimony of my own dirty nature," she rejects Doreen and turns to her opposite number:

> I made a decision about Doreen that night. I decided I would watch her and listen to what she said, but deep down I would have nothing to do with her. Deep down I would be loyal to Betsy and her innocent friends. It was Betsy I resembled at heart.

At the banquet next day Esther notices that Doreen, like Banquo, is missing from the place that they had set next to her "for some reason." She saves for Doreen the pocket mirror with the lacy script of her name on it. Esther tells Betsy how she has been unnerved that morning by Jay Cee. Esther cannot bring herself to go to a fur show with Betsy or to Coney Island with Doreen and Lenny. Feeling herself becoming immobilized and unable to do either what she should or shouldn't, Esther retreats to lying either in her bed or in the long grass in Central Park. She cannot explain to Jay Cee why all that she can do is "balk and balk like a dull cart horse." (The animal metaphors, reminiscent of Dostoevsky's *The Double*, will eventually be transferred to another of Esther's doubles, Joan Gilling). Beginning to feel more depersonalized, Esther finds herself replying to Jay Cee's questions as if she were a disembodied spirit listening to her own body speak.

In college Esther had enjoyed botany, where she innocently could explore the sex cycle of the fern through the expanded lens of a microscope, but she couldn't stand physics, where the professor, Mr. Manzi, was "shrinking everything into letters and numbers" and into hideous, cramped, "scorpion-lettered formulas." Growing larger, developing, appealed to her; but any shrinking experience, like the sensation of looking through the wrong end of a telescope, seemed to be a kind of dying.

Esther's evasion of both chemistry and her work on *Ladies' Day* makes her associate, in a hallucination, Mr. Manzi with Jay Cee, two surrogate parental figures. She wonders if someday she will become symbolically like her pseudo-mother in being reduced to the initials Ee Gee, but ambivalently she feels a certain security in aping her journalistic mentor: "I wished I had a mother like Jay Cee. Then I'd know what to do."

With Betsy and some other girls Esther goes to a movie, starring a nice blonde girl who looks like June Allyson and a sexy black-haired girl who looks like Elizabeth Taylor. They swoop across ballrooms in dresses out of *Gone With the Wind*. The nice girl wins the football hero, and the sexy girl is left marooned. Such a point of view, Esther thinks, would conform to the point of view of her mother. There in the dark, as Esther begins to feel sick from the poisoned crabmeat salad, she notices that the heads of others in the theater have a "silver" glow on them in front and a "black shadow" at the back, symbolic of the dual nature of her other double, Doreen.

Sick together in the taxi while returning to the Amazon, Esther and

Betsy hug each other, and then, upstairs, they part for opposite ends of the hall. Esther is simultaneously attracted toward and repelled by her innocent double. With Holden Caulfield's candor, Esther tells us, "There is nothing like puking with somebody to make you into old friends."

The ptomaine poisoning episode is the second in a series of symbolic deaths for the heroine. As she lies on the tiled bathroom floor, Esther feels that the summer has changed into winter, "and the big white hotel towel I had dragged down with me lay under my head numb as a snow-drift."

After Esther passes out a second time, she awakes with someone poking a white china cup of chicken broth under her nose. She mistakenly thinks it is Betsy, but ironically it is Doreen instead, whose face is now significantly in shadow. After she drinks from the pseudo-baptismal cup, Esther feels "purged and holy and ready for a new life," a *vita nuova*. Doreen then tells her that she had almost died. Having lost her exotic dinner to ptomaine poisoning, and having rested, Esther now feels "pure" again. As she opens presents sent by *Ladies' Day*, she gives Doreen her mirror place card and accepts in return the cup of broth that was meant for Doreen.

Then another double for Buddy Willard is heard in the voice of Constantin, the simultaneous translator from the UN. But before he appears on the scene there is a flashback via the story of the Jewish man and the nun who met at a fig tree where the little bird picked its way out of an egg. The birth of the bird is associated in Esther's mind with the time she saw a baby being born. Esther also associates Buddy's hypocrisy with that event. But birth was inextricably bound up in her mind with death. The table on which the woman had the baby looked to Esther like a torture table. She identified with Mrs. Tomolillo, the woman going through the agony of having a baby. She imagined herself on a delivery table, "dead-white," being vicariously reborn with her own child.

The first time Buddy had dated Esther was at college. He had come to the sophomore prom with Joan Gilling, but he left a letter with Esther, asking her to the Yale Junior Prom. She runs from the "bright white sun" on the porch into the "pitch-dark" house. What Esther finds she dislikes in Buddy is really what she dislikes most in herself, her "hang-up" about purity and her phobia about spending money. Ironically, they both suggest the medieval figures Esther is studying in history: Peter the Hermit and Walter the Penniless.

After Esther thinks she has discovered Buddy's supposed hypocrisy, his pretense, as she sees it, of being a virgin, she feels a perverse thrill in his being stricken down by TB and having to retreat, like one of Thomas Mann's characters, to the mountains. She thinks he has been living a "double life," and now she feels relieved in not having to explain to everybody why she has to study on Saturday nights.

Seeing another simultaneous translator with Constantin, a Russian girl who knew idioms in a language she could not begin to manage, makes Esther feel increasingly inferior, and she withdraws further into a vacuum of self-deprecation. She tells herself she cannot cook, do shorthand, dance, carry a tune, have a sense of balance, ride horseback, ski, speak German, read Hebrew, write Chinese, or understand maps. Her fig tree of expectation begins to wither and die.

While Esther is familiar with New York hamburger joints that sport glassy mirrors, Constantin takes her to a dimly lit, foreign restaurant in a cellar. Although she thought at first that Constantin was Mrs. Willard's protégé, he turns out to be the opposite of Buddy, and Esther plans to let him seduce her. But she supposes that, when she looks in a mirror the next day, she will see Constantin in miniature in her eye. Constantin, however, sees Esther as Mrs. Willard's protégé and falls asleep beside her, his arm "heavy as a dead man's."

When Esther awakes in a room under a ghostly light, Constantin seems insubstantial, as if his features were "drawn on fog." As characters symbolically die in this novel, their features become smudged and out of focus. Esther rejects Constantin, thinking that if she married him, she would become a kitchen mat like Mrs. Willard. In fact, her rejection of Buddy Willard's double makes her reject the idea of ever marrying.

Esther then relates in a flashback the time she had broken her leg while skiing with Buddy in the Adirondacks. Mr. Willard had driven her there, but he leaves because he cannot stand to see his son sick. Everything seems to have turned unexpectedly from green and slender to black and fat. Buddy seems to have metamorphosed into a physical opposite: "Everything concave about Buddy had suddenly turned convex." Buddy thinks Esther is neurotic to want to live in the country and the city at the same time. But she is scornful of his critcism of her split personality: "If neurotic is wanting two mutually exclusive things at one and the same time, then I'm neurotic as hell. I'll be flying back and forth between one mutually exclusive thing and another for the rest of my days."

Like Moses overlooking the Promised Land, Esther on skis looks down on Buddy from atop Mt. Pisgah. She hears music from *Kiss Me Kate* which she describes as "an invisible rivulet in a desert of snow." The speakers are playing, "Gazing down on the Jungfrau / From our [little] chalet for two . . ."—the alp "Jungfrau," of course, in German means Virgin.

After Esther's fall, the world seems to her like Cinderella's after "the stroke of a dull grandmother's wand." All love has magically disappeared. The dark figure of Buddy, who announces that she has broken her leg in two places, seems the polarized negative of the white winter sun toward which she now seems drawn.

Back at the magazine Esther is shocked by the dybbuk-like remark of Hilda, a mannequin in this tomblike world, who is glad that the Rosenbergs are going to die. Hilda's insensitivity to pain and death appears to echo Buddy's insensitivity to life. But Esther seems, unknowingly, to be entering deeper and deeper into this world of death. Later, being photographed for the magazine, Esther envisions herself as a ventriloquist's dummy. When everyone disappears, she feels spiritless, limp, and betrayed, like the "skin shed by a terrible animal." She looks in her compact mirror and sees a face that "seemed to be peering from the grating of a prison cell after a prolonged beating."

In her last days in New York, Esther becomes mulish and is unable to make decisions. She agrees to go on one more double date with Doreen who, with a nice touch, is "snowballing" all of Esther's clothes she can't stand the sight of under the bed. But Esther feels more and more depersonalized, "like an observer."

On the date Esther thinks the people with her are "empty as plates." Although Marco's diamond stickpin fascinates her and he gives it to her with casual generosity, Marco reminds her of a snake in the Bronx Zoo. When he dances with her, he says, to make her relax, "Pretend you are drowning." A woman hater, Marco is another evil double of Buddy Willard. He prodigally gives away his diamond, for a price, and lavishly feeds Esther's daiquiri to a potted palm. He blows "ghost-pale" smoke rings from his slim cigar and, of course, carries a "silver" bullet-shaped lighter. Esther discovers Marco is in love with his cousin, a nun, but, because he cannot have her, he assaults and tries to rape Esther, whom he calls a slut. She leaves Marco in the dark, looking for a "smaller darkness, that hid the light of his diamond from his eyes."

Back at the Amazon, Esther looks out over the city which seems "blackened, as if for a funeral." She lets her sexy New York wardrobe disappear piece by piece like bats floating off into the gloom or like scattering a loved one's ashes on the night wind. She has bequeathed the visible manifestations of her Doreen self to the "dark heart of New York," and ironically her wardrobe from *Ladies' Day* floats like white snowflakes into the night.

On the train home Esther looks again at her face in a mirror. This time she looks like "a sick Indian." Since she has returned to the innocent-twin side of her nature, Betsy has lent her an outfit to wear home. The frills on the blouse make her feel as if she had on "the floppy wings of a new angel." But she is still rather deathlike: "A wan reflection of myself, white wings, brown ponytail and all, ghosted over the landscape." She still has the blood-baptism marks from Marco, although she feels otherwise like Betsy, "Pollyanna Cowgirl."

Her mother meets her at Route 128 station in Dedham. She feels depressed by the suburbs whose summer breath on her, she thinks, is like the hand of death. Esther learns the bad news that she was not accepted into the writing course at Harvard Summer School. She sinks lower in the back seat of her mother's car which seems like a "prison van" and the equally spaced houses outside, like prison bars. Again like Golyadkin, she feels it is very important not to be recognized.

Back home her mother sleeps next to her in a twin bed, a curious variation on the theme of twins. The neighbor wheeling her sixth child along in front of the house makes Esther feel paranoid, as if it were done somehow for her benefit: "Children make me sick." Esther begins to have the same kind of conflicting feelings and instantaneous reversals of decisions as had Golyadkin. As soon as she rejects Jody's offer to join her at her Cambridge apartment and hangs up the phone, she changes her mind. Then she changes it again and again and again, until she is immobile as if she were colliding with a pane of glass. The bell jar is beginning to descend. A letter from Buddy Willard, speaking about a nurse, makes Esther reject him completely for his opposite number, the simultaneous interpreter to whom Buddy's mother had introduced her.

She decides to write a novel and feeds a "virgin" sheet of paper into her typewriter. But she is becoming gradually schizoid, seeing herself now from "another, distanced mind," like a doll in a doll's house. She makes up a name for her heroine with six letters like her own: Elaine. In her first attempt at writing an opening sentence, she compares the sweat crawling down her back to little slow insects. Like Gregor Samsa in Kafka's *Metamorphosis* or like Golyadkin in *The Double*, she is beginning to feel as insignificant as an insect. She also feels inert and infantile, as if she were regressing to childhood, wearing her mother's old yellow night-gown like a barefoot doll.

That night Esther is unable to sleep, and things move into a further warped perspective. Next day she tries to read *Finnegans Wake*, the hundred-letter word on the first page emerging like alphabet soup. The words seem like Arabic or Chinese or like "faces in a fun house mirror." All kinds of plans for the future zoom through her head, leaving her confused and exhausted. She feels as if a zombie were rising in her throat to choke her. Her aunt's sister-in-law recommends a psychiatrist, Dr. Gordon.

When she goes to the doctor's office, she sits curled in a "cadaverous leather chair." She tells him that she has been unable to sleep for a week and that she feels as if she "were being stuffed farther and farther into a black, airless sack with no way out." Paranoid and confused, she thinks the photograph of the doctor's children is there to let her know that she shouldn't get any ideas about him. They look like angels on a Christmas card, another unearthly image.

Although the still has on Betsy's clothes, she has written that morning a jerky letter to Doreen, asking to live with her in "West Virginia," and then she destroyed it. After her visit, her mother makes her feel guilty for having to once more visit a doctor who costs twenty-five dollars an hour.

Later, at the Boston Common, Esther gives a sailor her pseudonym from New York, Elly Higginbottom, and even considers taking on this other identity. Sensing that he is a young virginal sailor, Esther tries to play the vamp. But then she sees a woman who, in her paranoid state, she mistakes for Mrs. Willard. Of course Mrs. Willard is a double or surrogate for her own mother, whom now she unconsciously blames for all her wrong paths.

When her mother tells her that Dr. Gordon has recommended shock treatment, she feels curiously schizophrenic, as if she had "just read a terrible newspaper headline about someone else." She had seen a headline about a Mr. Polluci who attempted suicide. It was in a paper her mother called a scandal sheet, full of sex and violence; at home the family read only *The Christian Science Monitor*, which suppressed all mention of sex and violence.

Esther begins to have the hallucinatory feeling of Alice, getting larger and larger, everything appearing quite tiny, as if seen through a keyhole. She is obsessed with death; when she thinks of Japan the thought of hari kari comes to mind.

When Esther is taken by her mother to Dr. Gordon's hospital, all the people there seem mute and motionless as "shop dummies, painted to resemble people and propped up in attitudes counterfeiting life." Esther follows Dr. Gordon, who, like a perverse Virgil, is leading this innocent Dante through another labyrinthian level of hell. She is led to a room filled with locks and barred at the windows. She feels as if she were being electrocuted like the Rosenbergs. Later, she recalls a shock she received from her father's floor lamp. The scream that had come from her throat had seemed "like a violently disembodied spirit."

Esther has been conveyed to the sanitorium in Dodo Conway's black station wagon, "the dead spit of a hearse." Esther's mind is still going around in circles, pirouetting like a skater. She carries the smudged photograph of a dead girl in her pocketbook. In her paranoid condition she recalls all the criticism of her life and writing that anyone ever made and accepts the judgment that she is "factitious, artificial, sham." Unable to sleep, she longs to lose herself in a shadow. She thinks of committing suicide but looks again at her paralyzed image in the mirror.

After attempting futilely to cut herself with a razor blade, she goes to Deer Island Prison on the beach where she had once walked with her father. She walks out on the beach, but is again afraid of drowning and draws back.

Esther next double-dates Cal with Jody and Mark. She doesn't feel her "old self." She has been withdrawing to her room with the shades down and suspects that her mother has arranged this date to get her out. Having left the doll's house, Esther is now attracted to a discussion of Ibsen's *Ghosts*, because it deals with madness, mothers, and death.

Even on the beach Esther has the impression that she is in a modern Audenesque Inferno, where the smudgy skyline is filled with gas tanks, factory stacks, derricks, bridges, and the water with orange peels and candy wrappers. As if it were an academic question, Esther asks Cal how he would commit suicide but decides his method, shooting himself, is untrustworthy and impractical in her case. Again she tries to drown herself but fails. At home, she next tries hanging. Having read a little abnormal phychology, she thinks her mind is going soft like Oswald Alving's, and she fears above all the trauma of more shock treatment.

Working as a candy striper in the local hospital as a kind of therapy, Esther is still obsessed by morbid images, such as grimy water in the mop buckets, dying flowers, and a tomblike basin that suggests to Esther the hospital morgue. By contrast the women in the maternity ward seem like parrots in a parrot house. In a fury over the accusations, Esther leaves the hospital.

The pendulum swinging violently to her innocent side, Esther contemplates becoming a Catholic, even a nun. She thinks of throwing herself at a priest's feet and saying, "O father, help me." She is unconsciously lonely for her own father and actually seeks out his grave. She picks azaleas from the gateway bush and puts them on her father's grave. Then, for the first time, she cries over her inappeasable loss. Like Stephen Dedalus in *A Portrait of the Artist*, she feels she has squandered her prize money. Her New York funds almost exhausted, she buys a black mackintosh, reminiscent of the man in the brown mackintosh at the graveyard in *Ulysses*.

Sylvia's description of how Esther took the sleeping pills and crawled behind a woodpile in the cellar is an exact account of her own experience. The following year when she was writing her thesis, she was pleased to notice a coincidence in Golyadkin's experience; he also hid behind a woodpile. After speaking of how, at His Excellency's, Golyadkin pleads for his "father" to take his part, Sylvia gives this picture of the schizophrenic hero:

> The final scene shows Golyadkin hiding in shadow in Olsufy's yard, confusedly rationalizing his preposterous position. This instinct to hide in the dark, whether it is the dark of a carriage, a back stair, or a woodpile, reiterates Golyadkin's desire to be anonymous (therefore irresponsible and detached) and unseen (therefore nonexistent or dead). Just as he is attempting to reassure himself by denying any relationship whatsoever with the situation, he is aware that groups of people are at Olsufy's windows staring out at him. "The treacherous shadow had betrayed him" (608).
>
> Even as the shadow of the woodpile refuses to conceal him, so the projection of his own "shadow" in the Double refuses to conceal the complete nature of his identity.

The woodpile refuses also to hide Esther's location, her voice crying out, giving away her hiding place, as recorded also in the poem, "Stones."

Esther has entered her cellar, which seems illuminated by "a dim, undersea light." She is swept to sleep finally on a "surging tide." The water imagery and the drowning motif (Marco's suggestion while dancing) may have been suggested by Eliot's *Waste Land*, but were actually associated more in Sylvia's imagination with her father's death. Even though he died in a hospital, her father has metaphorical ties to the sea, as seen in "Daddy" and "Full Fathom Five," a motif, by the way, also used by both Joyce and Eliot.

At this point in the book Esther feels that she is symbolically reborn. Unearthed like a mummy, drawn down a long tunnel like Alice, she comes forth from the dark crying "Mother!"

As she comes to and begins to recover, Esther is visited by her mother and by a young intern, George Bakewell. When Esther looks at herself in a mirror, she thinks she sees the picture of a person whose face has a "supernatural conglomeration of bright colors," as if she were in fact an angel. She breaks the mirror in an attempt to destroy her double's identity.

Oddly enough, the woman in the next bed has the same name as the woman Esther had seen having a baby: Mrs. Tomolillo. Apparently she is supposed to be another mother double, for "every time my mother moved, Mrs. Tomolillo imitated her." Like the hallucinations of Golyadkin's mocking double, the woman in the next bed appears in Esther's paranoid eyes to be mocking her mother's movements.

A doctor, who seems a double for Doctor Gordon, looking very much like him "except that he has black skin where Doctor Gordon's skin was white," is given the distorted name of Doctor Pancreas, while Esther imagines that another doctor introduces himself as Doctor Syphilis. She has the paranoid feeling that doctors are taking down every word she says to her mother. Esther still wants to kill herself, like the son in *Ghosts*, and hopes somehow to get her mother's assistance.

Mrs. Tomolillo usually dishes up the food "like a little mother," but she leaves the hospital, and no one takes her twin bed in Esther's room. But her double appears in the form of a Mrs. Mole, who makes oinking noises and who overturns the beans. Esther thinks the Negro attendant is insolent, as Golyadkin had regarded Golyadkin Jr., but he is, rather, a black double for the Buddy Willard who betrayed her, renouncing her by calling her "Miss Mucky-Muck" under his breath. In effect, she gets even for Buddy's being responsible for her breaking her leg by kicking his Negro double in the shins.

Esther still retreats under her bedclothes, like the cowled, nunlike

Stephen Dedalus when he saw the overblown roses on the wall, and thinks of writing for E.C., "Are you not tired of ardent ways?" Esther purposely breaks the thermometers, scoops up the mercury, and returns to Mrs. Mole's old room. She is still in effect sharing a twin bed with her mother and unconsciously rejects being made over into her image. Playing with the ball of silver mercury in her cupped hand, she is unconsciously facing the dilemma of whether to allow herself to become more divided and finally shattered into madness or whether to get well: "If I dropped it, it would break into a million little replicas of itself, and if I pushed them near each other, they would fuse, without a crack, into one whole again." At this point in the narrative Sylvia may well have been thinking of a similar passage in Chapter Ten of Dostoevsky's *The Double*, where the hero has the dream of his own self splitting indefinitely:

> Beside himself with shame and despair, the utterly ruined though perfectly just Mr. Golyadkin plunged headlong, ready to go wherever fate might lead him; but at every step he took, at every tap of his foot on the granite of the pavement, there leaped up as though out of the earth a Mr. Golyadkin precisely the same, perfectly alike, and of a revolting depravity of heart. And all these precisely similar Golyadkins set to running after one another as soon as they appeared, and stretched in a long chain like a file of geese, hobbling after the real Mr. Golyadkin, so there was nowhere to escape from these duplicates—so that Mr. Golyadkin, who was in every way deserving of compassion, was breathless with terror; so that at last a terrible multitude of duplicates had sprung into being; so that the whole capital was at last chock-full of duplicate Golyadkins, and the police officer, seeing such a breach of decorum, was obliged to seize all these duplicates by the collar and to put them into the station house, which happened to be nearby. . . . Numb and frozen with horror, our hero would wake up, and, numb and frozen with horror, feel that his waking state was hardly more cheerful. . . .[2]

When Sylvia had been writing her thesis the following year from the time of the novel, she was immensely amused by a cartoon she came across—I believe in *The New Yorker*—of a man on a sidewalk in a black suit and black derby, selling mechanical men who were identical with him and who were running in all directions, wound up by a lever attached to a spring in their backs. The man himself has a lever in his back like the wound-up man in the Sheraton ad. Imitating the man in the cartoon, Mrs. Mole has apparently shattered, become an underground woman, gone to another ward. Esther hopes she herself will fuse and be well, but she is still stewing in her own sour air under her glass bell jar.

Taken by Philomena Guinea to a nicer hospital (McLean), Esther is assigned a woman psychiatrist, Dr. Nolan. At the hospital a nurse writes her name, E. Greenwood, on several adhesive tapes to be put in her clothes, the repetition of which has the unconscious effect on Esther of further splitting her identity. She continues to have paranoid feelings about things, such as the matches left behind by Dr. Nolan, which Esther hides in the hem of her bathrobe.

At the new hospital Esther acquires two doubles. The first is Miss Norris, who sits with her in "sisterly silence." There is also another girl, Valerie, who has achieved her marble calm through a prefontal lobotomy. Meanwhile Esther is having insulin injections to bring her around.

When Miss Norris is moved off to Wymark, the dormitory for the sicker patients, Esther is surprised that she is replaced by an old friend, who becomes the major double in the second half of the book. Joan Gilling came from her home town, went to the same college, and also dated Buddy Willard. Esther notices that Joan's room at the hospital is "the mirror image of my own." This early material about Joan Gilling is strictly biographical. The original was a girl named Jane whom Sylvia really admired. But here is one place where Sylvia materially altered her experience for the sake of the novel's structure. As the heroine's main double in McLean, Joan had to die, allowing the good side of the heroine to emerge cured.

Joan shows Esther "tarty" pictures of herself, taken at *Ladies' Day*. Esther was then like the "Doreen" side of herself. Joan represents the perverted Betsy or the inverted Victorian side of Esther, formed by people such as Mrs. Willard. But, like Esther's attraction to the decadent Doreen, she thinks for the first time she has something in common with Joan after she sees the welts on her wrists from her attempted suicide.

When Esther has a negative reaction to the insulin injections, she is soothed by a nurse, Mrs. Bannister, who is another pseudo-mother double. As Sylvia said, Esther tastes the hot milk luxuriously, "the way a baby tastes its mother." Again Esther likens her recovery of sanity to her own postnatal experience. But when her own mother brings her roses for her birthday, Esther dumps them in a wastebasket, telling her cruelly to save them for her funeral. Through Doctor Nolan's assistance, Esther comes gradually to understand her curious Electra complex, her suppressed love for her dead father and her irrational hatred of her mother.

Esther is soon moved to Belsize, the house for the patients who were nearly well. She is confused, for she knows that she is not yet better. Schizophrenically, she associates the place with her double, Joan, who seems to have progressed ahead of her. As Sylvia says for her heroine for the first time explicitly, "Joan was the beaming double of my old best self, specifically designed to follow and torment me." Still seeing life through Golyadkin's distorted lens, Esther thinks Joan sneers at her and treats her as an inferior. Esther is also paranoid about what people in Belsize are saying about her.

Joan informs Esther that her picture is in a magazine. When Esther sees the girl in the strapless gown, her "Doreen" self, she refuses to acknowledge that identity: "No, it's not me. Joan's quite mistaken. It's somebody else."

A nurse at Belsize also works at the institution, the state asylum next door. She tells Esther, "You wouldn't like it over there one bit, Lady Jane." Esther thinks: "I found it strange that the nurse should call me Lady Jane when she knew what my name was perfectly well." Here twin sounding names, Jane and Joan, like Shem and Shaun, become more meaningful when you know that the original of Esther's double was really named Jane. Trying to heal the splits in her own personality, Esther does not like to be characterized as Lady Jane. She is also chilled by the nurse's talk of the state institution, thinking again in a paranoid manner that the nurse is indicating what will happen to her if she falls like a burning star and sinks mentally to the bottom.

Ironically, Esther gets a little pleasure thinking of her China blue dishes. The identification earlier with a China man or woman suggested another distorted image of herself when not herself. Here she seems to be grasping at a new orientation for her dislocated self. Still somewhat "beside" herself, Esther thinks the nurse who comes in without a breakfast tray, indicating that the patient would have shock treatment that morning, must have made a mistake. With her blankets up over her head she feels as if she were in a cocoon. Light dazzles her from her own mirror and from the silver forks on the other patients' trays. Esther next tries to retreat to the far corner of an alcove with a blanket over her head. Dr. Nolan comes in and puts her arm around Esther, hugging her "like a mother." Esther feels betrayed by a person in whom she has put her complete trust. As Dr. Nolan takes Esther to the treatment room, they pass Joan Gilling. Esther holds on to the doctor's arm "like death." She feels as if she were going to her execution, like the girl at the end of "Johnny Panic and the

Bible of Dreams." A Mr. Anderson has to wait while Miss Huey, a giant "cadaverous" nurse with acne on her face like moon craters, prepares Esther for electrotherapy.

When Esther awakes, Doctor Nolan takes her through a door into the "fresh, blue-skied air." The bell jar seems now suspended a few feet above her head.

Returning to the daylight world and taking up her silver knife, Esther notices Joan now playing chopsticks on the piano with Dee Dee, whose husband was living with his mistress. Both Joan and Esther have received letters from Buddy Willard. Joan says that Mrs. Willard has been a virtual mother to her. Esther's view of Mrs. Willard is that with her maternal maxims she has mothered even her own husband. But the view given of Joan in the novel is that she was more attracted to Mrs. Willard than to Buddy. That prepares us for the lesbian scene between Joan and Dee Dee, when Esther enters Dee Dee's room looking for sheet music. Sylvia here changed Jane's nature (à la *The Children's Hour* or Golyadkin's "Judas kiss") in order to give Esther a reason for rejecting her double. But Esther is still fascinated by that which repels her: "Her thoughts were not my thoughts, nor her feelings my feelings, but we were close enough so that her thoughts and feelings seemed a wry, black image of my own."

Joan tells Esther that she likes her better than Buddy, but Esther rejects her mercilessly, telling her: "You make me puke, if you want to know." Biographically, the truth of the matter was that Sylvia did not dislike Jane, nor was there any *Children's Hour* business between Jane and any of the girls at the hospital.

Esther believes now she is gaining her symbolic freedom from her past by acquiring a diaphragm. She still has a phobia about having a baby, but Joan ironically makes it easier for Esther to gain freedom from her double and what she represents by visiting her at nurse Kennedy's in Cambridge.

Esther meets Irwin on the steps of Widener Library and has snails at Nuits St. George with the dragon, who turns out to be the priest chosen for the tribal rite of defloration. Irwin is the last in a series of mirror opposites or evil doubles for Buddy Willard. Her own evil double is still Joan, who has become a puritanical caricature of what Auden calls "ingrown virginity." The animal similes, like the insect ones, which Esther used to associate with herself are now transferred to her double (horse, owl, and cat) as if she were a totemic representation of the subhuman or animal in Esther's nature, which she has been able to purge.

When Dr. Quinn, Joan's psychiatrist, comes to see Esther, inquiring as to her patient's whereabouts, Esther has a sudden urge to dissociate herself from Joan completely. As she goes to sleep that night, Esther can hear Joan's voice and see Joan's face floating in the air, "bodiless and smiling, like the face of the Cheshire Cat." It is like Stephen Dedalus's vision of the decorated head of Cranly, who has been to the Christ-like Stephen both a John the Baptist and a Judas.

After Joan is found hanged near the frozen pond in the heart of winter, Esther is again symbolically reborn. A "fresh fall of snow" leaves on the asylum grounds "a pure, blank sheet." Now it is Esther's mother's face that floats before her like a "pale reproachful moon." Her mother thinks the whole experience should be forgotten like a bad dream, but Esther feels her nightmare inscape has been that of a regressed and paralyzed baby, almost like the bottled foeti she saw in the medical school; she feels "black and stopped as a dead baby." But, because of Doctor Nolan's shock therapy and talk, the bell jar is beginning to lift.

Now Esther, like Blake's risen hero, has regained a primal but higher innocence. The nurse who comes to tell her of Buddy Willard's visit looks snow-capped. Like the day she broke her leg, Buddy is still wearing khaki green, suggesting military regimentation of thought and a parallel lack of sensitivity. He now seems "unrelated" to her. Reversing roles because of his physical sickness, Esther does most of the work digging his car out of a snowdrift. She is back from her shadowy world, outside in a brilliant, sunny, "pristine expanse." The world for her seems to have "shifted slightly, and entered a new phase." People on adjoining walks glide by on casters, and Valerie has a "calm snow-maiden face." On the phone Irwin's voice means nothing to her. She feels free, not so much from him as from the repressive attitudes which she feels landed her in the asylum.

Esther attends Joan's funeral and wonders what she thought she was burying. In a neat reversal of associations, Joan's coffin is covered with the "snow-pallor of flowers—the black shadow of something that wasn't there." She thinks of the grave prepared for her double: "That shadow would marry this shadow." The soul or shadow of her double, the evil conscience within herself, has been exorcised, and she feels very much alive: "I am, I am, I am."

In the final scene, when Esther is about to face a board of doctors, similar to the scene where Esther faced her second shock treatments,

Doctor Nolan, her new mother, assures her that she will be there. Esther is "scared to death," like a baby in birth trauma. In a ritual of rebirth and marriage ("Something old, something new") she becomes a second-hand car recrossing the Lethe, "patched, retreaded, and approved for the road." Like the birth of America under the Pilgrims, Esther steps forth into a new land, leaving behind the "pocked and cadaverous face" of Miss Huey. Also, like Ariadne returning from the labyrinth of the Minotaur, or like a baby with an umbilical cord, Esther steps past the eyes and faces, guiding herself "as by a magical thread."

It has been my intention in this retelling of *The Bell Jar* not to pass judgment on its literary qualities. That is for someone else to do. I have merely tried to do the first part of a critic's job, as explained to me by one of Sylvia's and my teachers, Robert Gorham Davis—that is, to show what the author was attempting to do and, by sticking close to her imagery and similes, to show how well she performed her self-assigned task. I have concentrated mainly on the structuring device of the "doubles" to which Sylvia herself pointed the way in her Dostoevsky thesis. Upon emerging from McLean, Sylvia was naturally and intuitively attracted to this author of profound psychological insight, who gave her a better understanding of her own schizophrenic experiences than any psychoanalysis could have done.

In *The Brothers Karamazov*, you recall, Ivan's double, his bastard brother Smerdyakov, ends by hanging himself, but this greatest of Russian novels deals basically with parricide, as *Crime and Punishment* in effect deals with matricide, and both end with the moral that the hero is responsible for his ideas and not above the moral law. It was, I believe, a more biographical Dostoevsky novel, not discussed in Sylvia's thesis, which gave her the idea for the end of her novel. *The Possessed* (or *The Devils*, as it is sometimes called) ends with Stavrogin, a kind of double or surrogate for the ideas of Peter Verkhovensky, hanging himself as Peter escapes unharmed to Switzerland. Attempted expiation through the death of the double was not a new theme in that novel. Another conspirator, Kirilov, had shot himself, accepting the blame in a suicide note for the murder committed by Peter Verkhovensky.

The terrible irony of *The Bell Jar* is that the original of Joan Gilling, the double that Sylvia kills off so that Esther can live, is very much alive, and that it is Sylvia who has been successful in killing herself. Many critics have noted the irony that Sylvia prophetically sensed at the end of the novel that in Europe the bell jar might descend again. But it did not descend for her double. The girl whom Sylvia knew in Wellesley and at Smith College and whom she felt had followed her to McLean is actually very unlike the Joan Gilling who has lesbian leanings toward another inmate. In fact, Sylvia very much admired and liked the original girl. Was Sylvia, then, projecting her deepest fears onto the double of her heroine? After all, Esther gets a perverse thrill at Joan's funeral as she becomes stronger, more able to face the bright, snow-filled world. Knowing both Sylvia and the original of Joan Gilling well at the time of the events depicted in the novel and for several years afterward, I can testify that neither girl had inclinations in this direction. I think we must seek the roots of Sylvia's disturbance in another psychological area.

Otto Rank says that when a narcissist experiences the loss of a double it sometimes demonstrates only his intense interest in himself:

> Thus the apparent contradiction—the loss of the shadow-image or mirror-image represented as pursuit—is understood as a representation of the opposite, the recurrence of what is repressed in that which represses. . . .
> This same mechanism is shown by the denouement of madness, almost regularly leading to suicide, which is so frequently linked with pursuit by the double, the self. Even when the depiction does not measure up to Dostoevsky's unsurpassable clinical exactitude, it does become clear that it is a question of paranoid ideas of pursuit and influencing to which the hero is prey by reason of his double. Since Freud's psychoanalytic clarification of paranoia, we know that this illness has as a basis "a fixation in narcissism," to which corresponds typical megalomania, the sexual overrating of oneself. The stage of development from which paranoids regress to their original narcissism is sublimated homosexuality, against the undisguised eruption of which they defend themselves with the characteristic mechanism of projection. On the basis of this insight, it can easily be shown that the pursuit of the ill person regularly proceeds from the originally loved persons (or their surrogates).[3]

Sylvia never loved the original of Joan Gilling, but she did greatly admire her at one time. For Esther, Joan finally represents all the puritanical ethos present in the world of Buddy and Mrs. Willard. She has to be rejected, much as was the extravagantly wild double, Doreen, rejected earlier. But why did Sylvia feel the necessity to alter her experience and kill off this particular double?

Otto Rank explains:

The frequent slaying of the double, through which the hero seeks to protect himself permanently from the pursuits of his self, is really a suicidal act. It is, to be sure, in the painless form of slaying a different ego: an unconscious illusion of the splitting-off of a bad, culpable ego —a separation which, moreover, appears to be the precondition for every suicide. The suicidal person is unable to eliminate by direct self-destruction the fear of death resulting from the threat to his narcissism. To be sure, he seizes upon the only possible way out, suicide, but he is incapable of carrying it out other than by way of the phantom of a feared and hated double, because he loves and esteems his ego too highly to give it pain or to transform the idea of his destruction into the deed. In this subjective meaning, the double turns out to be a functional expression of the psychological fact that the individual with an attitude of this kind cannot free himself from a certain phase of his narcissistically loved ego-development.[4]

I have to conclude, then, that Sylvia was trying to free herself from certain negative attitudes she recognized within herself, puritanical attitudes which she associated with Mrs. Willard and which she projected in a perversion of sexual purity upon her double. Although Rank notes above that "the stage of development from which paranoids regress to their original narcissism is sublimated homosexuality," I do not think it applies to Sylvia. I knew her too well at the time of the incidents related in *The Bell Jar* ever to conclude that she had lesbian tendencies. Aside from the original of Buddy Willard, I am the only person, I believe, who has ever dated both Sylvia and the original of Joan Gilling. Although certainly neither girl was inclined toward lesbianism, Sylvia understood enough of the love-hate duality of rivals to suggest this characteristic in her artistic double.[5]

I feel that it was Sylvia's narcissism, developing from the loss of love, beginning at the time of her father's death, that caused her to project upon innocent and evil doubles her conflicting polarized selves. As an artist, she fully understood this inner conflict and, with Dostoevsky's help, created a vehicle for its expression. Had Otto Rank's *The Double* been translated before 1963, Sylvia might have understood and accepted the etiological conclusion that her incipient schizophrenia stemmed from narcissism and might have transformed it, as she transformed so much of her experience, into art.

1 3 The Deathly Paradise of Sylvia Plath

Constance Scheerer

> Green alleys where we reveled have become
> The infernal haunt of demon dangers;
> . . .
> Backward we traveled to reclaim the day
> Before we fell . . .
> All we find are altars in decay. . . .
>
> Sylvia Plath, "Doom of Exiles" (1954)

In Ted Hughes's "Notes on the Chronological Order of Sylvia Plath's Poems," included in *The Art of Sylvia Plath*, he refers to several written in 1956-1957, calling their vision of "the deathly paradise" a "chilling" one. The comment is haunting, also puzzling: how can "paradise" be "deathly"? Sylvia Plath was, Hughes adds, evolving her own pantheon of deities at the time, her special cosmic vision. Although she was inspired by the works of "primitive painters" from Henri Rousseau to Leonard Baskin, he explains, the vision was an internally felt experience and very much her own.

Paradise is, by definition, not deathly. A concept common to many myths and religions, it is invariably defined as the starting point for humanity, also as the time when human beings possessed the ideal life, including intimate contact with God or gods. In pagan or pre-Christian faiths or stories, the original state of innocence and bliss can be recaptured only by a return: this was often meant literally and forms the cyclical pattern of Oriental religions or pagan philosophers. With the coming of the Judaeo-Christian tradition, paradise, our first home, takes on an eschatological meaning as well. Its idyllic condition waits in some uncertain future time, a going-forward to a place or state won through God's redemptive power and grace. The word "paradise," of Persian origin, means simply "walled garden," and this aspect is retained with its traditional imagery and lavish beauty in many Plath poems as it is in paintings by Rousseau.

A deathly paradise is, however, of darkling, sinister import, presided over by presences divine but demonic—mythic figures of power, impersonalized archetypes without concern for what they create. Within the walls of such death-gardens ravaging figures sometimes prowl and destroy, like the tigers of Rousseau's mysterious canvases, or the archetypal sow who swills down the very cosmos itself as she wallows in the "walled garden" of her legendary sty in the Plath poem, "Sow." Although they contain by implication humanity's beginnings and endings, death, not life, is the ruling principle of these anti-Edens. Moreover, their inhabitants have no freedom of choice in the old Miltonic sense of having been made "Sufficient to have stood though free to fall." They are human but hapless, at the mercy of deity or deities. The deathly paradise, then, is deathly not only because it affirms death instead of life but also because it swallows up purpose and individuality. Its ultimate affirmation is a negation: the search for an identity means the search for nonidentity. The discovery of purpose discloses that there is no purpose.

On this paradox Sylvia Plath's vision is based. Having told us in "The Death of Myth-Making" (1959) what our world would be like—dull and mechanized—ruled only by the ugly, limiting vision of Reason and Common Sense, she demonstrates in her poetry how the mythic, in its immemorial pre-Christian (even pre-Graeco-Roman) dress of birth and death, seasonal and vegetative changes, moon and sea phases, and archaic concept of beginnings and endings, is the only way to express the cosmos, is, in fact, the only way the cosmos can express itself.

Early uncollected poems, scattered through Aurelia Plath's edition of her daughter's *Letters Home*, help us trace the poet's developing vision. A fragment about an archaic garden-figure of a boy, significantly described as "eyeless," tells us that his function is to make us forget our own mortality because his frozen, impersonal youth is eternal. "Doom of Exiles" is a "Paradise Lost" in minuscule, an apprehension of "fallen man" in a world without hope of salvation. In "the ramshackle meadow" of "Temper of Time," the snake lurks as a shadow while "apples go / Bad to the core." In the south of France, sketching the walled garden of a nunnery from the outside, Sylvia bursts into tears. "I knew it was so lovely *inside*," she writes her mother (italics mine). A Rousseau-painting poem, "Pursuit," is animated by "the terrible beauty of death." The panther, who symbolizes male sexuality as well as the death-lust, has an easy time of it, ravaging the land "Condemned by our ancestral fault"—the lost paradise again. But this poem goes further. No wall, it says, can keep death out of a paradise already spoiled, penetrated by a power at once fatal and erotically attractive.

These early poems prefigure the twenty-eight or thirty "garden" poems in *The Colossus*. Among them "Snakecharmer" deserves attention, partly because it is one of the poems Ted Hughes found especially "chilling," and partly because it is a more complete realization of the anti-Edenic vision than is found in earlier works. Inspired by Rousseau's "La Charmeuse de Serpents," "Snakecharmer" reaches back into an archaic world. Turning the painting's female snakecharmer into a male demigod, perhaps a principle of ageless, archetypal function, the poet creates a cultic figure possessing the secrets of life and death, creation and destruction. What this snakecharmer pipes, has forever piped, and will eternally pipe, is a *private* Eden, expressive of his personal, whimsical vision. He is uninterested in plan or purpose, in gods or men. He pipes a lush, green, watery world into existence, then, as the mood takes him, out of existence again. By his piping he not only creates this world but peoples it—with snakes. It seems at first as if his garden and its occupants exist only so long as he wills them to be.

When the snakecharmer tires, however, his creatures become part of "the simple fabric, / Of snake-warp, snake-weft"—in other words, there is an *idea* of snakes, almost in a Platonic sense, a "cloth" without whose prior existence no particular snakes could be given form. Soon, as the piper pipes, his snakes undergo change: they become "Leaf, become eyelid; snake-bodies, bough, breast / Of tree and human." The piper as creator-destroyer is actually piping the human race. This is a pre-Genesis as well as an anti-Genesis concept of paradise and human origins: humanity is not driven forth into the human condition by a stern yet just and compassionate God who is also prepared to redeem his children. Humanity, in this "paradise," is a ripple on a green, watery surface, a flick of a serpent tongue, an inhalation of a piper's breath. "Eden" is a painted backdrop, cool, silky, witty, amoral, perhaps a cosmic joke. Yet because of that "simple fabric," that preexistent "idea" of snake humanity, the vision is no literal "pipe-dream," and its "reality" is what gives the piece its "chilling" quality.

Like "Snakecharmer," the other garden poems of *The Colossus* present a garden that is off-center, strange, anti-Edenic. It may be a death-garden ("The Manor Garden"), or a garden combining death and the erotic ("The Beekeeper's Daughter"), or a garden without any potential for redemption ("The Burnt-out Spa"), or a garden in which the snake still burns like a jewel and has the last laugh, even though he has been slain by the yardman—a further symbolizing of humankind as incapable of overcoming the "snake," of keeping death out of paradise ("Medallion"). Perhaps it is a garden closed into a superegg, attainable only through peering in—the great Alice-in-Wonderland daughter on her knees at the tiny window behind which lives and looks sadly back at her the eye of the dead father ("The Beekeeper's Daughter"). It may be made along the lines of a mechanical model ("The Stones"), or created by or for an "Absolutely alien / Order" ("Mussel Hunter at Rock Harbor"). But in each case it is a frightening garden, one which traps without sheltering, rejects even when it entices.

Moreover, whoever controls the garden, however it is described, holds the secrets of origins and ends, of life and death. The presence, the persona, god or demigod, human or partly human, differs markedly from one poem to the next, but the control is always absolute, and the meaning (or meaninglessness) of each garden is at this power's discretion. As divorced from control of their own destiny as the snake-descended humanity of "Snakecharmer," the "controlled" are set apart in every poem. Sometimes they are voiceless appendages, sometimes helpless pleaders, occasionally welcomers crying out in greeting. But they are always placed in irreconcilable polar opposition to the "controller" or power.

"The Surgeon at 2 A.M." (CW) [1] is a rather different poem in this tradition. Again the central metaphor is the garden and its creator-lord. This time the garden is biological, within the body of a particular patient undergoing emergency surgery late at night, afterward in a ward where many patients lie recovering. The surgeon, the poem's power and persona, first presents a garden in his patient on the table: it is internal, beneath the skin, containing the "bell-bloom" that is the heart, the "tubers and fruits / Oozing their jammy substances," the "lung-tree." Snake imagery is present, too, but is equated by the surgeon with "orchids" and beauty. "I am so small," says the surgeon, "in comparison with these organs!" But the surgeon is not small in relation to his job:

he is playing God. He does not pretend to create human beings: he does re-create them. His skill at rearranging internal parts brings life out of death and saves the bodies in which the souls, invisible, are anchored. Next, orderlies are "wheeling off" the patient and putting him to bed in the ward. The surgeon, tagging along yet remote and detached, continues to muse, admiring the results of his craft and seeing himself as the divinely inspired "gardener." In a world where all is blue—light, linen, angelic atmosphere—he contemplates, not without considerable satisfaction, the drugged faces that "follow [him] like flowers." The garden concept has expanded from a particular patient to a ward filled with patients, saved, reborn, turning in concert to the doctor-as-God.

The poem, however, is more complex. Death imagery is introduced at the end. The sleepers are described as lying in "gauze sarcophagi." Blue, hue of heaven, gives way to red, symbol of anguish, wounds, death vividness, power. "I am the sun," the self-admiring surgeon comments. It is an Eden, this hospital, but an Eden man-made. The very purity (i.e., innocence) is artificial ("The white light . . . hygienic as heaven"). The presiding deity is a physician who saves bodies, not souls. Rebirth is physical, into a world of new teeth, a gall bladder extracted, a limb of flesh replaced by "clean, pink plastic." The soul, that reality which the surgeon posits while admitting he had never "seen" it, is not medicine's province. (Tonight, from the patient who has just undergone surgery, it has temporarily receded, like a ship's light, and stands watch.)

If it was the poet's intention to portray a compassionate figure in her surgeon, she did not succeed. He is detached, cool, admiring the body as "a Roman thing," a superb piece of engineering, and himself as its perfecter. A telling aspect of the poem is that neither on the operating table nor in the ward do patients have "faces" for the surgeon; on the ward, "Grey faces, shuttered by drugs," make an expressionless expanse of uniformity. In its own way, the garden-vision of this poem is fully as chilling as that of "Snakecharmer," its Eden as eerie and as limited. In this garden of the faceless, no seeds of redemption have been planted. The surgeon is pleased to accept responsibility for the total "garden," but not for the individual blooms. He is also attracted, actually, by human suffering, something he can control and manipulate at will without himself becoming part of it—an attitude found in several Plath poems. The "Adams" and "Eves" of his "Eden" are described in such terms as "A lump of Chinese white / With seven holes thumbed in" (a head), or "a pathological salami" (tissues awaiting analysis). There is a hint of medical school student humor here: there is depersonalization, too. And there is an implied irony: why go through surgery only to wake to a world of tubes and plastic, or artificial replacements? Is this our destiny—even our *physical* destiny? Moreover, the surgeon who equates the "snakes" in his patients with "orchids" and splendor ignores the "snake" in his own soul. A surgeon is not meant to be a father confessor, but this surgeon's pride is the real serpent in his hospital-garden. His is not the Eden of the caring God, but the Eden of a man who plays at being God, not humble before his powers but floating in exalted detachment ("I am the sun").

There is purpose and order in the surgeon's garden of life and death, but his control over it is startlingly akin to that of the snakecharmer. The surgeon is happy as he "worms" and "hacks"—he revels in lovely red blood. Perhaps he is the moral evocation of the snakecharmer; but for a mere hair which the centuries have drawn he might turn and "hack" his "flowers" to purposeless shreds. He does not, of course (although the theme still appears in "mad doctor" movies): the amorphous shimmer of the snakecharmer's world has been replaced by a clean, decent, ordered vision. But it is a paradise no less deathly in a nonphysical sense, because it is both man-made and man-redeemed. In a way, snakecharmer and surgeon inhabit the same mythic world. The snakecharmer belongs to the primal life before individual consciousness came into being—or became important: the surgeon is part of the Romantic or post-Renaissance world in which human individuality receives an emphasis little known in antiquity (although born with the birth of Christianity). But both personas are controlling figures alienated from their worlds—creators parted from their creatures. Both "garden poems" romanticize the alienated superfigure at the expense of faceless sufferers.

If we take the sequential publication of Sylvia Plath's poetry as a roughly accurate guide to the development of her thought and vision— we know, for instance, that the poems of *The Colossus* were completed by 1959, that the poems of *Crossing the Water* follow along in sequence more or less, and that the poems in *Winter Trees* are contemporaneous with those in *Ariel* and probably written during the last nine months or so of the poet's life—we note that garden imagery and metaphor grow less frequent. As the "garden" drops away, "the journey" takes its place—anything to get on board that train (ultimately the death train), to find the "terminus" for which the "suitcases" are packed, to ride that horse, churn with those churning pistons. Such garden poems as do appear are more decadent. For instance, in "Leaving Early" (CW) the garden has moved indoors into a cold, artificial atmosphere charged with crackling hatred. A mysterious "lady" appears, "creator" of a cluttered, degenerate, messy apartment, and later is seen (an aspect quite possibly never intended by the poet) as pathetic victim of the poem's persona in a cosmos of lacerating tensions whose "Eden" is not only deathly but "lousy." The poem, first printed in August, 1961, belongs to the same period as "I Am Vertical" (CW), an attempt to cancel the alienating barriers between self and nature, creature and creator. This poem's speaker longs for the death which will make her one with the garden, in this case the totality of Nature: it is restful, pleasant, but impersonal, and purity has no part in it. In "Among the Narcissi" (WT) we sense at once that the recuperating old man has not long to live as he hobbles among his "children," the white-paper flowers. But the garden's true response is not to the man but to an overpowering sense of cosmos or godhead—neutral, alien, fearsome. To it the flowers do obeisance; of it, frail old Percy remains innocently unaware.

It is not until the poem "Tulips" (A) that the metaphors of garden/Eden and purity/innocence cross one another for the first (and almost the last) time. This garden is an "excitable" mass of huge, intense, scarlet flowers, brought to the suffering speaker's hospital room where they oppress and disturb her. She does not simply *want* to die—that would be easy enough. She now feels that she is ready, *worthy*, by a process of preparation—"I am a nun now, I have never been so pure." But someone has brought her a red garden, forcing vivid life upon the peaceful death-whiteness of purified readiness. "Tulips" sets up a confrontation not only between life and death but between the faceless and the face-endowed as well, i.e., between the impersonal, nonindividuated, primal, and mythic, and the personal, individual, cared-for and caring, here-and-now. The speaker wishes to be effaced: the tulips will not let her. They not only force existence on the speaker but pain and self-awareness as well.

From this point on, the poems of *Ariel* pick up speed, merging into the imagery of the gallop, the piston, the mad journey, the agony. One last garden of death ("The Moon and the Yew Tree") presents a quiet graveyard of rest after despair, but is left behind like a way station receding into the distance while the themes of purity and redemption move harder and faster with the striking hooves, the turning wheels, the churn of pistons, "Ariel," "Getting There," "Fever 103°," "Totem," "Years," "Words"—all tell of cosmic trips without destination or even a clear point of origin, divorced from the human and the individualized. All the while the lusted-for goal (for which the self has been packed into its cosmic suitcase) is death—death in the form of sweeping away of identity, melding into the primal/impersonal.

There are no more gardens (perhaps a touch or two of garden imagery). There are no creator figures either, only machines on the move, and one pitiable old queen bee with "wings like torn shawls" who ascends, red and terrible, into the cosmos, taking the poet's self along with her, a lost and defeated identity in a world found more and more alien and alienating. In "Stings" there is a final hint, in the tradition of "Snakecharmer" or "The Surgeon at 2 A.M.," of a presiding, commanding, alien power who skips in from the mythic and skips out again, leaving a few tangible clues in the form of shed garments, symbolizing the concrete dropping away from the abstract and the continuing possibility of an eternal forming power in the cosmos. In "Edge," almost the last poem Sylvia Plath ever wrote, the themes of purity and the garden cross once again with a power and effect not found in "Tulips" as, in a series of marbleized images, "the woman," now "perfected" by death, folds her children back into herself and makes of her act a self-created garden, the "deathly paradise" come true.

Two things seem clear as we trace through the poetry of Sylvia Plath: she rejects both the primal and the eschatological paradise and seeks redemption elsewhere and in a different form; Edenic imagery and metaphor for the search for purity find different voices. The quest for the garden and the quest for the lost innocence are almost never the same quest. Sometimes her simpler nature poems hold out a kind of hope, resolution, promise, for example, "Black Rook in Rainy Weather" (CW). Certain mother-child poems hint at a similar transforming power: in "Child" (WT) the speaker comes closer to God in the clear beauty of her baby's eye than in any "paradise" (the glimpse is almost at once negated as she also sees in that same pure eye the reflection of the cosmos as "dark / Ceiling without a star"). A deeply mythic distrust of gardens as sources of purity is voiced in "Three Women" (WT): the wife, safely delivered of a healthy son and concerned with how to shield him from the world's pain, asks "How long can I be a wall around my green property?" "Not very long," is the implied reply, and it brings us face to face with the metaphysical basis of Sylvia Plath's distrust of Eden, of the paradise of life.

Her trouble lies not necessarily in the garden per se, but in the wall around it. Mythic or real, stylized like Pope's or roving into nature like Wordsworth's, gardens are designed to protect, to keep certain things in and other things out. Even though her poetry depicts a world of alienations—man from man, man from nature, man from God (perhaps mother and child form the one abiding exception)—alienation is what Sylvia Plath cries out against in most of her poetry. If we live in a garden, or seek one as a perfect spot, we are always closed in *with* something or *from* something. If evil has got in, like the tiger in Rousseau's paintings, we are trapped with it: if we are barred from the garden, on the outside, there is no way back in, no way to find the lost innocence. Paradise, ultimately, is deathly for Sylvia Plath, not because it is a source of death but because it promises or threatens to prevent death. Like that mysterious "birthday present" always "waiting," it will not "let down the veil," it keeps its wall up. As under the "bell jar" where one breathes only one's own self-poisoning air, one is trapped in and by a garden, or barred from it, unable to cope with one's sins. This is why many Plath poems express a world without help, refuge, salvation, redemption. For many, paradise is bliss with its confining order: for Sylvia Plath it was not. In one sense a daughter of Eve, the poet in a deeper sense is closer to Persephone who, as Milton wrote in effect, while gathering flowers became herself the flower gathered. Ravishment by Dis was the price Persephone paid for her aimless, primal flower-picking in which, as John Armstrong writes in *The Paradise Myth*, the girl surrenders to "the imperative need to counteract the oppressiveness of the idyllic confine. . . ."

A price has to be paid for the refusal of the garden's walls. In Sylvia Plath's poems we see the same price being paid over and over as her poetic voices seek yearned-for purity outside the "idyllic confine." Her personas continually express the cosmology of aliens in the world who are at the same time muffled and inaccessible behind the garden world. Her poems perpetually ask Alan Watts's questions: How far out can I get? How lost without being utterly lost? No sure answer is given, but there is a rejection of all experiences which may be likened to what the poet called a "shut box." The garden as first-and-final home is shunned. So is the body, another form of trap. In "Getting There" (A), the poet writes, "And I, stepping from this skin / Of old bandages . . . old faces. . . ." In "Apprehensions" (WT) it is the mind that is the prison, and in "Even" (WT) marriage is seen as a crippling confinement, turning into torment the bed once experienced as "paradise." "Last Words" (CW) envisions a "box" as a happy world, pretty sarcophagus with "a face on it," and one is tempted to see this as a clinging to the individual personality, to walls that protect selfhood—until one remembers that in the archaic, nonindividualized world, a magical use was made of objects but not of the body or the personality.

It is an unendurable paradox: Sylvia Plath, who could not tolerate the wall, the constriction, the garden, also felt lost and alien in the expansion of the unconfined universe. Does this mean that death was to her the ultimate expansion, therefore the ultimate restriction—the last, walled, confining garden? One begins to suspect that, despite the frantic need for freedom, motion, and wildness, this was so. The poet always sought purification, redemption in the dynamic, the active; and yet the purifying act, in her poems as in her life, took place in enclosures: the love of the dead father in the sugar-egg; the fruition of motherhood in the dark, closed, blooming womb; death in the cellar-ledge of her mother's basement; death, finally, in the "shut box" of the gas oven, as if her myths of origins and ends were finally translated into realities.

The origin of humanity's sense of being lost and alienated has been well defined by Alan Watts in his *Beyond Theology: The Art of Godsmanship:*

> Man is kicked out of Paradise, because Paradise is having a connection —roots in the garden, stem from the branch, current to the light. To be unaware of the connection is to have one's heart in the wrong place— far out in the fruit instead of within, in the tree. It is to feel that one's basic self is isolated within the body's envelope of skin, forgetting that the self is the whole circulating current from which embodiments come and go . . . endless variations upon one theme.

But Sylvia Plath's poems tell us that life in alienation, in perpetual polar tension with "other," is not worth it, and that wall-less life cosmically, mythically blended with the universe is simply not possible. The poet longs to creep back, not into the conventional womb, but into the archaic world of feeling, governed not by morality or stern justice and duty but by an indifferent, amorphous, mysteriously attractive, destructive/life-giving, goddesslike power which reveals no secrets as to our origins and makes no promises as to our ends. But surrender to this deathly paradise even as an act of imagination gives small comfort. The death-garden may not judge, neither does it save. It may promise rebirth, but not of the individual consciousness. And it appears to be totally without love.

When the garden poems with their controlling figures have faded from her work, one realizes that, because of the sheer number and variety of their personas—sacred or secular, human or demonic, male or female—no one accepted figure, power, or control exists. Even the moon, possibly the greatest single deity figure, only occasionally fulfills the controlling function, and her presence, too, is always charged with ambiguity since, like those dark mother-goddesses of primal times, she presents a fearsome combination of the destructive and the maternal. It begins to appear as if setting in motion a world and its inhabitants and ordering its meaning and their end is a game at which any number may play. It comes as no surprise when Sylvia Plath, no longer speaking through some persona but in a voice all too patently and painfully her own, decides to undertake the task herself.

Therefore, in "Edge," written a day or so before her death, she creates her own new myth. In the only other poem except "Tulips" in which images of purity cross those of the garden, the persona folds in upon herself and into herself (taking her children with her) and completes rites of purification which paradoxically convert self and children into a sealed garden, where neither hope, life, nor redress bloom and flourish, yet where a strange "perfection" waits. "Edge" states that the only real "journey" is a moveless, static infolding; the only garden the last, not the lost one. The marbleized Greek necessity of the poem's vision refuses to affirm the infinite value of human life or the existence of the divine and the transforming in the universe. "Edge" does away with the alien power of "other," but at a terrible cost. The primal and/or eschatological meaning of "garden" is denied, and the poetic persona *becomes* the garden, self-created. Self is the wall, the idol and monument, the creator, end, and aim of this garden. In its concept of the ultimate "home," "Edge" offers us the most "chilling" definition of "the deathly paradise," with the self as controlling deity, not from *hubris* but from the pathos of utter despair, in a world which can offer no place "to get to."

14   Sylvia Plath and the New Decadence

ARTHUR K. OBERG

The effects of Sylvia Plath's suicide and the posthumous publication of her second volume of poems, *Ariel*, have exceeded the 1965, 1966 British and American editions of that work. The last poems have become the property not only of the journals and little magazines, but of *Glamour* and *Time*. Earlier work of hers—published, unpublished, from the most minor to the most mature—continues to be reprinted. Articles about her self, her poetry, and her prose proliferate; and what began as a life has taken on the appearance of a legend or an art work concluded in death.

The poems in *Ariel* have succeeded almost too well. Their restless intelligence and agonizing, ordered intensity have marked them too tellingly. They are now in danger of becoming an anomaly instead of taking their place in a romantic, imagistic tradition extending back and beyond the official Romantic poets to Smart and Blake and Clare. A respect for the particular otherness of things and for the peculiar joy of the visionary moment places Sylvia Plath in a long line of poets often wrongly separated into romantic and unromantic camps: Yeats and Eliot, Roethke and Elizabeth Bishop, Thomas and Marianne Moore.

Yet, Sylvia Plath's curiosity and hunger for experience are continually transformed in her poems from a romantic poetry of observation into a poetry of annihilation and transcendence. Her poems strive toward a state of purity. There is an inclusiveness at once so exclusive and reticent that critics commonly have provided for her work a kind of Mc-Luhanized recreation of it. We have received running commentary and shorthand notes in place of systematic analysis. We have received bare juxtaposition (e.g., Plath with more Plath, Plath with Dickinson) and correlative-for-correlative reconstruction in place of elucidation of text.

The inclination to provide new distillation for an already distilled poetry becomes understandable in view of the creatures and objects in a Plath poem. However generous in her life or in the giving of her poetry, Sylvia Plath presents us with poems that, after long inspection, remain unfamiliar and increasingly disdainful of outer, human reference. In the history of poetry, language has seldom been so evidently in crisis, written so painfully *in extremis*.

What we discover in approaching Sylvia Plath's work is less a collection of poems than a distinctive decor that is related to a new decadence in art. The opening poem of *The Colossus*, her first book of verse (1960), initiates a reader into the dark, funereal world he has chosen to enter. However, for all the intimations in *The Colossus* of Sylvia Plath's later work, this first collection remains saner and brightly wittier than the poems she went on, with deadly competence, to perfect.

Linked to modern poetry by an unusual artistic accomplishment in sculpted form, Sylvia Plath looks to striking image and to prominent rhythm for the authority of her voice. "Death & Co.," one of the *Ariel* poems, establishes itself from the opening line with a matter-of-fact sureness that is typical of her later work:

> Two, of course there are two.
> It seems perfectly natural now—
> The one who never looks up, whose eyes are lidded
> And balled, like Blake's,
> Who exhibits
>
> The birthmarks that are his trademark—
> The scald scar of water,
> The nude
> Verdigris of the condor.
> I am red meat. His beak
>
> Claps sidewise: I am not his yet.
> He tells me how badly I photograph.
> He tells me how sweet
> The babies look in their hospital
> Icebox, a simple
>
> Frill at the neck,
> Then the flutings of their Ionian
> Death-gowns,
> Then two little feet.
> He does not smile or smoke.

The other does that,
His hair long and plausive.
Bastard
Masturbating a glitter,
He wants to be loved.

I do not stir.
The frost makes a flower,
The dew makes a star,
The dead bell,
The dead bell.

Somebody's done for.

There is an insistence here that borders on obsession and hysteria but that is never out of control. The logic ("then . . . then," "the one . . . the other"), the procession and progression of images (frost, flower, dew, star, bell) conclude the poem so ritually and insistently that we may forget the nightmarish confusions upon which "Death & Co." has built. Death, birth, and sex merge and are distorted in images that extend to untried and dangerous alignments of art and life.

No single image is adequate as metaphor. Alone and in combination, the images in "Death & Co." outdo one another in inventive brilliance. The deadly duo, the Blakean, eccentric detail, the Ionian flutings are perfectly, insistently right in their concretion and associational power. Image and rhythm give the sense of being self-generating and -sustaining from the start. "Two, of course there are two." This is the way it is, we are told, with an authority in which we acquiesce.

Combining lyricism with bald understatement, Sylvia Plath guys rhythm as she pursues a persuasive and controlled voice. Violence is never excluded, and in the virtuosity of the rhythms—exceeding even the jack-hammer rhythms of Lowell's early poetry—we sense what is being held down and held back. The rhythmical expertise of *Ariel* distinguishes poems that are in the tradition of Eliot's "fragments . . . shored against my ruins" and Frost's "momentary stay[s] against confusion." But Sylvia Plath lets in more horror than Eliot or Frost ever entertained in their most terrible poems. In turn, she was forced to create rhythms more compelling and compulsive than anything contemporary poetry has known.

In Sylvia Plath, rhythm and image, relentlessly extended as far as they will go, evolve into a poetry of breakdown and breakthrough. A woman watched and watching, Sylvia Plath writes out of a modern sensibility burdened by an excess of guilt and consciousness. She is married and suffering, and she shamelessly introduces us to her particular "totem," "medallion," "muses," and "lorelei." The company she keeps is both mentor and destroyer. Associated with madness, sex, sickness, and death, this company establishes her decor.

And decor and fetor often are one. Her helicon is a burnt-out spa, and there is no god of healing in her poems. Instead, there is a slow and indelible stain, scar, and smell that touches everything. In her several bee poems, it is a sting which is a source both of intrigue and fearful repulsion, the sweet taste and smell of life and death.

Despite the number of annihilatingly beautiful poems in her volumes —"The Colossus," "Blue Moles," "Flute Notes from a Reedy Pond," "Death & Co.," "Lady Lazarus," "Tulips," "Daddy"—we are more likely to remember a series of images rather than individual poems. Similarly, we are more likely to take away a vision of evil and corruption than an impression of particularized horrors. The Nazi concentration camps and Hiroshima are absorbed in grander intimations of destruction. What are recorded are processes of depletion and disintegration—of the poet's own self and of a world reduced to unrelated parts.

Although the closing lines of "The Stones" in *The Colossus* expressed an acceptance of imperfection as well as a hope for restoration, *Ariel* presents the recurrent tableau of "a country far away as health." As the later poems traffic in unfamiliar artistic and psychological states, movement is internalized. And meaning frequently turns elitist. In poems like "Berck-Plage" and "Fever 103°" there is a sensed loss of an available world. Yet, at the same time, what surprises us is how many of the poet's private signatures give up their meanings. As intimations of death increase, Sylvia Plath composes out of "limbs, images, shrieks" a poetry of anticipation—for perfection and for death.

Death is redolent in Sylvia Plath's moon poems, night poems, and bee poems. It inhabits poems that begin like domestic, occasional pieces but end in terror. What she seeks is a stance and a collection of selves that are fitted to an awareness of sublunar darkness and natural and unnatural danger. As she approaches moments of vision, Sylvia Plath is often reticent. But she is more often given up to a histrionic exhibition of herself and her wounds, and to a wish to undo herself.

At times suggestive of a queen of suffering or empress of Calvary,

Sylvia Plath pursues selves that vie with the most dramatic personas of Emily Dickinson. In "Lady Lazarus," Sylvia Plath compares herself to a strip-tease artist, and her body to a relic. The skill of the artist and the perfection of the art join in a dance of death. In claiming a kinship with a stripper or with Lady Godiva, Sylvia Plath reveals a pathological wish to die as well as a pathological direction that Lawrence Kubie in *Neurotic Distortion of the Creative Process* has found evidenced in the contemporary arts:

> In part the obscurities of modern art, literature, and music grow out of man's reticence about making a public show of his private neurosis except to a select and inner circle; and this reticence wars with the defiant impulse of Everyman (and Woman) to be Gypsy Rose Lee (p. 99).

Although presented with clinical objectivity, the death relived by Sylvia Plath in *Ariel* is her own death, unlike the parablelike presentations of it in poems of the first volume. The isolated, hermit's house of *The Colossus* becomes, in *Ariel*, a mausoleum and a wax museum. Concerned with the perfection of death, Sylvia Plath feels fear for and fascination with what will become. Stasis is at once attractive in its rest and repulsive as it strangles and suffocates. Hooks, both real and surrealist, reach out continually to destroy her. Figures of Lazarus in the grave, Gulliver tied down by the Lilliputians, and Isadora Duncan in her tragic, romantic death occur as embodiments of these fears. If her dreams bind her to such fears, they occasionally, as at the conclusion of "Lady Lazarus," free her from them.

An artistic and mental predilection for anesthesized states never excludes for Sylvia Plath the possibility of admitting enormity and danger in the process of reducing her poems to the fixity of stone. Although she can regard with humor the content of her poems—things "out of the dark's ragbag," "such collusion of mulish elements," "a content / Of sorts"—her attraction to the underside of things commonly turns infernal:

> I like black statements. ("Little Fugue")
> I am incapable of more knowledge. ("Elm")

On the one hand, there is the threat of material growing out of control and actively asserting itself:

> The blood jet is poetry,
> There is no stopping it. ("Kindness")

On the other hand, there is the threat of material continually being reduced to a frozen state, a movement that is finally more frightening
and dangerous to the poet. Words, once a lifeblood, bleed and become
deadly *objets d'art* in her last poems. Gautier's *Emmaux et Camées* and
Pound's "A catalogue, his jewels of conversation" find their death-stroke
in these final poems that Sylvia Plath came to write.

An association of the perfection of art and the death of life was
present from the beginning of her work. Fascination with the act and
art of suicide and with the figure of suicidal creatures marks both *The
Colossus* and *Ariel.* Revealing a decadent sensibility, Sylvia Plath's poem,
"Lesbos," and her sexual, aesthetic voyagings look back to Baudelaire's
"Lesbos" and to a Rimbaudean voyeur.

While Sylvia Plath's browned gardenia and ghastly orchid recall the
fin de siècle botanical catalogues, it is in her taste in sounds, colors,
jewels, music, painting, and literature that she shows herself to be a
contemporary decadent. Lowell's attraction to the personages of Nero
and Caligula, and Anne Sexton's to the distortions of Kafka and Van
Gogh, are outdone in Sylvia Plath—in her espousal of Brueghel, Swift,
and Leonard Baskin, in her choice of a snake for medallion, in her
method of "deranging by harmony," in her taste for the absolute blankness of black and white for sheer, primary red. And the contents of her
boudoir table and city of mending, while going back to the catalogues
of Swift and Ovid, rival any late nineteenth-century, decadent mélange.

Involved in breakthrough and breakdown, the poetry of Sylvia Plath
exposes its specifically decadent forebears as much as the directions that
have been indicated in modern art. Contemporary poetry, as it derives
from Yeats, Eliot, and Pound, has accepted both the need for masks
and the assumptions of a poetry judged on the criteria of sincerity and
intensity. If the difficulties of seeming "genuine" have increased for the
poet, the nature of Sylvia Plath's range and content becomes compre-
hensible in terms of literary as well as personal history. However, it is
in bringing whatever tendencies were either implicit or explicit in modern art to a deadly perfection that she evidences the confusion of life
and art which we associate with decadence.

For Sylvia Plath, "dying / Is an art." And the perfection of the art
becomes inseparable from the perfection of life in death. Both volumes
of her poems are involved in a movement toward stasis and purity, death
and perfection. Sylvia Plath is attracted to what is inhuman and tran-

scendent. What is preferred is the "elemental" and "pure." "Making stone out of everything," she is kin to the jewel-master, stone cutter, and sculptor of her poems. There is the distillation of all to the hardness of flint and to the fixity of mannequin and statue. *The Colossus* metaphorically comes to stand for her entire creation in life and in art. It is a creation which is also a ruin. Beyond the beautiful and the ugly, this structure, which she feared in *The Colossus* would always remain imperfectly incomplete, is perfected in such *Ariel* poems as "Contusion," "Edge," and "Words." Significantly, they were among the last poems she wrote.

In perfecting her art and herself as a woman, Sylvia Plath gave herself up to a rehearsal and preparation for death in poems like "A Birthday Present," "Daddy," and "Death & Co." These are poems that could only conclude in death. Dying over and over in her poems, she celebrated a black mass that lends to her last book the distinction of sacrament and desecration.

The poems of *The Colossus* and *Ariel* are related to those sequences which came to stand in some significant way for a poet's life—Whitman's *Leaves of Grass*, Pound's *Hugh Selwyn Mauberley* and *Cantos*, Lowell's *Life Studies*, Ginsberg's *Howl* and *Kaddish*, Berryman's *Dream Songs*, Anne Sexton's *To Bedlam and Part Way Back* and later volumes. But in the poetry of Sylvia Plath there is an absence of the kind of human, available world that impresses us with these sequences. However often these poets may join Sylvia Plath in reducing their words to things or in pursuing things "beyond the mundane order," they never arrive at the degree of infernal autonomy and ventriloquism that her last poems achieve.

Stasis. Perfection. Death. The associations are unmistakable, and they are increasingly, obsessively impressed upon us in Sylvia Plath's late work. Whatever light or sanity existed in *The Colossus*—the small, human corner of the Brueghel painting in "Two Views of a Cadaver Room," the release to fluid music at the conclusion of "Flute Notes from a Reedy Pond"—is overpowered in *Ariel* by images of screaming, bloodied babies and instruments of torture. As the images turn to stone, there is the reduction of words to fixed objects that neither the poetry of Pound nor Williams ever aspired toward, but that the decadent poetry of number and nightmare curiously did. Sylvia Plath's use of imagery looks back to the French Decadents and to their attempts to perfect color, sound, and sense in image and vowel.

The process and direction indicated in Sylvia Plath's poems dangerously approach a purity in which analogy and metaphor finally are abolished. In "The Night Dances," a poem that arose from observing the movements of her child Nicholas in his crib, paraphrasable meaning is deserted as the poem moves toward an associational perfection.

> And how will your night dances
> Lose themselves. In mathematics?
>
> Sure pure leaps and spirals—
> Surely they travel
>
> The world forever, I shall not entirely
> Sit emptied of beauties, the gift
>
> Of your small breath, the drenched grass
> Smell of your sleeps, lilies, lilies.
>
> Their flesh bears no relation.
> Cold folds of ego, the calla,
>
> And the tiger, embellishing itself—
> Spots, and a spread of hot petals.

Here, image, for all its ostensibly visual qualities, reaches toward a mathematical, abstract objectivity. Impersonal, it seeks, like the sculpture of Leonard Baskin whose work she admired, "a solider repose than death's"; the poet repeatedly associates fixity and perfection and death, and in her image in the poem, "Medallion," of "pure death's-metal," all three are momentarily joined.

Beyond ordinary criticism and human art, Sylvia Plath's poems so intractably link the perfection of art and the death of life—"Perfection is terrible, it cannot have children," she wrote—that they pass into our hands, only to go out of them, and for all time.

The poetry that Sylvia Plath sought and came to write is so pure and perfected that at her death several journals and newspapers printed her last poems as they stood, with little or no editorial comment, as her most suitable epitaph. They read as if they were expressly written to commemorate the occasion of her death. As epitaph, they attain the highest mark of a decadent art, the perfection of life in art in death.

But, as indicative of the confusion of art and life pursued in the writing of an absolute poetry, Sylvia Plath's last poems must also serve to remind us of the enormous risks, the human cost, as well as the waste that such decadence demands. Against whatever perfection she managed in her final poems must be placed the confusion and delusion which became explicit in her suicide. At her physical death, associations of woman-mother-poet, child-flower-poem suddenly broke down. The Lady Lazarus figure—part nine-lived cat and miracle bird—she imagined herself to be deserted her outside her poems. The children—beautiful, deadly—she imagined folded back into her could not be taken with her out of this life; both realizing and belying her, they remain: the two children by Ted Hughes, the *Ariel* poems left behind as grim reminders, gathered together in a posthumous volume that criticism can afford neither to falsify nor to neglect.

15   The Dark Funnel: A Reading of Sylvia Plath

ROBERT PHILLIPS

"Such a dark funnel, my father," Sylvia Plath cries out in her "Little Fugue." And Otto Plath is a funnel indeed, leading her psyche from the openness of youth down toward the small dark point of death. Jan B. Gordon has touched upon this mythos of the father in his important essay, "Who is Sylvia? The Art of Sylvia Plath." [1] But to date no one has traced the trajectory of her father's memory in the body of Plath's work. We suggest that a pattern of guilt over imagined incest informs all of Plath's prose and poetry. When Otto Plath died of natural causes in a hospital on November 2, 1940, he might just as well have been a lover jilting his beloved. Indeed, in all her poems Plath makes of this separation a deliberate desertion. In poem after poem the father drowns himself.

This act is the central myth of Plath's imagination. Critics have called hers a poetry of annihilation, and place it in context with that of John Berryman, Randall Jarrell, and Anne Sexton—three others who also took their lives. Horace Gregory even suggests these poets were possessed by an "Empedocles Complex"—with suicide constituting their final creative act, with the hope that, like Empedocles, in their violent disappearance they might be taken for gods. [2] Certainly Plath's suicide has gained for her attention she never had in life. Yet I would suggest that her suicide, like her poetry, must be set against a larger framework of a modern world which deliberately destroys—the Nazi genocide of Jews, the Kamikazes, Hiroshima. True, hers is an imagery of destruction; in one poem, even a train is said to eat its track. Also significant is a favorite image of the hook: from the bend in the road to the corner of her son's smile, everything is a trap, a snare, a hook for the unsuspecting. But such a world view springs from the writer's terrible, unforgiving nature. In feeling victimized first by her father's early death and later by an unsatisfactory marriage, she makes no distinction between her tragedy and those of Auschwitz or Nagasaki.

Indeed, in the poem "Daddy," Plath claims to become a Jew, an identification which reaffirms an earlier persona assumed in the auto-biographical novel, *The Bell Jar*, in which she chooses the name "Esther Greenwood" for the protagonist. That the heroine was, in experiential terms, "green wood," can be seen from such passages as, "How could I write about life when I'd never had a love affair, or a baby or seen anybody die?" [3] But it is the forename which is telling. Esther of the Old Testament was the Jewish queen who kept her nationality secret until the evil Haman conceived a plot to destroy all the Jews in the kingdom. It was Esther who saved the Jews by pleading with the king. Such an identification would also appear to confirm the Oedipal nature of Plath's work. Queen Esther (and the further identification with queen bees will be explored later) was more than a deliverer of the Jews. She was also the beautiful young virgin with whom King Ahasuerus united after his wife, Queen Vashti, treated him with contempt. Plath reveals in *The Bell Jar* that Mrs. Plath treated her husband's memory in similar fashion: "My mother had taught shorthand and typing to support us ever since my father died, and secretly she hated it and hated him for dying and leaving us no money because he didn't trust life insurance salesmen." [4]

The mother's contempt for the father is parallelled in the novel by Sylvia Plath's own violent distaste for men, a reaction triggered by her "abandonment" by the father. The novel's most heartless character, Buddy Willard, is—like her father—a scientist. (Dr. Plath was known for work in ornithology, entomology, ichthyology, and biology, and was author of a book on bumblebees.) [5] Instead of frogs and bees, Buddy dissects human cadavers. By extension he dissects the sensitive human fibers of Sylvia Plath's being. For her, Buddy clearly represents the male species, which she finds cruel and deceptive. Her attitude toward men is nowhere more clear than as echoed in the words of the second voice in her radio play, *Three Women:* "They are jealous gods / that would have the whole world flat because they are." This "flatness" is the same as insensitivity, which for the female—and especially for the female artist—is intolerable. (Dr. Plath was said to possess a coldly scientific mind. He also taught scientific German.) When Buddy makes Esther view a birth, and tells her the woman is on a drug which afterward will make her forget she has had any pain at all, Plath concludes, "it sounded just like the sort of drug a man would invent. Here was a woman in terrible pain, obviously feeling every bit of it or she wouldn't groan like that, and she would go straight home and start another baby, because the drug would make her forget how bad the pain had been." [6]

The Bell Jar is full of contempt for the hypocrisy of men and their double standard. Even Esther's friend and savior, Doctor Nolan—another scientist!—like her father, betrays her. But the real turning point of the novel comes, appropriately, when she goes looking for her father (her father's grave) and cannot at first find him. When she finally approaches his grave, the marker's insignificant appearance, coupled with the memories of her mother's remarks on how much "better off" he was in death than in life, cause the girl to collapse. In this love triangle it was obviously the daughter who loved Otto Plath more than the mother did.

That Sylvia Plath felt consciously rejected by the father in his lifetime is not apparent (though he as much as did so when it was revealed to him his newborn was not a boy. On October 27, 1932, the day she was born, he declared: "All I want from life from now on is a son born two and a half years to the day." With remarkable efficiency, Mrs. Plath gave him the wanted son on April 27, 1935. Professor Plath's teaching colleagues toasted him as "the man who gets what he wants when he wants it").[7] But while he lived Sylvia never felt second best. In her own words, she was never happier than when she "was about nine and running along the hot white beaches with my father the summer before he died." [8] That she felt rejected by him in his act of dying is documented in poem after poem. Had he lived, she elaborates in the novel, she was certain he would have taught her German and Latin and Greek, as well as everything there was to know about insects. She would even have become a Lutheran for him. In short, her life would have been totally different.[9]

That she tried to keep her dead father alive within her can be seen from her interests over the years. She began the study of German, though openly admitting a hatred for the language. According to her high school yearbook, she continuously played on the piano the "Bumble Boogie"—that frantic bit of pop music approximating the sound of bees. As a pet expression she used "God save the Queen," unconsciously incorporating bees into her conversations. And, after her marriage to Ted Hughes, she began beekeeping. The author of *Bumblebees and Their Ways* was with her yet. It is not surprising that, when she entered the casualty ward for removal of a splinter from one eye, she confesses to have been "babbling frantically about Oedipus." [10]

We suggest that Plath was a modern Electra. Her unnatural love for her father, who "abandoned" her in death, caused her subsequent hatred of all men, a hatred we shall document by examining the four collections of poems and the novel. (Electra, as no one needs reminding, took vengeance on her mother, Clytemnestra, for murdering Agamemnon, thereby robbing the girl of her beloved father.) Agamemnon was killed in his bath; in Plath's mythology her father died in water. This charge would appear to be substantiated in the overt and uncollected poem, "Electra on the Azalea Path," which reads in part, "Oh pardon the one who knocks for pardon at / Your gate, father—Your bound-bitch, daughter, friend. It was my love that did us both to death." [11] In another uncollected poem the father is like Thompson's hound of heaven, pursuing the daughter to her end: "There is a panther stalks me down: / One day I'll have my death of him: / His greed has set the woods aflame; / He prowls more lordly than the sun." [12]

Such is the case of a daughter having great difficulty freeing herself emotionally from her infantile milieu. In psychological terms, Plath's untoward attachment for her father precipitated a conflict and ultimately a psychotic disturbance. Her libido, already sexually developed, poured into the Oedipal (Electral) mold and "set," in her poems and radio play and novel, in feelings and fantasies which, until the time of composition, had been totally unconscious and more or less inchoate.[13]

Jung differentiates between two types of conscious behavior as a consequence of the formation of intense resistances against such "immoral" impulses resulting from the activated complex. The first is direct, in which the daughter displays violent resistances against the mother and a particularly affectionate and dependent attitude toward the father. The second is indirect—or "compensated"—in which the daughter displays, instead of resistance to the mother, a marked submissiveness combined with "an irritated, antagonistic attitude" toward the father. Jung also acknowledges that these direct and compensated consequences can sometimes alternate, as they seem to have done in Plath. The heroine of *The Bell Jar* seems a perfectly realized embodiment of Jung's first type of behavior; the protagonist of "Daddy" a violent example of his second. What we have is perhaps not so much an alternation of behavior as a development from one state into another. Certainly the poet of "Daddy" had grown into a depth of self-knowledge far beyond that possessed by the protagonist of the novel.

Naturally, if the sexual libido were to function unchecked in this manner, daughters would go about killing their mothers and sleeping with their fathers, or vice versa. Fortunately, in life the libido is forced to seek new love objects, as Plath did in marriage. These new subjects for affection, according to Jung, serve as a check against parricide and incest: "The continuous development of libido toward objects outside the family is perfectly normal and natural, and it is an abnormal and pathological phenomenon if the libido remains, as it were, glued to the family. Nevertheless, it is a phenomenon that can sometimes be observed in normal people." [14] Sylvia Plath's libido never became totally unglued. Only instead of ending in parricide ("Daddy"), her identification with her father grew so intense she committed suicide. It is with a great sense of irony, then, that we turn to the penultimate page of Plath's first book, "A Note on the Type," and read there the publisher's innocent note: *The text of this book is set in Electra.*[15]

Jung has also said that experience shows the unknown approach of death often casts an adumbratio—an anticipatory shadow—over the life and the dreams of the victim. Plath's poems in this sense were her dreams, and a preparation for death expressed through art—words not unlike tales told at primitive initiations or Zen koans. The *Ariel* poems, her greatest achievement, rather than conforming to Christian orthodoxy, are formulated more on primitive thought drawn from outside historical tradition and taken from the psychic sources which have nourished religious and philosophical speculation about life and death since prehistoric times. A case can be built stating that such an adumbratio informs Plath's imagery from the first, as if her future suicide were casting its shadow back by arousing in her certain archetypes which, usually dormant, were tripped by death's approach. And while the specific shape of the archetypes in Plath is very personal, albeit confessional, the general pattern of the archetypes is collective. Her use of the yew tree, the rose, the moon, and the bee—while deriving from autobiography—have universal implications. One encounters parallels in Dante and Leopardi as well as in Coleridge and Eliot.

The first collection, *The Colossus* (1960), contains the poems of a young woman whose mental disturbance can be detected in subject and image. Poet-critic Richard Howard even reads the poems' forms as unhealthy—the rhymes all slant, the end-stop avoided like a reproach—and calls the book a "breviary of estrangement." [16] More important, there are no people in this first book, only the poet's conflict between her need to reduce the demands of life to the unquestioning acceptance of a stone (what Howard calls "the lithic impulse") and the impulse to live on. Always in these first poems one observes Plath's identification with the lower forms of existence—mushrooms and moles, snakes and insects, stones and bones. Ultimately her search through the lower forms reaches an ultimate depth in whiteness and in death, not unlike Ahab's obsession with the whiteness of the whale. Every landscape in *The Colossus* is a nightmarescape—or, as Jan B. Gordon would have it, a psychescape—of dead sea creatures and boat wrecks. (In her transitional poems, those written between that collection and the maturity of *Ariel,* Plath's vision lifts from the earth's depths and surfaces to the moon's and the clouds beyond. But there is no psychic relief, and her mental sickness becomes personified in many physical images of surgery and bandages as well.)

The first line of the first book contains an image for death: "The fountains are dry and the roses over. / Incense of death. Your day approaches." [17] In Plath's beginning is her end. Reversing the usual cause/effect progression, in the second poem we are given the cause of the previously posited effect: a medical student in a dissection room ("Buddy Willard"?) cruelly hands her "the cut-out heart like a cracked heirloom." His act seems the kind of male role which causes the spiritual death imaged in the opening poem. The dissection room is a microcosm of the world, and Buddy is the ruling cold male intellect in a universe in which flesh, not spirit, prevails. Plath of course would beg that the male sees both function and beauty, both flesh and spirit. The poem parallels the later "Pheasant," from *Crossing the Water,* in which the male also is callous and a destroyer.

The male principle of power and thrust is symbolized in the silver factory's undershirted workers and machinery of "Night Shift." The obvious analogies with the physiological function of sex are contained in a later poem, "Blackberrying," in which Plath also speaks of silversmiths "Beating and beating at an intractable metal"—a more violent sexual metaphor. (In "Years" she exclaims, "The piston in motion— / My soul dies before it.") Even the poem "Sow," which appears to render a fecund earth-mother type, is really "about" the state of the female when reduced to pure reproductive functions, the sow a symbol of the transmutation of the higher order into the lower. That Sylvia Plath saw herself so reduced is evident in the title poem, "The Colossus," in which she becomes a broken idol and issues from her lips "mule-bray, pig-grunt, and bawdy cackles." (This translation of the typically male colossus figure, e.g., the Colossus of Rhodes, into the female is typical of Plath's inversions, as we shall see. In her rebellion against typical sexist attitudes she reverses conventional male-female roles.)

The lowered estate of the female is seen in "Strumpet Song," in which Plath positions the self as whore, made so perhaps because of her incestuous wishes, and in "Fever 103°," in which she calls all her selves "old whore petticoats." These denigrations of self finally give rise to a poetry of utter escape, and in both "The Eye-Mote" and "Ariel" Plath uses a horse as a symbol of freedom. Then she confesses a desire for a return to the purity she possessed before the fact of men: "What I want back is what I was / Before the bed, before the knife." Such an unspoiled world is shown in "Hardcastle Crags." Man is seen as the spoiler, and in "Faun" he is projected as a Pan-figure—Pan traditionally being a figure dreaded by maidens, and rightfully so, with his overt sensuality, horns, pug-nose, and goat-feet. (Goats held none of the charm for Plath that they have for Picasso; in "Departure" she depicts them as "rank-haired" and "morose.")

It is Plath's hatred of men and the unhealthiness of her mental condition, then, which is figured in the title poem, "The Colossus," in which the poetess identifies with a broken idol out of the stream of civilization, one whose "hours are married to shadow." No longer does she "listen for the scrape of a keel / on the blank stones of the landing." Man, personified by a ship, has no place in her scheme. The marriage to shadow is Plath's marriage to the memory of her father, and therefore to death itself. The pull toward that condition is the subject of "Lorelei" as well as the central symbol of "A Winter Ship." That Plath perceived the nature of her own condition is clear not only in the identification with the broken idol of "The Colossus," but the broken vase of "The Stones" as well.

Plath makes a metaphor for her reversed misogyny in "The Bull of Bendylaw," in which she transmogrifies that traditionally feminine body, the sea—la mer—into a brute bull, a potent symbol for the active, masculine principle. The bull here is a symbol of both destruction and power (as the figure of the bull clearly expresses in all palaeo-oriental cultures). Yet our own reading must not stop there. As with many of Plath's symbols, there is a complexity, a muchness. According to Leo Frobenius, for example, a black bull is linked in the unconscious with the lower heaven, that is, with death.[18] This could be substantiated, one supposes, by the historical fact that in India the bodies of princes were burned specifically in bull-shaped coffins. Yet Jung would disagree, claiming in his *Symbols of Transformation* that the bull, like the he-goat, is a symbol for the father. And while it is possible to read "The Bull of Bendylaw" with all these suggestions in mind, the bull which overpowers the existing order by devouring the royal rose must, primarily, be seen as the male principle, personified by her dead father—a presence so real to Plath it ultimately caused her destruction. In the world of her private mythology, the sea and her father and herself become one. If the single rose is taken as a symbol of completion and wholeness and perfection, Plath says in this poem that her father destroyed all that—her sanity—with the line, "the royal rose in the bull's belly." This was a charge she was to repeat in "Daddy" and other poems.

In "All the Dead Dears" Plath acknowledges outwardly and not meta-phorically the influence of relatives upon her own psyche:

> From the mercury-backed glass
> Mother, grandmother, great-grandmother
> Reach hag hands to haul me in.

But the pull of the past cannot be explored without further contemplation of the "draft father" who drowned himself, "With orange duck-feet winnowing his hair," an imaginative event explored at greater length in "Suicide Off Egg Rock," in which the father resolutely turns his back on the imperfect landscape.

The crime of renouncing his daughter is ultimately equated by Plath with the Nazi destruction of the Jews. The first manifestation of this occurs in "The Thin People," who are at once the Jews and the ghosts of the past which haunt her. Then in "Frog Autumn" the "fold" who "thin / lamentably" are both frogs and all withering races with which she identifies. "Mary's Song" (*Winter Trees*) continues the exploration of persecution, as does "Getting There" (*Ariel*). The subject receives its fullest and most sensational treatment in the poem "Daddy" in which, as I have said, Plath literally becomes a Jew, her father a Nazi.

"Mushrooms," a very Roethkesque poem of Keatsian negative capability, seems to mean not what it appears to say, that the meek shall inherit the earth, but rather that the parasites shall prevail. Her father, in her view, was one of the latter living off her blood, which is the reason why at the conclusion she must drive a stake through his heart—as she literally does at the end of "Daddy," killing the vampire memory.

"The Ghost's Leavetaking," in which to awaken in the morning is to experience the Fall, mourns Plath's lost innocence and childhood. "Full Fathom Five" lays that lost innocence once again at the feet of her father. Alluding as it does by title to Ariel's speech from *The Tempest*,

> Full fathom five thy father lies,
> Of his bones are coral made,
> Those are pearls that were his eyes . . .

the poem begins with a god-figure, perhaps that of Neptune, perhaps that of a god of that other dark deep place, the unconscious; then progresses to the death of her own father in his "Shelled bed" (never the hospital bed!). She concludes that she herself is like a fish, finding the air she breathes killing, and would breathe water with her father instead. Her search for such a father/god figure can only end in death.

In "Man in Black" the figure of the father clad in "dead / Black" balanced on the spit of stone in the sea is the figure of Death who stands on the shred of Plath's sanity, the balance of which can be tipped by evoking the father figure. Indeed, men in black pervade all of that later book, *Ariel*, as well, culminating in "Years" in which God is seen clad in "vacuous black." The search for the father and the search for The Father, as in Roethke and Kunitz, ultimately become one. And just as the impulse to enter water was seen in "Full Fathom Five" and "The Lorelei," Plath would become a mussel in "Mussel Hunter at Rock Harbor," a poem in which she pursues the Wholly Other. The body of the fiddler-crab, one who "saved / Face, to face the bald-faced sun," seems also a symbol for the father.

Only once in *The Colossus*, in "The Disquieting Muses," is the mother really portrayed. Then it is as one who is comforting but ineffectual in protecting the daughter from Mother Nature. ("Point Shirley," on the other hand, depicts Plath's genuine love for her grandmother.) Plath's attitude toward her mother is tempered, as I have said, by an unconscious feeling of rivalry and resentment. It also may derive from her feelings toward the institution of marriage generally, and particularly in her own case. Her fullest treatment of this in the first book is the veiled little poem, "Spinster," which is a literary curiosity. The overall tone and diction of the poem are clearly derived from John Crowe Ransom ("By this tumult afflicted . . ."; "a burgeoning / Unruly enough to pitch her five queenly wits / Into vulgar motley—"; and other Ransomed kidnappings). Yet Plath's story of the maiden who retreated from love is a neat parable of the necessity for a woman-poet to resist the temptation of "romance." Read in such a manner, the poem gives up undeniable echoes of Elinor Wylie ("Puritan Sonnet") in stanza three; and Edna St. Vincent Millay ("Spring," with its celebrated image of the season as a babbling idiot strewing flowers) in stanza four. In writing of the feminine artist's necessity for independence from the male, Plath invokes—purposefully, I would submit—the work of two very independent woman poets.

Perhaps the most overt of all incestuous poems is "The Beekeeper's Daughter," in which the father, "Hieratical" in his frock coat, is a father/priest who initiates the daughter into holy mysteries. The beehive is seen as the boudoir, a place rich in sexual suggestion and appealing so immensely to Plath's imagination because it ironically inverts the double standard, making the queen bee the goddess of the harem, the males all drones. Incestuous suggestions are found in the lines,

> Here is a queenship no mother can contest—
> A fruit that's death to taste; dark flesh, dark parings.

I suggest the latter word is a pun, conscious or unconscious, on dark "pairings"—pairings which can end only in insanity or death. That Plath sees the poem's sacred marriage as an incestuous one cannot be doubted:

> Father, bridegroom, in this Easter egg . . .
> The queen bee marries the winter of your year.

This is a poem of a defiant spirit, albeit an unhealthy one. Here too is the explanation for the situation of the volume's final poem, "The Stones," perhaps the only poem in the entire first volume which truly points the way to Plath's more mature style and approach. With its first sentence, "This is the city where men are mended," we are pitched into a mental institution where the poet finds herself after falling from grace into the "stomach of indifference." In the tenth stanza she recreates the experience of electric shock treatment. As in "The Colossus," Plath gives us an image for the broken self—this time a vase which must be mended. Like that earlier poem which eschewed the possibility or even the desirability of love, we are here told that "Love is the bone and sinew of my curse." The devoured rose of "The Bull of Bendylaw," here clearly a symbol of

Plath's spirit, is momentarily resurrected: "The vase, reconstructed, houses / the elusive rose." And in the last line she tells us, "I shall be good as new."

But of course she will not be, and knows that she will not be. A vase once broken is never totally new again. The seams always show, no matter how cleverly held together. The permanent damage to Plath's psyche is manifest in the other three volumes which follow.

The poems of *Crossing the Water*, written during 1960 and 1961, a transitional period between *The Colossus* and the late work of *Ariel* and *Winter Trees*, continue Plath's preoccupations with death, drowning, and terminations. The feminine protest against the masculine ego, will, and violence, seen in the earlier collections, is first manifest here in "Pheasant," in which Plath urges the aggressive male to "Let be. Let be." [19] (In *Three Women* Plath's one contented wife is compared to and empathizes with a pheasant.) In Plath, man's rage for order is as despicable as his violence. If woman gives in to man, she becomes the robotlike modern female of "An Appearance": "From her lips ampersands and percent signs / Exit like kisses." Elsewhere, in "A Birthday Present" (*Ariel*), Plath rails against the rigidity of "adhering to rules, to rules, to rules."

"I Am Vertical" announces, on the obvious level, the poet's death wish. But buried in the language is protest against the image of woman as seen by the male chauvinist pig:

> Nor am I the beauty of a garden bed
> Attracting my share of Ahs and spectacularly painted,
> Unknowing I must soon unpetal.

The real components of this statement are evident. The symbolic components only less so: "The beauty" who is "spectacularly painted" and who receives her share of "Ahs" from admirers is no flower, but modern woman who must dutifully "unpetal" for the male in that not-so-Edenic (garden) bed, the nuptial.

A new preoccupation emerges in this second collection, that of lost youth. "The Baby Sitters" is pure nostalgia, and indeed "Face Lift" is the fantasy of a woman who wishes to appear with her face rendered "Pink and smooth as a baby," perhaps a metaphor for Plath's desire to become again her daddy's little girl. "Parliament Hill Fields," the next poem, displays a sensibility numb to adult responsibilities and emotions; the death of the narrator's own infant is described as barely entering her consciousness—perhaps prompted by the narrator's own desire never to cease being a child herself, which the condition of motherhood would make impossible. The wish to return to childlike innocence is seen in "Child" (*Winter Trees*) as well. This theme of aging reaches its apogee in "Mirror":

> In me she has drowned a young girl, and in me an old woman
> Rises toward her day after day, like a terrible fish.

The earlier preoccupation with split personality, in "The Colossus" and "The Stones," is bettered by "In Plaster" which explores the dualities of sane/insane, saint/sinner, wife/daughter. It also repeats the symbol of the rose as soul. Surprisingly, the volume contains several poems in praise of heterosexual relations, such as "Love Letter" and "Widow"—a portrait of a woman's loss of identity without the company of a man. "Heavy Women," by way of contrast, portrays each mother as a Virgin Mary. But more often Plath is one with her own "Candles"—that is, "Nun-souled, they burn heavenward and never marry." (In "Small Hours" she describes herself as "nun-hearted.") When a baby is born to her, "a black gap discloses itself" and she feels "dismembered." She would like to conform to the world's expectations of her as a thoroughly modern mother, stated satirically as a "Mother of white Nike and several bald-eyed Apollos," to become part and parcel of the mechanized male-oriented world, and even to contribute to it. But she cannot. "The Tour" satirizes and ridicules the "normal" domestic scene, with its bald wife and exploding furnace, a machine gone wrong, a machine which, predictably true to Plath's mythology, disfigures the female.

The depersonalized male appears in "The Surgeon at 2 A.M." (a poem which should be compared in vision and intention with the earlier "Two Views of a Cadaver Room"). In the later poem a doctor sees human flesh as nothing more than "a pathological salami," something less efficient and desirable than "a ·clean, pink plastic limb." In his white coat he walks apparently godlike among the wards; in reality he is not human, let alone godly. He is as impersonal as the Danish jeweler in "On Deck," a man who "is carving / A perfectly faceted wife to wait / On him hand and foot, quiet as a diamond"—a vision the Women's Lib supporters will applaud. As doubtless they would applaud Plath's nightmare visions of the "Zoo-Keeper's Wife," that sensitive soul lost in a world of hairy, obscene beasts who copulate out of pure boredom. The animals and the male are here inseparable. As heartless as the earlier medical student, and later the surgeon, this Mellors figure of a zoo-keeper "checked the diet charts and took me to play / With the boa constrictor in the Fellow's Garden." The snake here is the powerful crushing phallic principle. The destructive element pervades the poem, nowhere more harrowingly than in the image of the "bear-furred, bird-eating spider / Clambering round its glass box like an eight-fingered hand." Plath is the bird devoured.

This then is Sylvia Plath's psychological view of life, and all the preoccupations of the first two books are summarized in the final lines of "A Life":

> Age and terror, like nurses, attend her,
> And a drowned man, complaining of the great cold,
> Crawls up out of the sea.

The ghost of her father is with her yet.

After these beginnings Plath played only theme variations with her two remaining books (*Ariel*, which was published soon after Plath's death; and *Winter Trees*, which was not, although its poems were written at the same time as those of *Ariel*, during the last nine months of her life).[20] The title poem, "Winter Trees," for instance, displays Plath's identification with trees (the name Sylvia, after all, is the feminine form of Sylvanus, "living in the wood") and her envy of them for their freedom from woman's fate of copulation, abortion, and bitchery. Tree weddings are seen as merely the quiet accretion of new growth-rings; their seedings are totally effortless, unlike the sweat and heave of human procreation. Like Leda, they are full of wings and other-worldliness. (When Zeus coupled with Leda, he did so in the form of a swan.) Yet we should not forget that in Plath's radio play, *Three Women*, one of the three equates winter trees with death, perhaps the natural conclusion of such inhuman congress. Another of the women cries that there "is a snake in swans." Sex in any form seems to repel.

The poem is followed by a series of bitter portraits of men. Unlike the zoo-keeper of the previous volume, the "Gigolo" in the poem of that title is repellent not for his sweat and animalism, but for his clean efficiency and glitter. He is possibly an animus figure for Plath, who elsewhere was concerned with female prostitutes. Yet he is no less repellent than the zoo-keeper, with his "way of turning / Bitches to ripples of silver." Here is yet another man who, in seeing women as mere instruments, becomes himself such an instrument. The gigolo is also the male as Narcissus, a new exhibit in Plath's chamber of horrors. He is soon joined by "Purdah," Sultan, who is "Lord of the mirrors." The poem's violent climax is the assassination of the male ego by one who has been too long a mere member of the harem.

"The Rabbit Catcher" performs the role of the male who snares his prey, in a world which is "a place of force." (We recall the passage from *The Bell Jar* about the male treachery of anesthesia in childbirth.) Like rabbits, women are caught to attend the brute violence; like hunters, men have minds "like a ring / Sliding shut on some quick thing." The rabbit, we assume, was chosen not only for its fecundity but also for its connotations of the world of subhuman instinct. Plath concludes with the confession that such constriction kills her as well. After which, as in "Stopped Dead," there is always "a goddamn baby screaming." (In "Lesbos" there is always "a stink of fat and baby crap.") The car stopped just short of the cliff's edge is a figure for Plath's life, especially her marriage, an event which left her suspended just above the abyss. We can only wonder that she did marry, and not have just one child but two. But then she herself gives us her own interpretation for her action in "Daddy," which I discuss shortly.

Such discord between the sexes is communicated not only by the male narcissism of "Gigolo" and "Purdah" but also through the absenteeism of the father in "For a Fatherless Son" and "By Candlelight." [21] The latter is a satirical poem, spoken somewhat in the chiding voice of "The Tour." The almighty male, reduced to a "little brassy Atlas" statue, is at best a poor heirloom. As a figure for the absent father and husband, he has no child or wife, nothing save his masculine bluster—bawdily synthesized in the image of his five brass balls, which he can use "To juggle with, my love, when the sky falls."

Another satirical male portrait is that of the friend's husband in "Lesbos," whose "Jew-Mama guards his sweet sex like a pearl" and whose wife used to play-act quick orgasms to thrill her lovers. In such a world the image of woman—traditionally identified with the moon—now is nothing more than a "bloody bag." The logical conclusion is that "Every woman's a whore." (The statement has been made implicitly earlier in "Strumpet Song.")

The roles women must play, then, is the theme of "Winter Trees": daughter, beloved, wife, mother, girl friend, sister, friend of girls—they are all explored in the "Poem for Three Voices," (*Three Women*), which concludes the volume. Plath chooses three different attitudes to be embodied by her characters. The first is a woman who is gladly a mother. The second, one who loses her child through miscarriage. And the third is one who gives her child, unwanted, away.

The mother who retains her child accepts her lot as naturally as a seed breaks. It is the second and the third who seem to speak for Plath, however, the second finding men flat as cardboard, a flatness which she herself caught like some fatal disease:

> That flat, flat, flatness from which ideas, destructions,
> Bulldozers, guillotines, white chambers of shrieks
> proceed . . .

And the third envisioning women as victims of men's torturing:

> They hug their flatness like a kind of health.
> And what if they found themselves surprised, as I did?
> They would go mad with it.

Indeed, this unlikely shared vision of male "flatness" by both women can be seen as a shortcoming of the play. Plath stacks her deck too high. Clearly all three women are, in many ways, aspects of Plath's personality. Even the docile mother-wife confesses that she too is too open: "it is as if my heart / Put on a face and walked into the world." In a prayer echoing "Born Yesterday," a poem of Philip Larkin's, she begs that her child be unexceptional, for "It is the exception that interests the devil. / It is the exception that climbs the sorrowful hill."

Sylvia Plath, an exceptional individual, climbed that hill to the summit. The full revelation of her agony comes in *Ariel*, her most famous book, and the one which contains her most striking poems. What one must realize, however, is that the poems in all four books were written between 1959 and her death in February, 1963. As the shapes of the poems grow sparer and sparer, the tones darker and darker, she follows her father into the small end of the funnel. The poems are all part of one great confession. The publication, seven years after *Ariel*, of the poems in *Crossing the Water* and *Winter Trees*, shows us how wholly obsessed with her themes Plath really was. *Ariel* was no one-shot love affair with death. She courted it all her life, and won.

Ariel is filled with poems of marriage, estrangement, and suicide—a pattern which follows that of Plath's life. In the marriage poems the modern wife is "A living doll" who performs mechanical functions ("It can sew, it can cook, / It can talk, talk, talk"). Here the mechanistic images of "A Vision" (*Crossing the Water*) become more pointed and satirical. In "Tulips" the wife sees the smiles of her husband and child as "hooks"—that is, as lures to snare and catch her. She would rather return to her nunlike state, being afraid of human emotions and feelings.

Ironically, emotion is strong in Plath's poems of estrangement. Her estrangement from her own children is the subject of "Morning Song"; and that from her husband the subject of "The Couriers." In the latter the wedding band is tested and found to be nothing but fool's gold:

> A ring of gold with the sun in it?
> Lies. Lies and a grief.

Here as in "A Winter Ship," Plath employs the sun as the symbol of unattainable happiness. Finally, the theme of estrangement from the father is pursued, with parables of the lost lamb looking for the promised land and the Good Shepherd serving as vehicles for her own search for the earthly father. She fears, in "Sheep in Fog," that her own search will lead instead to a "starless and fatherless" heaven, into dark waters. Such dark waters are the subject of "Lady Lazarus," a much-quoted poem in which Plath compares herself to that biblical figure once resurrected by Christ, and also to a cat with its nine lives, because she has been "resurrected" from attempted suicide three times. The poem is also an act of revenge on the male ego.

> Out of the ash
> I rise with my red hair
> And I eat men like air.

Emasculation of the female occurs in "Cut," in which the lacerated thumb is a "little pilgrim" whose scalp has been axed by an Indian. Plath is the pilgrim, her husband (or all men) the savage, an Indian as well as a Kamikaze man or Ku Klux Klanner—any man violent and unmindful of humane values and depriving the female. In "Elm" we find another outward symbol for Plath's inner injuries, with that poem's concluding two stanzas presenting an implicit image of the Medusa, whose "snaky acids kiss." The Medusa is introduced here also for its connotations of guilt. In mythology she was a once-beautiful maiden whose hair was changed into snakes by Athena in consequence for her having had carnal knowledge of Poseidon in one of Athena's temples.

The act resulted in the birth of both Chrysaor and Pegasus. Plath develops this theme of guilt more completely in the poem titled "Medusa," in which she communicates with her unconscious, becoming the poetess with a divining rod who summons the image of the Father-God who is "always there, / Tremulous breath at the end of my line." If Plath is at the end of her rope, it is, she feels, the father's fault. The lust in the temple is incest in the sacred home, an obscenity instead of something sacred. This attitude toward sex permeates "Berck-Plage" as well.

The male predator becomes Death the predator in "Death & Co." Because she feels continually victimized, Plath can identify with the Jews in "Getting There." Ideally she would unite this male element with the female, the bestial with the poetic, as she does symbolically in "Ariel." In that poem she is a woman poet riding Pegasus (offspring of Medusa!). But as a woman riding the godly horse, Plath becomes a female centaur, another inversion of the usual male order, with the creature half-man, half-horse becoming half-woman, half-horse. This inversion is related to the image of the order of the beehive, another sexually inverted symbol. A. Alvarez is correct in noting of "Ariel" that "the detail is all inward. It is as though the horse itself were an emotional state." [22] But Alvarez is too simplistic in saying the poem is "about tapping the roots of her own inner violence." Rather, mounted on Ariel, hers is at once the drive toward death, toward God, the moth toward the flame and the red eye of morning.

The drive toward God is explored in "The Moon and the Yew Tree," in which Plath identifies with the moon and longs for religious belief. The moon identification is simple to comprehend, with its connotations of the imagination and the maternal, its mysterious connection between the lunar cycle and the menstrual cycle. Like woman, the moon is the celestial body which suffers painful changes in shape (as did Plath in pregnancy). There is also a parallel between Plath's being subject to changes as is the moon, with both hiding their dark sides. The moon is a female symbol because it is the passive sphere, only reflecting the glory of the male sun, a state of being similar to Plath's view of the conventional roles assigned wife and husband.

The poem's other central symbol, the yew tree, is also a conventional one, traditionally implying inexhaustible life and immortality. The ancient tree also seems to me to function here as a representative of the growth and development of Plath's psychic life as distinct from the instinctual life symbolized by animals such as the rabbit and the horse Ariel. That it is an important symbol to her is implicit in the fact that the yew appears in other poems, "Little Fugue" and "The Munich Mannequins" as well. In "The Moon and the Yew Tree" the tree's "Gothic shape" reinforces the implication that Plath aspired toward Christian belief and the Church, a quest which was to end only in coldness and blackness. There is no comfort to be found in institutional Christianity. Yet she repeats her desire to see, and therefore to enter the temple of God, in "A Birthday Present," the poem which follows. But ultimately religion fails her, and only through hallucination does she achieve Paradise, as in "Fever 103°," of which Plath herself wrote, "This poem is about two kinds of fire—the fires of hell, which merely agonize, and the fires of heaven, which purify. During the poem, the first sort of fire suffers itself into the second." [23]

The only way Plath was to achieve relief, to become an independent self, was to kill her father's memory, which in "Daddy" she does by a metaphorical murder of the father figure. Making her father a Nazi and herself a Jew, she dramatizes the war in her soul. It is a terrible poem, full of blackness, one of the most nakedly confessional poems ever written. From its opening image onward, that of the father as a "black shoe" in which the daughter has lived for thirty years—an explicitly phallic image, according to Freud—the sexual pull and tug is manifest, as is the degree of Plath's mental suffering, supported by references to Dachau, Auschwitz, and Belsen. (Elsewhere in Plath the references to hanged men also are emblems of suffering while swinging. In Jungian psychology the swinging motion would be symbolic of her ambivalent state and her unfulfilled longing as well.) Plath then confesses that, after failing to escape her predicament through suicide, she married a surrogate father, "A man in black with a Meinkampf look" who obligingly was just as much a vampire of her spirit—one who "drank my blood for a year, / Seven years, if you want to know." (Sylvia Plath was married to the poet Ted Hughes for seven years.) When Plath drives the stake through her father's heart, she not only is exorcising the demon of her father's memory, but metaphorically is killing her husband and all men as well.

It is a poem of total rejection. And when she writes that "The black telephone's off at the root," she is turning her back on the modern world as well. Such rejection of family and society leads to that final rejection, that of the self. Plath's suicide is predicted everywhere in the book, in poems of symbolic annihilation such as "Totem" and statements of human fascination with death, such as "Edge"—in which to be dead is to be perfected. Plath's earlier terror at death becomes a romance with it, and her poems themselves are what M. L. Rosenthal called "yearnings toward that condition." [24] Freud believed the aim of all life is death, and for Plath life was poetry. By extension, then, poetry for Plath became death, both conditions inseparable. She herself as much as said so: "The blood jet is poetry, / There is no stopping it." In the act of committing her confession to paper, she was committing her life to death. The source of her creative energy was her self-destructiveness. She did not have Sexton's or Roethke's humor to save her. (Instead of committing suicide, Roethke continually became a child again.)

And what burden of her life led Plath to cancel it? Many, surely. But none so overpowering as the psychological necessity to link herself with her father, spiritually and physically. Suicide then became a sexual act, the deathbed the marriage bed. This obsession is nowhere more apparent than in the four bee poems which, as an informal group, are the glory of the concluding pages of *Ariel*. Plath's fascination with bees, of course, is yet another attempt to reconstruct her father's life. Not only that Otto Plath was the author of a book on bumblebees, as I have noted; but also bees themselves, with the monarchic organization, are a potent symbol for order and obedience. To be a bee is to report to an authority figure.

"The Bee Meeting" opens with a vivid imaging of Plath's vulnerability before the hive. In the poem all the villagers but her are protected from the bees, and she equates this partial nudity with her condition of being unloved. In the symbolic marriage ceremony which follows, a rector, a midwife, and Plath herself—a bride clad in black—appear. Plath seems always to remember that even the arrows which Eros used to shoot into the ground to create new life were poisoned darts. And just as her search for a Divine Father was tempered by her fear there was none, so too her search for consolation from her earthly father created an intensity of consciousness in which she no longer had any guarantee of security. Eros was for her ever accompanied by the imminence of death. We are reminded here of the frequent word play in Italian literature between amore, love, and morte, death.[25] Certainly every mythology relates the sex act to the act of dying, most clearly perhaps in the tale of Tristan and Iseult. And in nature the connection is even more explicit. Sylvia Plath's personal mythology of the hive anticipates this: the male bee always dies after inseminating the queen. When the central figure of authority, the queen, is her father, the daughter/worker must die after the incestuous act, as she does at the conclusion of "The Bee Meeting." The long white box in the grove is in fact her own coffin; only in this light can she answer her own questions, "what have they accomplished, why am I cold?"

In the second bee poem, "The Arrival of the Bee Box," the coffin analogy is made again, and Plath confesses she "can't keep away from it." The unintelligible syllables of the bees are the mystery of the unknown, the cipher of her life and her father's. In "Stings" she herself becomes the queen, the self that needs recovering captured in a wax house, a mausoleum. The queen is the father and the daughter united, for by assuming his body she effectively kills him (just as Freud assured us the joining of the bodies in sexual congress results in a kind of death, speaking of the "likeness of the condition of that following complete sexual satisfaction to dying, and for the fact that death coincides with the act of copulation in lower animals. These creatures die in the act of reproduction because, after Eros has been eliminated through the process of satisfaction, the death instinct has a free hand for accomplishing its purpose").[26] Such a symbolic death of her father provided for Plath enormous psychic and physical release, and the occasion for one final invective against men ("Wintering"):

> The bees are all women,
> Maids and the long royal lady.
> They have got rid of the men,
>
> The blunt, clumsy stumblers, the boors.[27]

Sylvia Plath ended her life in the early morning of February 11, 1963. At the time she was living separately from her husband.

16 The Death Throes of Romanticism: The Poetry of Sylvia Plath

JOYCE CAROL OATES

> I am not cruel, only truthful—
> The eye of a little god . . .
>
> Plath, "Mirror"

Tragedy is not a woman, however gifted, dragging her shadow around in a circle, or analyzing with dazzling scrupulosity the stale, boring inertia of the circle; tragedy is cultural, mysteriously enlarging the individual so that what he has experienced is both what we have experienced and what we need not experience—because of his, or her, private agony. It is proper to say that Sylvia Plath represents for us a tragic figure involved in a tragic action, and that her tragedy is offered to us as a near-perfect work of art, in her books *The Colossus* (1960), *The Bell Jar* (1963), *Ariel* (1965), and the posthumous volumes published in 1971, *Crossing the Water* and *Winter Trees*.

This essay is an attempt to analyze Plath in terms of her cultural significance, to diagnose, through Plath's poetry, the pathological aspects of our era that make a death of the spirit inevitable—for that era and all who believe in its assumptions. It is also based upon the certainty that Plath's era is concluded and that we may consider it with the sympathetic detachment with which we consider any era that has gone before us and makes our own possible: the cult of Plath insists she is a saintly martyr, but of course she is something less dramatic than this, but more valuable. The "I" of the poems is an artful construction, a tragic figure whose tragedy is classical, the result of a limited vision that believed itself the mirror held up to nature—as in the poem "Mirror," the eye of a little god who imagines itself without preconceptions, "unmisted by love or dislike." This is the audacious hubris of tragedy, the inevitable reality-challenging statement of the participant in a dramatic action he does not know is "tragic." He dies, and only we can see the purpose of his death—to illustrate the error of a personality who believed itself godlike.

The assumptions of the essay are several: that the artist both creates and is created by his art, and that the self—especially the "I" of lyric poetry—is a personality who achieves a kind of autonomy free not only of the personal life of the artist but free, as well, of the part-by-part progression of individual poems; that the autobiographical personality is presented by the artist as a testing of reality, and that its success or failure or bewilderment will ultimately condition the artist's personal life; that the degree to which an audience accepts or rejects or sympathetically detaches itself from a given tragic action will ultimately condition the collective life of an era; and that the function of literary criticism is not simply to dissect either cruelly or reverentially, to attack or to glorify, but to illustrate how the work of a significant artist helps to explain his era and our own. The significance of Plath's art is assumed. Her significance as a cultural phenomenon is assumed. What needs desperately to be seen is how she performed for us, and perhaps in place of some of us, the concluding scenes in the fifth act of a tragedy, the first act of which began centuries ago.

Narcissi

Lawrence said in *Apocalypse* that when he heard people complain of being lonely he knew their affliction: ". . . they have lost the Cosmos." It is easy to agree with Lawrence, but less easy to understand what he means. Yet if there is a way of approaching Plath's tragedy, it is only through an analysis of what Plath lost and what she was half-conscious of having lost:

> I am solitary as grass. What is it I miss?
> Shall I ever find it, whatever it is?
>
> ("Three Women")

We must take this loss as a real one, not a rhetorical echoing of other poets' cries; not a yearning that can be dismissed by the robust and simple-minded among us who like that formidably healthy and impossible Emerson, sought to dismiss the young people of his day "diseased" with problems of original sin, evil, predestination, and the like by contemptuously diagnosing their worries as "the soul's mumps, and measles, and whoopingcoughs" ("Spiritual Laws"). Emerson possessed a consciousness of such fluidity and explorative intelligence that any loss of the cosmos for him could seem nothing more serious than an adolescent's perverse rebelliousness, at its most profound a doubt to be answered with a few words.

These "few words" in our era are multiplied endlessly—all the books, the tradition at our disposal, the example of a perpetually renewed and self-renewing nature—and yet they are not convincing to the Sylvia Plaths of our time. For those who imagine themselves as filled with emptiness, as wounds "walking out of hospital," the pronouncements of a practical-minded, combative, "healthy" society of organized individuals are meaningless. Society, seen from the solitary individual's viewpoint, is simply an organization of the solitary, linked together materially—perhaps, in fact, crowded together but not "together," not vitally related. One of Plath's few observations about larger units of human beings is appropriately cynical:

> And then there were other faces. The faces of nations,
> Governments, parliaments, societies,
> The faceless faces of important men.
>
> It is these men I mind:
> They are so jealous of anything that is not flat! They are
>   jealous gods
> That would have the whole world flat because they are.
>
> ("Three Women")

And, in a rapid associative leap that is typical of her poetry—and typical of a certain type of frightened imagination—Plath expands her sociological observation to include the mythical figures of "Father" and "Son," who conspire together to make a heaven of flatness: "Let us flatten and launder the grossness from these souls" ("Three Women"). The symbolic figures of "Father" and "Son" do not belong to a dimension of the mind exclusive, let alone transcendent, of society; and if they embody the jealous assumptions of an imagined family of "parent" and "child," they are more immediate, more terrifyingly present, than either.

"Nations, governments, parliaments, societies" conspire only in lies and cannot be trusted. Moreover, they are male in their aggression and their cynical employment of rhetoric; their counterparts cannot be women like Plath, but the creatures of "Heavy Women," who smile to themselves above their "weighty stomachs" and meditate "devoutly as the Dutch bulb," absolutely mute, "among the archetypes." Between the archetypes of jealous, ruthless power, represented by the Father/Son of religious and social tradition, and the archetypes of moronic fleshly beauty, represented by these smug mothers, there is a very small space for the creative intellect, for the employment and expansion of a consciousness that tries to transcend such limits. Before we reject Plath's definition of the artistic self as unreasonably passive, even as infantile, we should inquire why so intelligent a woman should assume these limitations, why she should not declare war against the holders of power and of the "mysteries" of the flesh—why her poetry approaches but never crosses over the threshold of an active, healthy attack upon obvious evils and injustices. The solitary ego in its prison cell is there by its own desire, its own admission of guilt in the face of even the most crazily ignorant of accusers. Like Eugene O'Neill, who lived into his sixties with this bewildering obsession of the self-annihilated-by-Others, Plath exhibits only the most remote (and rhetorical) sympathy with other people. If she tells us she may be a bit of a "Jew," it is only to define herself, her sorrows, and not to involve our sympathies for the Jews of recent European history.

Of course, the answer is that Plath did not like other people; like many who are persecuted, she identified in a perverse way with her own persecutors, and not with those who, along with her, were victims. But she did not "like" other people because she did not essentially believe that they existed; she knew intellectually that they existed, of course, since they had the power to injure her, but she did not believe they existed in the way she did, as pulsating, breathing, suffering individuals. Even her own children are objects of her perception, there for the restless scrutiny of her image-making mind, and not there as human beings with a potentiality that would someday take them beyond their immediate dependency upon her, which she sometimes enjoys and sometimes dreads.

The moral assumptions behind Plath's poetry condemned her to death, just as she, in creating this body of poems, condemned it to death. But her moral predicament is not so pathological as one may think, if conformity to an essentially sick society is taken to be—as many traditional moralists and psychologists take it—a sign of normality. Plath speaks very clearly a language we can understand. She is saying what men have been saying for many centuries, though they have not been so frank as she, and, being less sensitive as well, they have not sickened upon their own hatred for humanity: they have thrived upon it, in fact, "sublimating" it into wondrous achievements of material and mechanical splendor. Let us assume that Sylvia Plath acted out in her poetry and in her private life the deathliness of an old consciousness, the old cor-rupting hell of the Renaissance ideal and its "I"-ness, separate and dis-tinct from all other fields of consciousness, which exist only to be con-quered or to inflict pain upon the "I." Where at one point in civilization this very masculine, combative ideal of an "I" set against all other "I's" —and against nature as well—was necessary in order to wrench man from the hermetic contemplation of a God-centered universe and prod him into action, it is no longer necessary, its health has become a path-ology, and whoever clings to its outmoded concepts will die. If romanti-cism and its gradually accelerating hysteria are taken as the ultimate ends of a once-vital Renaissance ideal of subject/object antagonism, then Plath must be diagnosed as one of the last romantics; and already her poetry seems to us a poetry of the past, swiftly receding into history.

The "I" that is declared an enemy of all others cannot identify with anyone or anything, since even nature—or especially nature—is antago-nistic to it. Man is spirit/body but, as in the poem "Last Things," Plath states her distrust of the spirit that "escapes like steam / In dreams, through the mouth-hole or eye-hole. I can't stop it." Spirit is also intel-lect, but the "intellect" exists uneasily inside a prison house of the flesh; a small, desperate, calculating process (like the ego in Freud's psychol-ogy) that achieves only spasmodic powers of identity in the constant struggle between the id and the superego or between the bestial world of fleshly female "archetypes" and hypocritical, deathly male authori-ties. This intellect does not belong naturally in the universe and feels guilt and apprehension at all times. It does not belong in nature; nature is "outside" man, superior in brute power to man, though admittedly inferior in the possibilities of imagination. When this intellect attempts its own kind of creation, it cannot be judged as transcendent to the biological processes of change and decay, but as somehow conditioned by these processes and, of course, when found in poetry "Stillborn," lamenting the deadness of her poems, forcing them to compete with low but living creatures?— "They are not pigs, they are not even fish . . ."

It is one of the truly pathological habits of this old consciousness that it puts all things into immediate competition: erecting Aristotelian categories of x and non-x, assuming that the distinction between two totally unconnected phases of life demands a kind of war, a superior/inferior grading.

For instance, let us examine one of Plath's lighter and more "positive" poems. This is "Magi," included in the posthumous *Crossing the Water*. It summons up literary affiliations with Eliot and Yeats, but its vision is exclusively Plath's and, in a horrifying way, very female. Here, Plath is contemplating her six-month-old daughter, who smiles "into thin air" and rocks on all fours "like a padded hammock." Imagined as hovering above the child, like "dull angels," are the Magi of abstraction—the intellectual, philosophical concepts of Good, True, Evil, Love, the products of "some lamp-headed Plato." Plath dismisses the Magi by asking "What girl ever flourished in such company?" Her attitude is one of absolute contentment with the physical, charming simplicities of her infant daughter; she seems to want none of that "multiplication table" of the intellect. If this poem had not been written by Sylvia Plath, who drew such attention to her poetry by her suicide, one would read it and immediately agree with its familiar assumptions—how many times we've read this poem, by how many different poets! But Plath's significance now forces us to examine her work very carefully, and in this case the poem reveals itself as a vision as tragic as her more famous, more obviously troubled poems.

It is, in effect, a death sentence passed by Plath on her own use of language, on the "abstractions" of culture or the literary as opposed to the physical immediacy of a baby's existence. The world of language is condemned as only "ethereal" and "blank"—obviously inferior to the world of brute, undeveloped nature. Plath is saying here, in this agreeable-mannered poem, that because "Good" and "Evil" have no meaning to a six-month-old infant beyond the facts of mother's milk and a belly-ache, they have no essential meaning at all—to anyone—and the world of all adult values, the world of complex linguistic structures, the world in which Plath herself lives as a normal expression of her superior intellect, is as "loveless" as the multiplication table and therefore must be rejected. It is extraordinary that the original romantic impulse to honor and appreciate nature, especially mute nature, should dwindle in our time to this: a Sylvia Plath willfully admitting to herself and to us that she is inferior to her own infant! The regressive fantasies here are too pathetic to bear examination, but it is worth suggesting that this attitude is not unique. It reveals much that is wrong with contemporary intellectuals' assessment of themselves: a total failure to consider that the undeveloped (whether people or nations) are not sacred because they are undeveloped, but sacred because they are part of nature, that and the role of the superior intellect is not to honor incompletion, in itself or in anything, but to help bring about the fulfillment of potentialities. Plath tells us that a six-month-old infant shall pass judgment on Plato; and in the poem "Candles" she asks, "How shall I tell anything at all / To this infant still in a birth-drowse?" It is impossible, of course, for her to tell the infant anything, if she assumes that the infant possesses an intuitive knowledge superior to her own. And yet, and yet . . . she does desire to "tell" the infant and us. But her "telling" cannot be anything more than a half-guilty assertion of her own impotence, and she will ultimately condemn it as wasteful. The honoring of mute nature above man's ability to make and use language will naturally result in muteness; this muteness will force the individual into death, for the denial of language is a suicidal one and we pay for it with our lives.

Back from the maternity ward, resting after her painful experience, the most "positive" of Plath's three women is reassured when she looks out her window, at dawn, to see the narcissi opening their white faces in the orchard. And now she feels uncomplex again; she is relieved of the miraculous pain and mystery of childbirth and wants only for herself and for her child "the clear bright colors of the nursery, / The talking ducks, the happy lambs." She meditates:

> It is the exception that interests the devil.
> I do not will [my baby] to be exceptional.
> . . . .
> I will him to be common.

It seems to us pitiful that Plath should desire the "common"—should imagine that her loving words for her infant are anything less than a curse. But her conviction that "the exception interests the devil" is very familiar to us, an expression of our era's basic fear of the intellect; the centuries-old division between "intellect" and "instinct" has resulted in a suicidal refusal to understand that man's intelligence is instinctive in his species, simply an instinct for survival and for the creation of civilization. Yet the "loving of muteness" we find in Plath is understandable if it is seen as a sensitive revulsion against the world of strife, the ceaseless battle of the letter "I" to make victories and extend its territory. Even the highest intelligence, linked to an ego that is self-despising, will utter curses in the apparent rhythms of love:

> . . . right now you are dumb.
> And I love your stupidity,
> The blind mirror of it. I look in
> And find no face but my own. . . .
>
> ("For a Fatherless Son")

The narcissi of the isolated ego are not really "quick" and "white" as children (see "Among the Narcissi") but victimized, trampled, and bitter unto death. Plath's attitude in these gentler poems about her motherhood is, at best, a temporary denial of her truly savage feelings—we are shocked to discover her celebration of hatred in "Lesbos" and similar poems, where she tells us what she really thinks about the "stink of fat and baby crap" that is forcing her into silence, "hate up to my neck."

The poems of hatred seem to us very contemporary, in their jagged rhythms and surreal yoking together of images, and in their defiant expression of a rejection of love, of motherhood, of men, of the "Good, the True, the Beautiful. . . ." If life really is a struggle for survival, even in a relatively advanced civilization, then very few individuals will win; most will lose (and nearly all women are fated to lose); something is rotten in the very fabric of the universe. All this appears to be contemporary, but Plath's poems are in fact the clearest, most precise (because most private) expression of an old moral predicament that has become unbearable now. And its poignant genesis is very old indeed:

> And now I was sorry that God had made me a man. The beasts, birds, fishes, etc., I blessed their condition, for they had not a sinful nature; they were not to go to hell after death. . . .
>
> (John Bunyan, *Grace Abounding*)
> "I"/"i"

Male/Female
Nature as Object and as Nightmare

All this involves a variety of responses, though behind them is a single metaphysical belief. The passive, paralyzed, continually surfacing and fading consciousness of Plath in her poems is disturbing to us because it seems to summon forth, to articulate with deadly accuracy, the re-gressive fantasies we have rejected—and want to forget. The experience of reading her poems deeply is a frightening one: it is like waking to discover one's adult self, grown to full height, crouched in some long-forgotten childhood hiding place, one's heart pounding senselessly, all the old rejected transparent beasts and monsters crawling out of the wallpaper. So much for Plato! So much for adulthood! Yet I cannot emphasize strongly enough how valuable the experience of reading Plath can be, for it is a kind of elegant "dreaming-back," a cathartic experi-ence that not only cleanses us of our personal and cultural desires for regression, but explains by way of its deadly accuracy what was wrong with such desires.

The same can be said for the reading of much of contemporary poetry and fiction, fixated as it is upon the childhood fears of annihilation, persecution, the helplessness we have all experienced when we are, for one reason or another, denied an intellectual awareness of what is hap-pening. For instance, the novels of Robbe-Grillet and his imitators em-phasize the hypnotized passivity of the "I" in a world of dense and apparently autonomous things; one must never ask "Who manufactured these things? Who brought them home? Who arranged them?"—for such questions destroy the novels. Similarly, the highly praised works of Pynchon, Barthelme, Purdy, Barth (the Barth of the minimal stories, not the earlier Barth), and countless others are verbalized screams and shudders to express the confusion of the ego that believes itself—perhaps because it has been told so often—somehow out of place in the universe, a mechanized creature if foolish enough to venture into Nature; a too-natural creature for the mechanical urban paradise he has inherited but has had no part in designing. The "I" generated by these writers is typically a transparent, near-nameless personality; in the nightmarish works of William Burroughs, the central consciousness does not explore a world so much as submit pathetically to the exploration of himself by a comically hostile world, all cartoons and surprising metamorphoses. Plath's tentative identity in such poems as "Winter Trees," "Tulips," and even the robustly defiant "Daddy" is essentially a child's conscious-ness, seizing upon a symbolic particularity (tulips, for instance) and then shrinking from its primary noon, so that the poems—like the fiction we read so often today—demonstrate a dissolution of personality. As Jan B. Gordon has remarked in a review of *Winter Trees* (*Modern*

Poetry Studies, vol. 2, no. 6, p. 282), Plath's landscapes become pictorial without any intermediate stage, so that we discover ourselves "in una selva obscura where associations multiply endlessly, but where each tree looks like every other one. . . ." That is the danger risked by those minimal artists of our time whose subject is solely the agony of the locked-in ego: their agonies, like Plath's landscapes, begin to look alike.

But if we turn from the weak and submissive ego to one more traditionally masculine, activated by the desire to name and to place and to conquer, we discover a consciousness that appears superficially antithetical:

> Average reality begins to rot and stink as soon as the act of individual creation ceases to animate a subjectively perceived texture.
>
> (Vladimir Nabokov, from an interview)

> The obscure moon lighting an obscure world
> Of things that would never be quite expressed,
> Where you yourself were never quite yourself
> And did not want nor have to be,
>
> Desiring the exhilarations of changes:
> The motive for metaphor, shrinking from
> The weight of primary noon,
> The A B C of being . . .
>
> (Wallace Stevens, "Motive for Metaphor")

Where in Plath (and in countless of our contemporaries) the ego suffers dissolution in the face of even the most banal of enemies, in such writers as Nabokov and Stevens the ego emerges as confident and victorious. Yet we see that it is the same metaphysics—the same automatic assumption that there is an "average" reality somehow distinct from us, either superior (and therefore terrifying) or inferior (and therefore saved from "rot" and "stink" only by our godly subjective blessing). This is still the old romantic bias, the opposition between self and object, "I" and "non-I," man and nature. Nabokov and Stevens have mastered art forms in which language is arranged and rearranged in such a manner as to give pleasure to the artist and his readers, excluding any referent to an available exterior world. Their work frees the ego to devise and defend a sealed-off universe, inhabited chiefly by the self-as-artist, so that it is quite natural to assume that Nabokov's writing is about the art of writing and Stevens's poems about the art of writing;

that the work gives us the process of creativity that is its chief interest. Again, as in Plath, the work may approach the threshold of an aware- ness of other inhabitants of the human universe, but it never crosses over because, basically, it cannot guarantee the existence of other human beings: its own autonomy might be threatened or at least questioned. The mirror and never the window is the stimulus for this art that, far from being overwhelmed by nature, turns from it impatiently, in order to construct the claustrophobic *Ada* or the difficult later poems of Stevens, in which metaphors inhabit metaphors and the "weight of pri- mary noon" is hardly more than a memory. The consciousness discern- ible behind the works of Nabokov and Stevens is like that totally auton- omous ego imagined—but only imagined—by Sartre, which is self- created, self-named, untouched by parental or social or cultural or even biological determinants.

Since so refined an art willfully excludes the emotional context of its own creation, personality is minimal; art is all. It is not surprising that the harsh, hooking images of Plath's poetry should excite more interest, since Plath is always honest, perhaps more honest than we would like, and her awareness of a lost cosmos involves her in a perpetual question- ing of what nature is, what the Other is, what does it want to do to her, with her, in spite of her . . .? Nabokov and Stevens receive only the most incidental stimuli from their "average reality" and "obscure world," but Plath is an identity reduced to desperate statements about her dilemma as a passive witness to a turbulent natural world:

> There is no life higher than the grasstops
> Or the hearts of sheep, and the wind
> Pours by like destiny, bending
> Everything in one direction.
> . . . .
> The sheep know where they are,
> Browsing in their dirty wool-clouds,
> Grey as the weather.
> The black slots of their pupils take me in.
> It is like being mailed into space,
> A thin, silly message.
>
> ("Wuthering Heights")

And, in "Two Campers in Cloud Country," the poet and her companion experience a kind of comfort up in Rock Lake, Canada, where they "mean so little" and where they will wake "blank-brained as water in the dawn." If the self is set in opposition to everything that excludes it, then the distant horizons of the wilderness will be as terrible as the kitchen walls and the viciousness of hissing fat. There is never any integrating of the self and its experience, the self and its field of perception. Human consciousness, to Plath, is always an intruder in the natural universe.

This distrust of the intellect in certain poets can result in lyric-meditative poetry of an almost ecstatic beauty, when the poet acknowledges his separateness from nature but seems not to despise or fear it:

> O swallows, swallows, poems are not
> The point. Finding again the world,
> That is the point, where loveliness
> Adorns intelligible things
> Because the mind's eye lit the sun.
> (Howard Nemerov, "The Blue Swallows")

Nemerov shares with Stevens and Plath certain basic assumptions: that poems are "not the point" in the natural universe, and that the poet, therefore, is not in the same field of experience as the swallows. Poetry, coming from the mind of man, not from the objects of mind's perception, is somehow a self-conscious, uneasy activity that must apologize for itself. In this same poem, the title poem of Nemerov's excellent collection *The Blue Swallows*, the poet opposes the "real world" and the "spelling mind" that attempts to impose its "unreal relations on the blue swallows." But despite Nemerov's tone of acquiescence and affirmation, this is a tragic assumption in that it certainly banishes the poet himself from the world: only if he will give up poetry and "find again the world" has he a chance of being saved. It is a paradox that the poet believes he will honor the objects of his perception—whether swallows, trees, sheep, bees, infants—only by withdrawing from them. Why does it never occur to romantic poets that they exist as much by right in the universe as any other creature, and that their function as poets is a natural function?—that the adult imagination is superior to the imagination of birds and infants?

In art this can lead to silence; in life, to suicide.

The Deadly Mirror: The Risks of Lyric Poetry

Among the lesser known of Theodore Roethke's poems is "Lines Upon Leaving a Sanitarium," in which the poet makes certain sobering, unambiguous statements:

Self-contemplation is a curse
That makes an old confusion worse.
....
The mirror tells some truth, but not
Enough to merit constant thought.

Perhaps it is not just Plath's position at the end of a once-energetic tradition and the circumstances of her own unhappy life that doomed her and her poetry to premature dissolution, but something in the very nature of lyric poetry itself. What of this curious art form that, when not liberated by music, tends to turn inward upon the singer, folding and folding again upon the poet? If he is immature to begin with, of what can he sing except his own self's immaturity, and to what task can his imagination put itself except the selection of ingenious images to illustrate this immaturity? Few lyric poets, beginning as shakily as the young Yeats, will continue to write and rewrite, to imagine and reimagine, in a heroic evolution of the self from one kind of personality to another. The risk of lyric poetry is its availability to the precocious imagination, its immediate rewards in terms of technical skill, which then hypnotize the poet into believing that he has achieved all there is to achieve in his life as well as in his art. How quickly these six-inch masterpieces betray their creators! The early successes, predicated upon ruthless self-examination, demand a repeating of their skills even when the original psychological dramas have been outgrown or exhausted, since the lyric poet is instructed to look into his heart and write and, by tradition, he has only his self to write about. But poetry—like all art—demands that its subject be made sacred. Art is the sacralizing of its subject. The problem, then, is a nearly impossible one: How can the poet make himself sacred? Once he has exposed himself, revealed himself, dramatized his fantasies and terrors, what can he do next? Most modern poetry is scornful, cynical, contemptuous of its subject (whether self or others), bitter or amused or coldly detached. It shrinks from the activity of making the world sacred because it can approach the world only through the self-as-subject; and the prospect of glorifying oneself is an impossible one. Therefore, the ironic mode. Therefore, silence. It is rare to encounter a poet like Robert Lowell, who, beginning with the stunning virtuosity of his early poems, can move through a period of intense preoccupation with self (*Life Studies*) into a period of exploratory maneuvers into the personalities of poets quite unlike him (*Imi-*

tations) and, though a shy, ungregarious man, write plays and participate in their productions (*The Old Glory*) and move into a kind of
existential political-historical poetry in which the self is central but unob-
trusive (*Notebook*). Most lyric poets explore themselves endlessly, like
patients involved in a permanent psychoanalysis, reporting back for
each session determined to discover, to drag out of hiding, the essential
problem of their personalities—when perhaps there is no problem in their
personalities at all, except this insane preoccupation with the self and
its moods and doubts, while much of the human universe struggles simply for survival.

If the lyric poet believes—as most people do—that the "I" he inhabits
is not integrated with the entire stream of life, let alone with other
human beings, he is doomed to a solipsistic and ironic and self-pitying
art, in which metaphors for his own narcissistic predicament are snatched
from newspaper headlines concerning real atrocities. The small enclosed
form of the typical lyric poem seems to preclude an active sanctifying
of other people; it is much easier, certainly, for a novelist to investigate
and rejoice in the foreign/intimate nature of other people, regardless
of his maturity or immaturity. When the novel is not addressed to the
same self-analysis as the lyric poem, it demands that one look out the
window and not into the mirror; it demands an active involvement with
time, place, personality, pasts, and futures, and a dramatizing of emotions. The novel allows for a sanctification of any number of people,
and if the novelist pits his "I" against others, he will have to construct
that "I" with care and love; technical virtuosity is so hard to come by
—had Dostoevsky the virtuosity of Nabokov?—that it begins to seem
irrelevant. The novelist's obligation is to do no less than attempt the
sanctification of the world!—while the lyric poet, if he is stuck in a
limited emotional cul-de-sac, will circle endlessly inside the bell jar of
his own world, and only by tremendous strength is he able to break free.[1]

The implications of this essay are not that a highly self-conscious art is
inferior by nature to a more socially committed art—on the contrary, it is
usually the case that the drama of the self is very exciting. What is a risk
for the poet is often a delight for his reader; controlled hysteria is more
compelling than statements of Spinozan calm. When Thomas Merton cau-
tioned the mystic against writing poems, believing that the "poet" and
the "mystic" must never be joined, he knew that the possession of any
truth, especially an irrefutable truth, cannot excite drama. It may be a

joy to possess wisdom, but how to communicate it? If you see unity beneath the parts, bits, and cogs of the phenomenal world, this does not mean you can make poetry out of it—

> All leaves are this leaf,
> all petals, this flower
> in a lie of abundance.
> All fruit is the same,
> the trees are only one tree
> and one flower sustains all the earth.
> ("Unity," from *Manual Metaphysics*
> by Pablo Neruda; trans. Ben Belitt)

—not Neruda's best poetry.

By contrast, Plath's poems convince us when they are most troubled, most murderous, most unfair—as in "Daddy," where we listen in amazement to a child's voice cursing and rekilling a dead man, in a distorted rhythmic version of what would be, in an easier world, a nursery tune. An unforgettable poem, surely. The "parts, bits, cogs, the shining multiples" (*Three Women*) constitute hallucinations that involve us because they stir in us memories of our own infantile pasts and do not provoke us into a contemplation of the difficult and less dramatic future of our adulthood. The intensity of "Lesbos" grows out of an adult woman's denying her adulthood, her motherhood, lashing out spitefully at all objects—babies or husbands or sick kittens—with a strident, self-mocking energy that is quite different from the Plath of the more depressed poems:

> And I, love, am a pathological liar,
> And my child—look at her, face down on the floor,
> Little unstrung puppet, kicking to disappear—
> Why, she is schizophrenic,
> Her face red and white, a panic . . .
> . . . .
> You say I should drown my girl.
> She'll cut her throat at ten if she's mad at two.
> The baby smiles, fat snail,
> From the polished lozenges of orange linoleum.
> You could eat him. He's a boy . . .

Though Plath and her friend, another unhappy mother, obviously share the same smoggy hell, they cannot communicate, and Plath ends the poem with her insistence upon their separateness: "Even in your Zen heaven we shan't meet."

A woman who despises herself as a woman obviously cannot feel sympathy with any other woman; her passionate love/hate is for the aggressors, the absent husbands or the dead fathers who have absorbed all evil. But because these male figures are not present, whatever revenge is possible must be exacted upon their offspring. The poem "For a Fatherless Son" is more chilling than the cheerful anger of "Daddy" because it is so relentless a curse. And if it hints of Plath's own impending absence, by way of suicide, it is a remarkably cruel poem indeed. Here the mother tells her son that he will presently be aware of an absence, growing beside him like "a death tree . . . an illusion, / And a sky like a pig's backside. . . ." The child is temporarily too young to realize that his father has abandoned him, but

> one day you may touch what's wrong
> The small skulls, the smashed blue hills,
> the godawful hush.

This is one of the few poems of Plath's in which the future is imagined, but it is imagined passively, helplessly; the mother evidently has no intention of rearranging her life and establishing a household free of the father or of his absence. She does not state her hatred for the absent father, but she reveals herself as a victim, bitter and spiteful, and unwilling to spare her son these emotions. Again, mother and child are roughly equivalent; the mother is not an adult, not a participant in the world of "archetypes."

So unquestioningly is the division between selves accepted, and so relentlessly the pursuit of the solitary, isolated self by way of the form of this poetry, that stasis and ultimate silence seem inevitable. Again, lyric poetry is a risk because it rarely seems to open into a future: the time of lyric poetry is usually the present or the past. "This is a disease I carry home, this is a death," Plaths says in *Three Women*, and, indeed, this characterizes most of her lines. All is brute process, without a future; the past is recalled only with bitterness, a stimulus for present dismay.

When the epic promises of "One's-self I sing" is mistaken as the singing of a separate self, and not the universal self, the results can only be tragic.

Crossing the Water

Plath understood well the hellish fate of being Swift's true counterpart, the woman who agrees that the physical side of life is a horror, an ungainly synthesis of flesh and spirit—the disappointment of all the romantic love poems and the nightmare of the monkish soul. Since one cannot make this existence sacred, one may as well dream of "massacres" or, like the Third Voice in the play *Three Women*, express regret that she had not arranged to have an abortion: "I should have murdered this," she says in a Shakespearean echo, "that murders me." "Crossing the water"— crossing over into another dimension of experience—cannot be a liberation, an exploration of another being, but only a quiet movement into death for two "black, cut-paper people":

> Cold worlds shake from the oar.
> The spirt of blackness is in us, it is in the fishes.
> . . . .
> Are you not blinded by such expressionless sirens?
> This is the silence of astounded souls.
>   ("Crossing the Water")

In most of the poems and very noticeably in *The Bell Jar*, Plath exhibits a recurring tendency to dehumanize people, to flatten everyone into "cut-paper people," most of all herself. She performs a kind of reversed magic, a desacralizing ritual for which psychologists have terms—reification, rubricization. Absolute, dramatic boundaries are set up between the "I" and all others, and there is a peculiar refusal to distinguish between those who mean well, those who mean ill, and those who are neutral. Thus, one is shocked to discover in *The Bell Jar* that Esther, the intelligent young narrator, is as callous toward her mother as the psychiatrist is to her, and that she sets about an awkward seduction with the chilling prevision of a machine—hardly aware of the man involved, telling us very little about him as an existing human being. He does not really exist, he has no personality worth mentioning. Only Esther exists.

"Lady Lazarus," risen once again from the dead, does not expect a sympathetic response from the mob of spectators that crowd in to view her, a mock-phoenix rising from another failed suicide attempt: to Plath there cannot be any connection between people, between the "I" who performs and the crowd that stares. All deaths are separate, and do not evoke human responses. To be really safe, one must be like the young man of "Gigolo," who has eluded the "bright fish hooks, the smiles of women," and who will never age because—like Plath's ideal self—he is a perfect narcissus, self-gratified. He has successfully dehumanized himself.

The cosmos is indeed lost to Plath and her era, and even a tentative exploration of a possible "God" is viewed in the old terms, in the old images of dread and terror. "Mystic" is an interesting poem, on a subject rare indeed to Plath, and seems to indicate that her uneasiness with the "mill of hooks" of the air—"questions without answer"—had led her briefly to thoughts of God. Yet whoever this "God" is, no comfort is possible because the ego cannot experience any interest or desire without being engulfed:

> Once one has seen God, what is the remedy?
> Once one has been seized up
>
> Without a part left over,
> Not a toe, not a finger, and used,
> Used utterly . . .
> What is the remedy?

Used: the mystic will be exploited, victimized, hurt. He can expect no liberation or joy from God, but only another form of dehumanizing brutality. Plath has made beautiful poetry out of the paranoia sometimes expressed by a certain kind of emotionally disturbed person who imagines that any relationship with anyone will overwhelm him, engulf and destroy his soul. (For a brilliant poem about the savagery of erotic love between lovers who cannot quite achieve adult autonomy or the generosity of granting humanity to each other, see Ted Hughes's "Lovesong" in *Crow*, not inappropriate in this context.)

The dread of being possessed by the Other results in the individual's failure to distinguish between real and illusory enemies. What must be in the human species a talent for discerning legitimate threats to personal survival evidently never developed in Plath—this helps to explain why she could so gracefully fuse the "evil" of her father with the historical outrages of the Nazis, unashamedly declare herself a "Jew" because the memory of her father persecuted her. In other vivid poems, she senses enemies in tulips (oxygen-sucking tulips?—surely they are human!) or sheep (which possess the unsheeplike power of murdering a human being) or in the true blankness of a mirror, which cannot be seen as recording the natural maturation process of a young woman but must be reinterpreted as drawing the woman toward the "terrible fish" of her future self. Plath's inability to grade the possibilities of danger is reflected generally in our society and helps to account for peculiar admissions of helplessness and confusion in adults who should be informing their children:

if everything unusual or foreign is an evil, if everything new is an evil, then the individual is lost. The political equivalent of childlike paranoia is too obvious to need restating, but we have a cultural equivalent as well that seems to pass unnoticed. Surely the sinister immorality of films like *A Clockwork Orange* (though not the original English version of the Burgess novel) lies in their excited focus upon small, isolated, glamorized acts of violence by nonrepresentative individuals, so that the unfathomable violence of governments is totally ignored or misapprehended. Delmore Schwartz said that even the paranoid has enemies. Indeed he has enemies, but paranoia cannot allow us to distinguish them from friends.

In the summer of 1972 I attended a dramatic reading of Plath's *Three Women*, given by three actresses as part of the International Poetry Conference in London. The reading was done in a crowded room, and unfortunately the highly professional performance was repeatedly interrupted by a baby's crying from another part of the building. Here was—quite accidentally—a powerful and perhaps even poetic counterpoint to Plath's moving poem. For there, in the baby's cries from another room, was what Plath had left out: the reason for the maternity ward, the reason for childbirth and suffering and motherhood and poetry itself.

What may come to seem obvious to people in the future—that unique personality does not necessitate isolation, that the "I" of the poet belongs as naturally in the universe as any other aspect of its fluid totality, above all that this "I" exists in a field of living spirit of which it is one aspect—was tragically unknown to Plath, as it has been unknown or denied many. Hopefully, a world of totality awaits us, not a played-out world of fragments; but Sylvia Plath acted out a tragically isolated existence, synthesizing for her survivors so many of the sorrows of that dying age—romanticism in its death throes, the self's ship, *Ariel*, prematurely drowned.

> It is so beautiful, to have no attachments!
> I am solitary as grass. What is it I miss?
> Shall I ever find it, whatever it is?
>   ("Three Women")

17 The Plath Celebration: A Partial Dissent

Irving Howe

I

A Glamour of Fatality hangs over the name of Sylvia Plath, the glamour that has made her a darling of our culture. Extremely gifted, her will clenched into a fist of ambition, several times driven to suicide by a suffering so absolute as to seem almost impersonal, yet in her last months composing poems in which pathology and clairvoyance triumphantly fuse —these are the materials of her legend. It is a legend that solicits our desires for a heroism of sickness that can serve as emblem of the age, and many young readers take in Sylvia Plath's vibrations of despair as if they were the soul's own oxygen. For reasons good and bad, the spokesmen for the sensibility of extreme gesture—all the blackness, confession, denial, and laceration that are warranted by modern experience but are also the moral bromides of our moment—see in Sylvia Plath an authentic priestess. Because she is authentic, the role would surely displease her; dead now for a decade, she can offer no defense.

Quantities of adoring criticism pile up around her, composed in a semi-mimetic frenzy designed to be equivalent in tone to its subject. The result is poor criticism, worse prose. In a collection of essays devoted to Sylvia Plath, the editor writes—almost as if he too were tempted by an oven: "The courting of experience that kills is characteristic of major poets." [1] Is it? Virgil, Petrarch, Goethe, Pope, Hugo, Wordsworth, Bialik, Yeats, Stevens, Auden, Frost?

In dissenting a little from the Plath celebration, one has the sense not so much of disagreeing about the merits of certain poems as of plunging into a harsh *kulturkampf*. For one party in this struggle Sylvia Plath has become an icon, and the dangers for those in the other party are also considerable, since it would be unjust to allow one's irritation with her devotees to spill over into one's reponse to her work. So let us move quickly to the facts about her career and then to the poems she wrote toward the end of her life, crucial for any judgment of her work.

Her father, a professor of biology and (it's important to note) a man of German descent, died when she was nine. The reverberations of this event are heavy in the poems, though its precise significance for Sylvia Plath as either person or poet is very hard to grasp. She then lived with her mother in Wellesley, Massachusetts; she went to Smith, an ardent student who swept up all the prizes; she suffered from psychic disorders; she won a Fulbright to Cambridge University, then met and married a gifted English poet, Ted Hughes. In 1960 she published her first book of poems, *The Colossus*—it rings with distinguished echoes, proclaims unripe gifts, contains more quotable passages than successful poems (true for all her work). She had two children, in 1960 and 1962, to whom she seems to have been fiercely attached and about whom she wrote some of her better poems. She was separated from her husband, lived one freezing winter in London with her children, and, experiencing an onslaught of energy at once overwhelming and frightening, wrote her best-known poems during the last week of her life. On February 11, 1963, she killed herself.

Crossing the Water contains some of the poems she wrote between the early work of *The Colossus* and the final outburst that would appear posthumously in 1965 as *Ariel*. There are graphic lines in *Crossing the Water*, but few poems fully achieved. "The desert is white as a blind man's eye, / Comfortless as salt . . ." we read in a poem not otherwise notable. The drive to self-destruction that would tyrannize the last poems is already at work in these "middle" ones:

> If I pay the roots of the heather
> Too close attention, they will invite me
> To whiten my bones among them.

The poems in *Crossing the Water* are, nevertheless, more open in voice and variable in theme than those for which Sylvia Plath has become famous; they have less power but also less pathology. She writes well, in snatches and stanzas, about the impersonal moments of personal experience, when the sense of everything beyond one's selfhood dominates the mind. She writes well, that is, precisely about the portion of human experience that is most absent in the *Ariel* poems; such poems as "Parliament

Hill Fields," "Small Hours," and a few others in *Crossing the Water,* unheroic in temper and unforced in pitch, can yield familiar pleasures. The flaws in her work she describes charmingly in "Stillborn," though it's characteristic that, after the vivid opening stanza, the poem should itself seem stillborn:

> These poems do not live; it's a sad diagnosis.
> They grew their toes and fingers well enough,
> Their little foreheads bulged with concentration.
> If they missed out on walking about like people
> It wasn't for any lack of mother love.

II

At a crucial point in her career Sylvia Plath came under the influence of Robert Lowell's *Life Studies,* and it is this relationship that has led many admirers to speak of her late work as "confessional poetry." The category is interesting but dubious, both in general and when applied to Sylvia Plath.

In *Life Studies* Lowell broke into a new style. He abandoned the complex interlacings of idea and image, the metaphysical notations and ironic turnings of his earlier work, and instead wrote poems that were to deal immediately with his own experience: his time as CO, his nervous breakdowns, his relations with his wife. When he wrote "I" it was clear he really did mean his private self, not a persona created for the poem's occasion. To the small number of people who read poetry at all, *Life Studies* came as a valued, perhaps overvalued, shock—a harsh abandonment of the Eliotian impersonality that had previously dominated American poetry. Inevitably, this new style was widely imitated and its inherent difficulty frequently ignored. The readiness with which Lowell exposed his life caused people to admire his courage rather than scrutinize his poems. Candor was raised to an absolute value, such as it need not often be in either morals or literature. Our culture was then starting to place an enormous stress on self-exposure, self-assault, self-revelation—as if spontaneity were a sure warrant of authenticity, and spilling out a sure road to comprehension. The bared breast replaced the active head.

Insofar as a poem depends mainly on the substance of its confession, as blow or shock revealing some hidden shame in the writer's experience, it will rarely be a first-rate piece of work. It will lack the final composure that even the most excited composition requires. Insofar as it makes the confessional element into something integral to the poem, it ceases, to that extent, to be confessional. It becomes a self-sufficient poem, not dependent for its value on whatever experience may have evoked it. Perhaps the greatest achievement of this kind in English is the group of poems Thomas Hardy wrote in 1912-1913 after the death of his first wife: they are full of the regrets of wasted life, missed opportunities, shamed quarrels, but they take on an autonomous life, beyond the rawness of confession.

Now this is dogma and, as such, suspect—even by those who may agree with it. For obviously there are cases where residues of personal confession can be detected, yet the poem constitutes more than a mere notation of incident or memory. I would also add that the short lyric is a form likely to resist confessional writing, since it does not allow for the sustained moral complication, the full design of social or historical setting, than can transform confession from local act to larger meaning. The confessions of Augustine and Rousseau are long works, and they are in prose.

A flaw in confessional poetry, even the best of it, is one that characterizes much other American poetry in the twentieth century. It is the notion that a careful behavioral notation of an event or object is in itself sufficient basis for composing a satisfactory poem: the description of an orange, a wheelbarrow, a woman's gait. What such poems depend on, for their very life, is the hope of creating an aura, a network of implication, that will enlarge the scope of their references. Sometimes, as in Frost's "Spring Pools," this feat is managed; too often, what we get is a mere verbal snapshot, a discrete instance, that has little reverberation. And this holds true even if the snapshot records an event that rouses our curiosity or dismay.

Robert Lowell's poem, "Man and Wife," shook many readers when it first appeared in 1952. When you read a poem that begins—

> Tamed by Miltown, we lie on Mother's bed;
> the rising sun in war paint dyes us red;
> in broad daylight her gilded bedposts shine,
> abandoned, almost Dionysian.

—some feeling of involvement, even pain, is likely to be invoked through the very announcement of its subject. There is the compressed suggestibility of "Mother's bed," the vividness of the "war paint" in the second line. But the poem as a whole no longer seems quite so remarkable as I once thought. In the middle—and the middle is where confessional poems get into trouble, once the subject has been declared and something must now be done with it—Lowell declines into a recollection about the time he "outdrank the Rahvs in the heat / Of Greenwich Village." Most readers do not know "the Rahvs," and the reference is therefore lost upon them; those few who do may find it possible to resist the poet's intention. Here the poem has slipped into self-indulgence. At the end, Lowell does achieve a recovery with several lines describing his wife's invective after a quarrel, presumably before Miltown "tamed" them both:

> your old-fashioned tirade—
> loving, rapid, merciless—
> breaks like the Atlantic Ocean on my head.

These lines move the center of the poem away from the confessing, preening self of the poet and reveal a counteraction: that's not just a prop lying there in bed with him, it's another human being. True, the reference remains local and thereby, perhaps, open to the kind of criticism I made earlier of confessional poetry as a whole. But through severe detail Lowell has managed to suggest reverberations that move the poem beyond the edges of his personal wound.

At times Sylvia Plath also wrote confessional poetry, as in the much-praised "Lady Lazarus," a poem about her recurrent suicide attempts. Its opening lines, like almost all her opening lines, come at one like a driven hammer:

> I have done it again.
> One year in every ten
> I manage it—
>
> A sort of walking miracle, my skin
> Bright as a Nazi lampshade,
> My right foot
>
> A paperweight,
> My face a featureless, fine
> Jew linen.

The tone is jeeringly tough, but at least partly directed against herself. There is a strain of self-irony ("a sort of walking miracle") such as poetry of this kind can never have enough of. Still, one must be infatuated with the Plath legend to ignore the poet's need for enlarging the magnitude of her act through illegitimate comparisons with the Holocaust (a point to which I will return later).

Sylvia Plath's most notable gift as a writer—a gift for the single, isolate image—comes through later in the poem when, recalling an earlier suicide attempt, she writes that they had to "pick the worms off me like sticky pearls." But then, after patching together some fragments of recollection, she collapses into an archness about her suicide attempts that is shocking in a way that she could not have intended:

> I do it so it feels like hell.
> I do it so it feels real.
> I guess you could say I've a call.
>
> It's easy enough to do it in a cell,
> It's easy enough to do it and stay put.

As if uneasy about the tone of such lines, she then drives toward what I can only see as a willed hysteric tone, the forcing of language to make up for an inability to develop the matter. The result is sentimental violence:

> A cake of soap,
> A wedding ring,
> A gold filling . . .
>
> Out of the ash
> I rise with my red hair
> And I eat men like air.

In the end, the several remarkable lines in this poem serve only to intensify its badness, for in their isolation, without the support of a rational structure, they leave the author with no possibility of development other than violent wrenchings in tone. And this is a kind of badness that seems a constant temptation in confessional poetry, the temptation to reveal all with one eye nervously measuring the effect of revelation.

There's another famous poem by Sylvia Plath, entitled "Cut," in which she shows the same mixture of strong phrasing and structural incoherence. "Cut" opens on a sensational note, or touch:

> What a thrill—
> My thumb instead of an onion.
> The top quite gone
> Except for a sort of hinge

> Of skin,
> A flap like a hat,
> Dead white.
> Then that red plush.

This is vivid, no denying it. Morbid, too. The question is whether the morbidity is an experience the writer struggles with or yields to, examines dispassionately or caresses indulgently.

There is a saving wit in the opening lines ("My thumb instead of an onion") and this provides some necessary distance between invoked experience and invoking speaker. But the poem collapses through Sylvia Plath's inability to do more with her theme than thrust it against our eyes, displaying her wound in all its red plushy woundedness.

> The stain on your
> Gauze Ku Klux Klan
> Babushka
> Darkens and tarnishes . . .

The bandage is seen as a babushka, an old lady's scarf. All right. But the Ku Klux Klan? And still more dubious, the "Ku Klux Klan Babushka?" One supposes the KKK is being used here because it is whitely repressive, the Babushka-bandage is "repressing" the blood, and in the poem's graphic pathology, the flow of blood from the cut is attractive, fruitful, perhaps healthy ("a celebration, this is," runs one line). But even if my reading is accurate, does that help us very much with the stanza? Isn't it an example of weakness through excess?

Sylvia Plath's most famous poem, adored by many sons and daughters, is "Daddy." It is a poem with an affecting theme, the feelings of the speaker as she regathers the pain of her father's premature death and her persuasion that he has betrayed her by dying:

> I was ten when they buried you.
> At twenty I tried to die
> And get back, back, back to you.

In the poem Sylvia Plath identifies the father (we recall his German birth) with the Nazis ("Panzer-man, panzer-man, O You") and flares out with assaults for which nothing in the poem (nor, so far as we know, in Sylvia Plath's own life) offers any warrant: "A cleft in your chin instead of your foot / But no less a devil for that. . . ." Nor does anything in the poem offer warrant, other than the free-flowing hysteria of the speaker,

for the assault of such lines as, "There's a stake in your fat black heart /
And the villagers never liked you." Or for the snappy violence of

> Every woman adores a Fascist,
> The boot in the face, the brute
> Brute heart of a brute like you.

What we have here is a revenge fantasy, feeding upon filial love-hatred,
and thereby mostly of clinical interest. But seemingly aware that the
merely clinical can't provide the materials for a satisfying poem, Sylvia
Plath tries to enlarge upon the personal plight, give meaning to the personal outcry, by fancying the girl as victim of a Nazi father:

> An engine, an engine
> Chuffing me off like a Jew.
> A Jew to Dachau, Auschwitz, Belsen.
> I began to talk like a Jew,
> I think I may well be a Jew.

The more sophisticated admirers of this poem may say that I fail to see
it as a dramatic presentation, a monologue spoken by a disturbed girl not
necessarily to be identified with Sylvia Plath, despite the similarities of
detail between the events of the poem and the events of her life. I cannot
accept this view. The personal-confessional element, strident and undisci-
plined, is simply too obtrusive to suppose the poem no more than a dramatic picture of a certain style of disturbance. If, however, we did accept
such a reading of "Daddy," we would fatally narrow its claims to emotional or moral significance, for we would be confining it to a mere vivid
imagining of pathological state. That, surely, is not how its admirers
really take the poem.

It is clearly not how the critic George Steiner takes the poem when
he calls it "the 'Guernica' of modern poetry." But then, in an astonishing
turn, he asks: "In what sense does anyone, himself uninvolved and long
after the event, commit a subtle larceny when he invokes the echoes and
trappings of Auschwitz and appropriates an enormity of ready emotion
to his own private design?" The question is devastating to his early comparison with "Guernica." Picasso's painting objectifies the horrors of
Guernica, through the distancing of art; no one can suppose that he shares
or participates in them. Plath's poem aggrandizes on the "enormity of
ready emotion" invoked by references to the concentration camps, in
behalf of an ill-controlled if occasionally brilliant outburst. There is some-

thing monstrous, utterly disproportionate, when tangled emotions about one's father are deliberately compared with the historical fate of the European Jews; something sad, if the camparison is made spontaneously. "Daddy" persuades once again, through the force of negative example, of how accurate T. S. Eliot was in saying, "The more perfect the artist, the more completely separate in him will be the man who suffers and the mind which creates."

III

The most interesting poems in Ariel are not confessional at all. A confessional poem would seem to be one in which the writer speaks to the reader, telling him, without the mediating presence of imagined event or persona, something about his life: I had a nervous breakdown, my wife and I sometimes lie in bed, sterile of heart, through sterile nights. The sense of direct speech addressed to an audience is central to confessional writing. But the most striking poems Sylvia Plath wrote are quite different. They are poems written out of an extreme condition, a state of being in which the speaker, for all practical purposes Sylvia Plath herself, has abandoned the sense of audience and cares nothing about—indeed, is hardly aware of—the presence of anyone but herself. She writes with a hallucinatory, self-contained fervor. She addresses herself to the air, to the walls. She speaks not as a daylight self, with its familiar internal struggles and doubts, its familiar hesitations before the needs and pressures of others. There is something utterly monolithic, fixated about the voice that emerges in these poems, a voice unmodulated and asocial.

It's as if we are overhearing the rasps of a mind that has found its own habitation and need not measure its distance from, even consider its relation to, other minds. And the stakes are far higher than can ever be involved in mere confession. She exists in some mediate province between living and dying, and she appears to be balancing coolly the claims of the two, drawn almost equally to both yet oddly comfortable with the perils of where she is. This is not the by-now worn romanticism of Liebestod. It is something very strange, very fearful: a different kind of existence, at ease at the gate of dying. The poems Sylvia Plath wrote in this state of being are not "great" poems, but one can hardly doubt that they are remarkable. For they do bring into poetry an element of experience that, so far as I know, is new, and thereby they advance the thrust of literary

modernism by another inch or so. A poem like "Kindness" is set squarely
in what I have called the mediate province between living and dying:

> What is so real as the cry of a child?
> A rabbit's cry may be wilder
> But it has no soul.

And then a few lines later:

> The blood jet is poetry,
> There is no stopping it.

The poems written out of this strange equilibrium—"Fever 103°,"
"Totem," "Edge"—are notable, and the best of them seems to me "Edge":

> The woman is perfected.
> Her dead
> Body wears the smile of accomplishment,
> The illusion of a Greek necessity
> Flows in the scrolls of her toga,
> Her bare
> Feet seem to be saying:
> We have come so far, it is over.
> Each dead child coiled, a white serpent,
> One at each little
> Pitcher of milk, now empty.
> She has folded
> Them back into her body as petals
> Of a rose close when the garden
> Stiffens and odours bleed
> From the sweet, deep throats of the night flower.
> The moon has nothing to be sad about,
> Staring from her hood of bone.
> She is used to this sort of thing.
> Her blacks crackle and drag.

The vision of death as composure, a work done well, is beautifully
realized in the first four stanzas. The next several, with "Each dead child
coiled, a white serpent," seem to me to drop into a kind of sensationalism
—not the kind one finds in the confessional poems, with their alternating
archness and violence, but one that invokes the completion that may come
once death is done and finished. The penultimate stanza is very fine; the
last lines again seem forced.

Even in this kind of poetry, which does strike an original note, there
are many limitations. The poems often shock; they seldom surprise. They

are deficient in plasticity of feeling, the modulation of voice that a poet writing out of a controlled maturity of consciousness can muster. Even the best of Sylvia Plath's poems, as her admirer Stephen Spender admits, "have little principle of beginning or ending, but seem fragments, not so much of one long poem, as of an outpouring which could not stop with the lapsing of the poet's hysteria."

Perhaps the hardest critical question remains. Given the fact that in a few poems Sylvia Plath illustrates an extreme state of existence, one at the very boundary of nonexistence, what illumination—moral, psychological, social—can be provided of either this state or the general human condition by a writer so deeply rooted in the extremity of her plight? Suicide is an eternal possibility of our life and therefore always interesting; but what is the relation between a sensibility so deeply captive to the idea of suicide and the claims and possibilities of human existence in general? That her story is intensely moving, that her talent was notable, that her final breakthrough rouses admiration—of course! Yet in none of the essays devoted to praising Sylvia Plath have I found a coherent statement as to the nature, let alone the value, of her vision. Perhaps it is assumed that to enter the state of mind in which she found herself at the end of her life is its own ground for high valuation; but what will her admirers say to those who reply that precisely this assumption is what needs to be questioned?

After the noise abates and judgment returns, Sylvia Plath will be regarded as an interesting minor poet whose personal story was poignant. A few of her poems will find a place in anthologies—and when you consider the common fate of most talent, that, after all, will not be a small acknowledgment.

Notes

1. In Search of Sylvia: An Introduction
Edward Butscher

1. "The Stones" is part of a seven-poem sequence, "Poem for a Birthday," which appeared intact only in the British edition of *The Colossus*.
2. *The Art of Sylvia Plath*, ed. Charles Newman (Bloomington: Indiana University Press, 1970).
3. Professor Plath's book was published by Macmillan in 1934.
4. The teacher, Addie I. Willard, is now retired and living in Florida.
5. The memoir can be found in *The Art of Sylvia Plath*, pp. 266-72.
6. *Sylvia Plath: Method and Madness* (New York: Seabury Press, 1976).
7. Philip McCurdy recalled Mrs. Plath's shocked reaction to the poem.
8. Some critics have been put off by my Freudian references, not realizing that Sylvia herself insisted upon their elemental validity in terms of self and literature. However artificial appearing or scientifically abstract Freud's constructs—and I would be the first to concede the need for modifications—they remain important blueprints of the unconscious.
9. The appearance of Nancy Hunter Steiner's memoir made an interview superfluous. See *A Closer Look at Ariel* (New York: Harper's Magazine Press, 1973).
10. Olive (Higgens) Prouty, the author of several best-selling novels, including *Stella Dallas* and *Now, Voyager*, had endowed the scholarship Sylvia won to Smith and took a personal interest in Sylvia's career, although she was subsequently pilloried as Philomenia Guinea in *The Bell Jar*.
11. Other poets she read and admired were mostly women: Isabella Gardner, Emily Dickinson, Edith Sitwell, Sara Teasdale, and Marianne Moore.
12. Olwyn has established her own press, Rainbow Press, and uses it to print expensive editions of Sylvia's uncollected works, among other things.
13. Irving Howe and Marjorie Perloff would obviously not agree, having relegated Sylvia to the dungeon of "minor" status, and others might think Emily Dickinson more worthy of the title, but her constricting, somewhat virginal whimsy prevented her, despite real brilliance, from ever establishing an entire world in her poetry, at least for me.
14. For Mailer's perceptive essay on Miller, see *American Review 24:* 1-40.

15. Sylvia herself admitted this during a 1962 interview for the BBC, claiming Blake as a new mentor and rejecting her own poetry before 1960.
16. The allusion was to Alvarez's sensationalist article in *The Observer* (November 14, 1971) in which he first advanced the notion that Sylvia's suicide was a gamble that failed. A second installment, due to appear the following week, was canceled at the insistence of the Hugheses.

5. Recollections of Sylvia Plath
Dorothea Krook

1. Since this was written, Irene V. Morris ("I.V.M."), Sylvia's tutor, has given her own charming account of the episode in her "Sylvia Plath at Newnham—a Tutorial Recollection," published in the *Newnham College Roll: Letter 1975*, pp. 45-47.

6. "Gone, Very Gone Youth": Sylvia Plath at Cambridge, 1955-1957
Jane Baltzell Kopp

1. *The Bell Jar* (New York: Harper & Row, 1971), p. 19.
2. "Fallgrief's Girl-Friends" and two untitled poems with the first lines, respectively, "Whenever I am got under my gravestone" and "If I should touch her she would shriek and weeping."
3. *Newnham College Roll: "Letter"* (January, 1975), pp. 45-47.

10. Architectonics: Sylvia Plath's Colossus
Pamela Smith

1. Anne Sexton, "The Barfly Ought to Sing," in *The Art of Sylvia Plath: A Symposium*, ed. Charles Newman (Bloomington: Indiana University Press, 1970), p. 175.
2. Sylvia Plath, *The Colossus and Other Poems* (New York: Vintage Books, 1968). Quoted with permission of Alfred A. Knopf and Miss Olwyn Hughes.
3. Sexton, "The Barfly Ought to Sing," p. 177.
4. Sylvia Plath, *Ariel* (New York: Harper & Row, 1966).
5. "Sylvia Plath," in Newman, p. 58.
6. "The Poetry of Sylvia Plath: A Technical Analysis," in Newman, p. 136.
7. Ibid., p. 146. The ten should include: "Manor Garden," "Night Shift," "The Eye-mote," "Faun," "The Bull of Bendylaw," "Suicide Off Egg Rock," "I Want, I Want," "A Winter Ship," "Blue Moles," and "Sculptor."
8. Ibid.
9. *The Bell Jar* (New York: Harper & Row, 1971), p. 69. The similarity is remarked by Lois Ames, "Notes Toward a Biography," in Newman, pp. 222-23.

10. Sylvia Plath, "Electra on Azalea Path," *Hudson Review* 13 (Autumn, 1960): 414-45.
11. Nims, in Newman, p. 147.
12. William Ruland, *Legends of the Rhine*, 11th ed. (Kolm Am Rhein: Verlag Von Hoursch & Bechstedt, n.d.).
13. *The Collected Poems* (New York: New Directions, 1957), p. 21.
14. Ted Hughes, "The Chronological Order of Sylvia Plath's Poems," in Newman, p. 189.
15. Nims, in Newman, pp. 140-41.
16. *Collected Poems, 1930-1960* (New York: Oxford University Press, 1960), p. 53.
17. Nims, in Newman, p. 139.
18. "Book Reviews," *London Magazine* OS 8 (March, 1961): 70.
19. Ames, in Newman, p. 160.
20. Hughes, in Newman, p. 188.
21. "The Tranquilized Fifties," *Sewanee Review* 70 (Spring, 1962): 216.
22. Peter Orr, ed., *The Poet Speaks* (New York: Barnes & Noble, 1966), p. 170.

11. On the Road to *Ariel:* The "Transitional" Poetry of Sylvia Plath
Marjorie G. Perloff

1. *Crossing the Water* (New York: Harper & Row, 1971); *Winter Trees* (London: Faber and Faber, 1971). *Ed. note:* The American edition of *Winter Trees* appeared from Harper & Row in 1972 and was not available to Professor Perloff at the time she wrote this essay.
2. Douglas Dunn, *Encounter* 37 (August, 1971): 68; Ted Hughes, "Sylvia Plath's *Crossing the Water:* Some Reflections," *Critical Quarterly* 13 (Summer, 1971): 165. Lyman Andrews's comment is reprinted on the dust jacket of *Crossing the Water*.
3. One can easily check the dates of magazine publication of Plath's poems by consulting the Plath Bibliography by Mary Kinzie, Daniel Lynn Conrad, and Suzanne D. Kurman in *The Art of Sylvia Plath*, ed. Charles Newman (London: Faber and Faber, 1970), pp. 305-19. The bibliography makes clear that the following poems were published before the end of 1960: "Candles," "Black Rook in Rainy Weather," "Metaphors," "Maudlin," "Ouija," "Two Sisters of Persephone," "Who," "Dark House," "Maenad," "The Beast," "Witch Burning." Of these, the two earliest are "Two Sisters of Persephone," first published in the January, 1957, issue of *Poetry*, and "Black Rook in Rainy Weather," originally published in *Granta* in May, 1957. All the rest, except for "Candles," which appeared in *The Listener* on November 17, 1960, were first published in the British edition of *The Colossus* in the late fall of 1960. Five of these poems— "Who," "Dark House," "Maenad," "The Beast," and "Witch Burning"—

were originally part of the seven-poem sequence, *Poem for a Birthday,* written at Yado in late 1959. The remaining two poems in this sequence— "Flute Notes from a Reedy Pond" and "The Stones"—were published as separate poems in the U.S. edition of *The Colossus* (1962).

I believe that the following poems were written before 1960: "Private Ground," "Sleep in the Mojave Desert," "Two Campers in Cloud Country," "On Deck," "Crossing the Water," and "Finisterre." (*Ed. note:* For a more recent treatment of Plath's published works in their British and American editions, see Edward Butscher, *Sylvia Plath: Method and Madness,* pp. 378-82.)

4. Ted Hughes calls "In Plaster" the "weaker twin" of "Tulips" and says that it was written "at the same time and in almost identical form." "The Chronological Order of Sylvia Plath's Poems," *The Art of Sylvia Plath,* p. 193.

5. See Lois Ames, "Notes Toward a Biography," Ibid., p. 170.

6. *The Divided Shelf* (1960; reprint Pelican Books, 1965), p. 110.

7. I have discussed this aspect of Plath's poetry in "Angst and Animism in the Poetry of Sylvia Plath," *Journal of Modern Literature* 1 (First Issue, 1970): 57-74.

8. "Sylvia Plath's *Crossing the Water,*" *Critical Quarterly,* p. 166.

9. *New Statesman,* June 4, 1971, p. 774.

10. See *The Savage God: A Study of Suicide* (New York: Random House, 1972), p. 21. Alvarez writes of Plath's last work, "These months were an amazingly creative period, comparable, I think, to the 'marvelous year' in which Keats produced nearly all the poetry on which his reputation finally rests."

11. I discuss the novel at length in "A Ritual for Being Born Twice: Sylvia Plath's *The Bell Jar,*" *Contemporary Literature* 13 (Fall, 1972).

12. The Double in Sylvia Plath's *The Bell Jar*
Gordon Lameyer

1. In her college thesis Sylvia speaks of the desecration of the father image by Robert Louis Stevenson's Mr. Hyde, the "bastard brother" or evil nature of Dr. Jekyll, who, she says, accuses his evil double of "destroying the picture of my father."

2. Fyodor Dostoevsky, *The Double,* in *Three Short Novels of Dostoevsky,* trans. Constance Garnett (New York, 1960), pp. 115-16.

3. Otto Rank, *The Double,* trans. Harry Tucker, Jr. (Chapel Hill: University of North Carolina Press, 1971), p. 74.

4. Ibid., pp. 79-80.

5. Cf. "Lesbos" in the American edition of *Ariel.*

13. The Deathly Paradise of Sylvia Plath
    Constance Scheerer

1. Where the source is not otherwise clear from the context, editions of Plath's work are designated in parentheses by the following symbols: (A) *Ariel;* (C) *The Colossus* (American ed.); (CW) *Crossing the Water;* (WT) *Winter Trees.*

15. The Dark Funnel: A Reading of Sylvia Plath
    Robert Phillips

1. *Modern Poetry Studies* 1: 1 (Fall, 1970): 6-34.
2. Quoted in a letter from Marya Zaturenska to Robert Phillips, May 29, 1972.
3. References are to the Faber edition of *The Bell Jar* (London, 1963), p. 128.
4. Ibid., p. 40.
5. Biographical facts are taken from Lois Ames, "Notes Toward a Biography," in *The Art of Sylvia Plath*, ed. Charles Newman (Bloomington: Indiana University Press, 1970), p. 156.
6. *The Bell Jar*, p. 68.
7. *The Art of Sylvia Plath*, p. 156.
8. *The Bell Jar*, p. 77.
9. Ibid., p. 175.
10. Ibid.
11. *Hudson Review* 13: 3 (Fall, 1960): 414-15.
12. *Atlantic* 199: 1 (Jaunary, 1957): 65.
13. See Jung's "The Oedipus Complex," in *Freud and Psychoanalysis*, in *Collected Works of C. G. Jung*, vol. 4, ed. G. Adler et al., trans. R. F. C. Hull (Princeton: Princeton University Press, 1961).
14. Ibid., p. 155.
15. For this and other observations I am indebted to Judith Bloomingdale.
16. *Alone with America: Essays on the Art of Poetry in the United States since 1950* (New York: Atheneum, 1969), p. 413.
17. *The Colossus* (New York: Alfred A. Knopf, 1962), p. 3. All quotations are from the first American edition.
18. *Histoire de la Civilisation africaine* (Paris, 1952).
19. *Crossing the Water* (London: Faber and Faber, 1971), p. 13. All quotations are from the first British edition.
20. *Winter Trees* (London: Faber and Faber, 1971).
21. After I had worked out this segment of this essay I was fortunate to read in manuscript Raymond Smith's excellent review of *Winter Trees*, written for volume 2 of *Modern Poetry Studies*. Dr. Smith confirms and elaborates upon these images of absence and narcissism.

22. *Beyond All This Fiddle* (New York: Random House, 1969), p. 49.
23. Quoted in *The Art of Sylvia Plath*.
24. *The New Poets* (New York: Oxford University Press, 1967), p. 88.
25. Rollo May, *Love and Will* (New York: W. W. Norton, 1969). May's discussion of the relationship between love and death is directly reflected in several of my conclusions.
26. Sigmund Freud, "The Two Classes of Instincts," in *The Ego and the Id*, Standard Edition (London: Hogarth Press, 1961), p. 47.
27. All quotations from *Ariel* are from the Faber edition (London, 1965).

16. The Death Throes of Romanticism: The Poetry of Sylvia Plath
Joyce Carol Oates

1. Since completing this essay I have come upon Roy Fuller's complex consideration of Nietzschean "tragedy" and its relationship to the literature of the present day, "Professors and Gods," in the Times Literary Supplement, March 9, 1973. He acknowledges that poetry in our time has lost much to the novel, but that it need not surrender entirely what the art of the novel forces upon the novelist—"a viewpoint not always his own and a regard for the situation of others." Fuller's distinction between the dramatized "tragedy" of the individual and the higher, more formal, and far more idealistic "tragedy" of the community is an important one, helping to explain why tragedy as an art form is so difficult and, in execution, so often disappointing in our time.

17. The Plath Celebration: A Partial Dissent
Irving Howe

1. *The Art of Sylvia Plath*, ed. Charles Newman (Bloomington: Indiana University Press, 1970).